Drone imaginaries

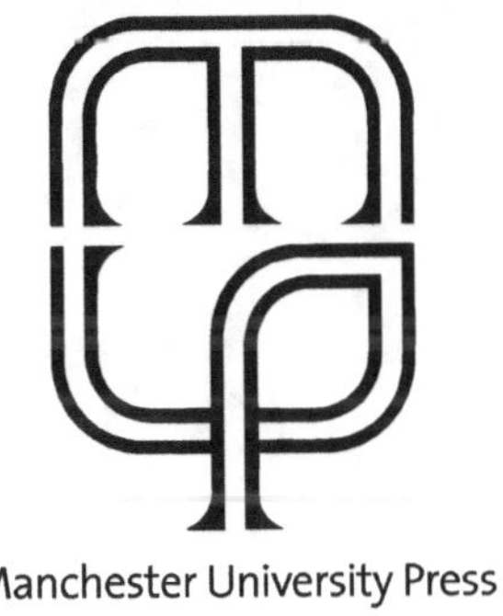

Manchester University Press

Drone imaginaries

The power of remote vision

Edited by

Andreas Immanuel Graae and Kathrin Maurer

MANCHESTER UNIVERSITY PRESS

Published by Manchester University Press
Oxford Road, Manchester M13 9PL

www.manchesteruniversitypress.co.uk

British Library Cataloguing-in-Publication Data
A catalogue record for this book is available from the British Library

ISBN 978 1 5261 4593 2 hardback
ISBN 978 1 5261 7898 5 paperback

First published 2021

Typeset by
Servis Filmsetting Ltd, Stockport, Cheshire

Contents

Part III: Communities

List of figures

List of contributors

Svea Braeunert is DAAD Visiting Associate Professor in German Studies at the University of Cincinnati. Her research interests include twentieth- and twenty-first-century art, literature, and film, media theory and visual culture, concepts of memory, trauma, and deferred action, and gender studies. She is the author of *Gespenstergeschichten: Der linke Terrorismus der RAF und die Künste* (Kadmos, 2015), and co-author and co-curator of *To See Without Being Seen: Contemporary Art and Drone Warfare* (University of Chicago Press, 2016) and *Method: Sasha Kurmaz* (Kehrer, 2016). She is currently working on a book project on *Media Cultures of Drone Warfare*.

Rasmus Degnbol is an award-winning Danish artist, documentary photographer and filmmaker focusing on worldwide political issues and storytelling. He was a masterclass mentee at the world-renowned VII Photo Agency in New York (2014–2015) and a member of REDUX Pictures agency in New York. He works on his own long-term projects and for international media clients like *New York Times*, *The Economist* and *National Geographic*. His recent work 'Europe's New Borders' has been exhibited at various galleries and museums around the world, including MoMA in New York, NYU Shanghai and Manchester Museum.

Andreas Immanuel Graae is Assistant Professor at the Royal Danish Defence College and has a PhD from the University of Southern Denmark with the dissertation *The Cruel Drone: Imagining Drone Warfare in Art, Culture, and Politics* (2019). He has published several articles on drones and is co-editor of a theme issue on drone warfare in the Danish journal *Politik* (2017) as well as co-author of a chapter in the anthology *Remote Warfare: New Cultures of Violence* (University of Minnesota Press, 2020). His current research focuses on military technology and aesthetics, exploring how drones, artificial intelligence and lethal autonomous weapon systems are about to transform current and future battlefields.

Arthur Holland Michel is Associate Researcher at the United Nations Institute for Disarmament Research and senior fellow at the Carnegie Council. He was founder and co-director of the Center for the Study of the Drone at Bard College, an interdisciplinary research institute, and the author of *Eyes in the Sky: The Secret Rise of Gorgon Stare and How it Will Watch Us All* (Houghton Mifflin Harcourt). His writing has appeared in *The Atlantic*, *Wired*, an *Oxford Research Encyclopedia*, *Slate*, *Vice*, *Fast Company*, *Motherboard*, *Al Jazeera America*, *The Verge*, *U.S. News*, *Bookforum* and *Mashable Spotlight*.

Tomas van Houtryve is a conceptual artist, photographer and author whose major works interweave investigative journalism, philosophy and metaphor. Van Houtryve makes images using a wide range of processes, ranging from nineteenth-century wet plate collodion to thermal imaging and augmented reality. His projects challenge our notions of identity, memory and power, often by highlighting the slippage of wartime structures into everyday life. Van Houtryve's works are widely exhibited, for example at the International Center for Photography Museum, New York (2017), Museum für Fotografie, Berlin (2017), and the British Museum, London (2016). In 2014, van Houtryve's *Blue Sky Days* series was published in *Harper's*. His recent monograph, *Lines + Lineage*, was published by Radius Books in 2019. The work takes aim at America's collective amnesia of history, addressing the missing photographic record of the period when Mexico ruled what we now know as the American West.

Caren Kaplan is Professor Emerita of American Studies at the University of California at Davis. Her research draws on cultural geography, landscape art, and military history to explore the ways in which undeclared, as well as declared, wars produce visual cultures of atmospheric politics. Selected publications include *Aerial Aftermaths: Wartime from Above* (Duke, 2018), *Life in the Age of Drone Warfare* (Duke University Press, 2017), *Between Woman and Nation: Transnational Feminisms and the State* (Duke University Press, 1999), *Questions of Travel: Postmodern Discourses of Displacement* (Duke University Press, 1996) and *Scattered Hegemonies: Postmodernity and Transnational Feminist Practices* (Minnesota 1994).

Claudette Lauzon is Assistant Professor of Contemporary Art History at Simon Fraser University in Vancouver, Canada. She is the author of *The Unmaking of Home in Contemporary Art* (University of Toronto Press, 2017) and co-editor of *Through Post-Atomic Eyes* (McGill-Queens University Press, 2020) and *Sustainable Tools for Precarious Times: Performance Actions in the Americas* (Palgrave McMillan, 2019). She is currently working on a SSHRC-funded illustrated technobestiary of drone warfare.

Kathrin Maurer is Professor of Humanities and Technology and leader of the Center for Culture and Technology at the University of Southern Denmark. Her research areas include cultures of surveillance, drone technology, visual culture, and nineteenth-century German literature. She has published the books *Visualizing War: Emotions, Technology, Communities* (Routledge, 2018, anthology), *Visualizing History: The Power of the Image in German Historicism* (Walter de Gruyter, 2013) and *Discursive Interaction: Literary Realism and Academic Historiography in Nineteenth-Century Germany* (Synchron, 2006). She has also published articles on drone warfare and culture, drone art, and the aerial perspective in nineteenth-century culture. She is the leader of the research cluster *Drone Imaginaries and Communities* and of the network *Drones and Aesthetics* (sponsored by the Danish Research Council).

Jan Mieszkowski is Professor of German and Comparative Literature at Reed College. He is the author of three books: *Crises of the Sentence* (University of Chicago Press, 2019), *Watching War* (Stanford University Press, 2012) and *Labors of Imagination: Aesthetics and Political Economy from Kant to Althusser* (Fordham University Press, 2006). Mieszkowski's recent articles explore a range of topics in Romanticism, Modernism and critical theory. He has also published and lectured widely on the spectacles of the permanent war economy. He is currently at work on a study of botany's importance for modern political philosophy.

Thomas Stubblefield is Associate Professor of Art History and Interim Associate Dean of the College of Visual and Performing Arts at the University of Massachusetts, Dartmouth. His first book, *9/11 and the Visual Culture of Disaster* (Indiana University Press, 2015), was awarded the Rollins Prize. In February 2020, his book, *Drone Art: The Everywhere War as Medium*, was published by the University of California Press.

Jutta Weber is an STS scholar, philosopher of technology and Professor of Media Sociology at the University of Paderborn. Her research focuses on computational technoscience culture(s) asking how and for whom the non/human actors work. Recent publications include *Technosecurity Cultures*, special issue of 'Science as Culture' (with Katrin Kämpf, 2020), *Tracking and Targeting: Sociotechnologies of (In)security*, special issue of 'Science, Technology & Human Values' (co-edited with Karolina Follis and Lucy Suchman, 2017), 'Human-Machine Autonomies' in Nehal Bhuta et al. (eds),

Autonomous Weapon Systems (Cambridge University Press, 2016, with Lucy Suchman).

Lauren Wilcox is Senior Lecturer in Gender Studies, Deputy Director of the University of Cambridge Centre for Gender Studies, and a fellow of Selwyn College, Cambridge. She won a prestigious Philip Leverhulme Prize for Politics and International Relations in 2018. Her first book, *Bodies of Violence: Theorizing Embodied Subjects in International Relations*, was published with Oxford University Press in 2015. Her current research project, War Beyond the Human, focuses on the political and technological assemblages of bodies that are both the subjects and objects of political violence to create an account of political violence that builds upon gender and sexuality theory to address the relationship between violence, desire, embodiment, race, sex, and gender in late liberal societies.

Introduction

Andreas Immanuel Graae and Kathrin Maurer

In December 2019, something strange appeared in the airspace over the Colorado and Nebraska prairie: drones. Lots of them. As a *New York Times* article reported, 'they come in the night [...] flying in precise formations.'[1] Nobody knew where they were coming from, who was controlling them or why they were there. Residents in the region were puzzled and slightly frightened. 'It's creepy',[2] a Nebraskan farmer said after witnessing drones hovering over her farm, blinking red in the dark. Rumours circulated about who might be responsible for the drones: The government? Drug cartels? Gas companies? Even though the unusual drone activity was investigated by the Federal Aviation Administration and multiple government agencies, their appearance remained unexplained and the mystery may never be unravelled. 'It's the fear of the unknown',[3] the Nebraskan farmer explained, expressing her unease about the mysterious drones and her discomfort at not knowing who or what was watching her from above. This uncertainty and creepy feeling embodies a common human reaction to drones, namely the sense of being watched or controlled by some unknown, uncanny, machinic, self-intelligent power.

This book explores the cultural and aesthetic imaginaries of drones, and how these imaginaries reflect the societal transformations that come with this burgeoning technology. Although we are growing accustomed to the extensive use of drones for mapping, farming and photography, the mysterious appearance of stray drones above the Nebraskan prairie was puzzling. The speculations about the unexplained drones suggest that the cultural formations and aesthetic configurations of drones are still up for negotiation, raising multiple questions. How are drones imagined in art and culture, as well as through political and military discourses? What kind of power regimes do these imaginaries of drones suggest? How do drones change the way we perceive and control human bodies? In what ways are they transforming our communities?

These questions cannot be answered by an academic approach that nestles solely in the social sciences; they also call the humanities to task. In this book, we address the impact of drones on human identity and society from a humanities point of view, conjoining approaches from literary, cultural, visual, aesthetic and media studies by investigating aesthetic representations of civilian and military drones in visual art, photography and literature. Central to our understanding of drones is their dual identity as both objects of representation and vision machines that introduce new ways of seeing. On the one hand, the escalating hype about drones in art, media and politics – the ongoing 'drone-o-rama', as Caren Kaplan has put it so aptly[4] – has turned them into aesthetic objects that are both fetishised and criticised in art, media and popular culture. On the other hand, drones are vision machines that offer new ways of perceiving and mediating the world (from above, from a distance, and from remote, crewless, machinic platforms). Specifically, the drone as a vision machine has become an efficient tool for the military and the security industry, which take advantage of its remote sensing capabilities and its powerful gaze from above.

Originally developed as a military technology, drones have therefore been closely linked in dominant conceptions to the realm of warfare, security and surveillance. Yet the recent explosion in popular usage of civilian drones has enabled a proliferation of aerial views outside of military institutions, turning the drone into an artistic medium. Artists, journalists and photographers alike now apply the drone's vertical gaze to present astounding new perspectives on landscapes, as well as on the social life of humans. This book investigates the power of this remote drone vision – in military operations as in critical artistic practices – by focusing on drones as both potent sensorial platforms and aesthetic objects of representation.

These heterogenous visualities and aesthetic representations embody 'drone imaginaries', a cultural storage of images and narratives about drone technology through which the complex interplay between drone technology and society can be analysed. The drone imaginary designates negotiations between personal, emotional experiences and the broader social imagination in the form of collective imaginings including affects, desires and fantasies. The ability of artistic or literary representations to critically reflect and reconfigure these shared ideas and fantasies remains crucial. Aesthetic works have a distinct potential to communicate cultural sensations of institutional changes or groundbreaking trends – such as new technologies and their influence on our social practices – in an independent and non-instrumentalised way. This is evident, for instance, in elin o'Hara slavick's painting *Afghanistan I, 1979 and Infinite Reach, 1998*, shown on the cover of this anthology. By means of intense colours, ornamental lines and a strange sense of beauty, her painting acts as a powerful aesthetic intervention and counteraction against the cold and dehumanised view of the drone and its aerial vison regime of surgical strikes.[5]

Also central to this book's enquiries into drones is the ambition to historicise the technology, a strategy to defetishise the drone by questioning the hype and supposed novelty surrounding it. By tracing historical continuities and early prototypes of crewless, remotely operated or aerial technologies, we can better understand how drones are transforming our contemporary communities and social practices. This trajectory of historical drone imaginaries – which include, for instance, historical documents or literary accounts, such as reports on nineteenth-century ballooning and imaginings of early robotic insect-machines in fiction – forms a reservoir of cultural knowledge, on the basis of which contemporary drone representations can be examined. However, the aim of this book is not to create a coherent history of drones, but rather to investigate how certain formations of the drone imaginary shape the aesthetic configuration of drones today. Altogether, these cultural forms and historical archives constitute what we understand as a drone imaginary: a prism of cultural knowledge through which the power of remote vision can be explored.

Aesthetic drone imaginaries and the social imaginary

As the various reactions to the stray Nebraskan drones imply, sensation-driven news media and popular culture have already made drones into something more than simple technological merchandise. Indeed, they are 'shrouded in fantasy', as essayist Adam Rothstein has noted,[6] indicating that they are 'not real' but rather are cultural constructs fuelled by political imagination. Central to this understanding of drone technology is the human capacity to produce images. Originating from the Latin word *imaginatio*, an equivalent of the Greek word *phantasia*, the notion of imagination goes as far back as Aristotle.[7] He sees *phantasia* as a combination of *aisthêsis* (sensation) and *doxa* (judgement), from which ideas are constructed as images based on sensory input. For Aristotle, even the most basic mental operations depend on images in order to produce ideas, which makes the imaginary an essential condition for all thought. As human beings we are therefore first and foremost 'imaginal animals',[8] which means that we need unifying images in order to maintain communal life and keep the political order running.

The aesthetic representations of drones investigated in this book are therefore not pure fictions or fantasies, but rather are part of a larger set of social imaginaries. Inspired by Charles Taylor's influential concept of the social imaginary,[9] we treat the realm of drone imaginaries as an intermediary field that fluctuates between social practices and abstract ideas. Social imaginaries form a background structure that gives meaning to the common practices that constitute a society. Seen in this light, the drone imaginary can be taken as part of a larger domain of shared meaning that guides the way crewless aerial technologies are thought of and operationalised in political thinking and the public sphere. Yet whereas Taylor defines the social imaginary in the broadest sense as an 'inarticulate understanding of our whole situation',[10] this book focuses more concretely on visual and discursive manifestations of drones and how they come to reflect social practices. In short, we investigate the realm of drone imaginaries as an aesthetic configuration of drones that exposes new modes of vision and powerful ways of producing images and worlds.

The latter capacity to imagine alternative or future worlds was especially revitalised and militarised in the aftermath of the September 11 attacks and the subsequent introduction of drones into the military toolbox. As described by the 9/11 Commission in July 2004, one of the major failures leading to the 9/11 disaster was 'one of imagination', which alluded to 'a mind-set that dismissed possibilities'.[11] In response to this alleged lack of imagination, a strategy to counter the possibility of future attacks emerged as a new security paradigm that was all about evoking images of imminent threats from an imaginary pool of virtual futures. In this paranoid hunt for future insecurities, armed drones soon became an important military technology, which could not only see but also 'foresee' and pre-empt future threats. In other words, the world-making power of the drone imaginary is closely tied to the drone's capacity to generate providence and future worlds through persistent surveillance and lethal weapons systems.

But the drone imaginary also has a more direct connection to the increasingly prominent role images play in military operations. As a weaponised vision machine, the drone produces images that are 'operational'[12] in more than one sense: on the one hand, they are images produced *by* the drone (which are hardly legible to humans); on the other hand, they are projections that are humanly interpreted and made operational as they enter into the larger social system of political decision-making, military practice and public perception. Whereas some chapters in this anthology engage with drone machine vision, most of them examine aestheticised drone imaginaries. The aesthetic archive of cultural drone representations provides a rich resource through which ethical dilemmas and common assumptions can be critically scrutinised. As condensed extracts of their time, the aesthetic drone imaginaries in this book thus constitute a privileged field of representation that can provide unique insights into our increasingly militarised culture, and into the embodied experiences of drone warfare that tend to be overlooked in more politico-juridical areas of academic drone research.

The buzz of critical drone studies

Since it became publicly known that the US government under the Obama administration was radically escalating the usage of armed drones in military operations, there has been a boom in academic research on drones. Among the fields that have been particularly productive in illuminating and conceptualising the various aspects of drone warfare are the disciplines of law, political science, anthropology and geography.[13] While each of these different fields has its own distinct vocabularies, methods and approaches, there are certain overarching terms and themes that together make the academic field of drone studies highly cross-disciplinary. In both legal and political drone studies, terms such as 'asymmetrical warfare' remain key to the discussion of how and why drones mark a new military paradigm of 'riskless war' in which states are able to project power without vulnerability.[14] These debates often raise the question of whether drone operations can be categorised within the legal framework of 'just war' (*jus ad bellum*), or whether they in fact represent an alternative mode of 'unjust' forever war or what Paul W. Kahn has called 'statecraft as the administration of death'.[15] While the chapters in this volume draw broadly on these well-established but diverse concepts of drone research, our objects of study differ from those of most drone studies, as we see the drone through the prism of aesthetic artworks.

In this endeavour, we situate our contributions in the slipstream of the growing number of humanistic drone researchers, particularly centred within the disciplines of philosophy, media studies and cultural studies. Above all, Grégoire Chamayou's seminal book *A Theory of the Drone* (2015) has had a huge impact on scholarly discourses and imaginaries related to drone warfare. Although Chamayou has been criticised for mythologising the drone[16] by situating it in the metaphysical context of ancient Greek, Nordic and Christian narratives of invincibility, this critique can also be contested, as his work is certainly self-reflexive about these myths. As opposed to Chamayou's mythical but also cultural, historical, philosophical and ideological rendering of the drone, a broad range of studies within the humanities has engaged with the more technical aspects of drone vision and its representation in art and visual culture. As these studies are typically rooted in visual art and media studies,[17] they often highlight the technical dimension of the drone as a medium, and therefore focus less on how drones are configured through art and culture as well as through language and narratives.

However, an exception is the ambitious anthology *Life in the Age of Drone Warfare* (2017) edited by Lisa Parks and Caren Kaplan, a work that does indeed span the breadth of humanities disciplines to include historical, colonial, gendered and networked perceptions of drones. While the contributions to Parks's and Kaplan's volume engage with non-Western representations of drone war, this perspective is even more thoroughly unfolded in Ronak K. Kapadia's recent book *Insurgent Aesthetics: Security and the Queer Life of the Forever War* (2019), which conceptualises the world-making power of contemporary art responses to US militarism in the Middle East. There is no doubt that Parks's and Kaplan's volume and Kapadia's book cover an impressive variety of perspectives on military drones, focusing on both artistic representations and the postcolonialism and racialised politics of drones warfare; yet the imaginative infrastructure of drones, such as the historical precursors and speculative futures of this technology, is not always to the fore. In this book, we engage more directly with the aesthetics, cultures and histories of drones in order to investigate how these diverse imaginaries can confront, question and critique the assumed power of drone vision and politics.

Thus, the chapters in this volume build on well-established drone research to further explore the aesthetic configurations of drones within larger political narratives and the social imaginary. While other scholars have used the term 'drone imaginary' to designate this larger political, social and military imagination into which drones inevitably enter, it has not always been entirely clear what exactly is implied by this notion.[18] With this book, we therefore wish to contribute new analytical insights to the dynamic field of drone imaginaries as hovering between aesthetic configuration and social imagination. Our conceptualisation of the drone imaginary is both narrow and broad in scope. It is narrow in its focus on the figural representations of drones – that is, how they are rendered sensible through aesthetic representations, and how they become aesthetically configured as they enter into larger social dynamics. It is broad in its focus on the imaginary as a domain of shared meaning which is shaped by, and continuously shapes, the figural representations of drones in the larger social imagination, including ordinary cultural practices as well as political institutions and military operations. In other words, the contributions to this volume oscillate between careful close readings of specific aesthetic drone representations and larger claims about the political world they enter into. To reflect the distinct layers through which this imaginary dialectic takes place, the book is divided into three parts that in turn mirror the most important or powerful dimensions of the military drone imaginary as we see them: vision, bodies and communities.

Vision: flattening, abstraction and patterns

Since the Napoleonic Wars and their media machines, we have known that military power is more than just munitions, troops and weapons.[19] Paul Virilio has shown that power in war is about vision, such as the cameras employed to execute war, the images mediated from the battlefield, and the perception of war by soldiers, victims and the public.[20] Researchers on military drones have extensively investigated the relationship between vision and power, in which the drone as a technology of seeing executes biopolitical and governmental control. This connection between drone vision and power is also an important vantage point of this book.[21] Its chapters explore how the drone's vision – that is, the way a drone and its pilot together perceive and grasp the world – is reflected and negotiated in drone imaginaries. According to Derek Gregory, drone vision embodies a 'militarized regime of hypervisibility'[22] that executes a vertical and synoptic view of the surveilled area. Eyal Weizman, Lisa Parks, Alain Bousquet and Ronak K. Kapadia have discussed this hypervisibility of the drone gaze as a martial regime of imperial power.[23] In these works, drone vision is portrayed as a mode of asymmetrical seeing in which the perpetrator/soldier/drone operator remains invisible to the target.

While our work builds on these approaches, which connect drone vision and vertical systems of power, it is our goal to show that the optical regime of the drone can also emit visual configurations beyond the vertical. Chapter 1, by Kathrin Maurer, traces the visual mode of flattening as a key marker of drone vision. Maurer shows that instead of pursuing hierarchical and vertical oppositions, drones can flatten the world into abstract patterns, topographical maps and clusters. In order to prove this point, she engages in an experimental comparison between the gas balloon and the drone as technologies of aerial seeing. Analysing late eighteenth-century poetic literature about ballooning by the early Romantic literary author Jean Paul, her chapter shows that the balloon view triggered new forms of spatial perception, which in turn can also be found in the drone. Her historicisation of the drone view is an attempt not only to rewrite the aerial view beyond the vertical paradigm, but also to defetishise the drone as a radically new and unprecedented technology. Its location in the same family as the non-steerable, whimsical balloon makes us wonder about the drone's reputation as a precise instrument of vision.

However, it is important to understand that flattened aerial vision nevertheless executes power: its configurations and dynamics are merely different from the vertical mode of vision. Zygmunt Bauman and David Lyon have already pointed out that the drone's visual field of surveillance is in fact far more powerful than the panopticon, since it requires neither spatial partitions nor fixed architectural demarcations. Drones embody what they call a 'liquid technology', no longer perpendicularly ordered, but a-central, flexible and fluid.

Thomas Stubblefield discusses this shift from the vertical to the liquid and flattened surveillance of drones in his chapter on contemporary drone art. Rather than establishing oppositions, drones operate via network-centric systems that dissolve visible hierarchies. This kind of flattening can execute power by penetrating the world directly, shifting drone power from the symbolic to the ontological. By turning to network theory, Stubblefield demonstrates that the drone's world-making power lies in precisely its ability to conflate clear distinctions and dualisms.

Indeed, flattened vision and network power push the connection between drones and vision to its limits. When we address the world-making power of drones, we need to talk about more than vision. Jan Mieszkowski's chapter on drones and data does precisely that. The camera of a drone and the screen where the drone operator sits are only parts of a larger technical–human apparatus. Drones deliver data streams, which in turn are evaluated in ground data centres by human agents and algorithms. Drones go beyond the visual, and they sense via datafication, data networks and algorithms. Mieszkowski's chapter investigates the drone's data by connecting the flattening of drone perception to the abstraction processes of datafication. Thereby he pursues an aesthetic approach that explores the sublimity of drone big data in the post-vision age, and considers its implications for an emerging drone aesthetics and post-photography.

The conceptual artist, photographer and author Tomas van Houtryve is also interested in the power of drone vision, discussed in the interview with Svea Braeunert in this anthology. His collection *Blue Sky Days* (2013) is a black-and-white photo series that was shot by a drone filming scenes and places in the US, such as playgrounds, weddings and leisure sports. With a nod to the drone art of Martha Rosler and Omer Fast, his images bring the war home to US territory by applying the martial drone perspective to domestic territories. In so doing, Houtryve emphasises the abstraction of drone photography, but these processes of formalisation do not neglect the human figure. Rather, they work as an aesthetic practice to produce images that differ from the stream of images in today's media landscape, and which thus still have the power to speak to us and make us empathise.

The body, intimacy and closeness

Although drone vision is about distance, abstraction and flattening, it nevertheless also embodies closeness. Despite being detached, military drone pilots often get extremely close to their targets, and can see the killing up close on their screens. Instead of a numbed gaming mentality, drone killing entails a 'sense of intimacy', as Derek Gregory has noted.[24] The whole discourse on drone pilots and post-traumatic stress disorder raises this aspect of traumata and psychological damage, which in turn also shows that drone warfare touches upon the human body[25] – not only the body of the drone pilot, but even more so the bodies of the targets. Svea Braeunert's chapter traces the visual representation of the human body and target in contemporary artworks that deal with drone warfare. She shows that although drone images portray abstracted flattened landscapes, they also trace the human body. Thereby she engages with the genre of the tilted image, which plays with background and foreground and in which two images are present at the same time (such as images of a duck and a rabbit, or a young and an old woman). Analysing artworks by James Bridle, the online campaign #NotaBugSplat and Seth Price, her chapter reveals the dynamic of appearance, disappearance and reappearance of the human body, which in turn demonstrates the body's precariousness and vulnerability.

Drones not only upset the dichotomies of distance and closeness, absence and presence, remoteness and intimacy; they also challenge the gendered aspect of war. As war has been considered one of the most gendered of all human activities, Lauren Wilcox's chapter suggests that perhaps one of the reasons that drone warfare is so troubling and difficult to classify is precisely because it defies the gendered categories that have constituted theories of war and political violence. Inspired by feminist critiques of the war/peace distinction in terms of sexualised violence against women, she draws on queer and black feminist thought to analyse not only how the drone challenges our understanding of what war is, but also how it must be understood as a gendering and racialising technology. Given the much-noted voyeuristic intimacy of the drone, and its fetishised, even sublime qualities of predator/prey, Wilcox argues that in order to understand the gender politics of the drone we must examine the constitution of the concept of gender as simultaneously both a technology of embodiment and a racialising technology.

The various ways in which human bodies are rendered precarious by the drone also inspire the photographer and visual artist Rasmus Degnbol in his ongoing project *Europe's New Borders* (2015–). In an interview with Andreas Immanuel Graae, Degnbol explains how he used a drone to photograph refugees arriving at the edge of Europe on the Greek island of Lesbos in the summer of 2015. With its distancing gaze on the humanitarian crises unfolding across the borders of Europe, Degnbol found the drone uniquely capable of mediating the scale and dehumanisation of European migration politics. According to Degnbol, this distanced governmental view is mirrored in the drone gaze, and through this perspective the figure of the individual human body dissolves into cool statistics, landscapes and topographies. From the governmental perspective of the drone, there are thus no individual bodies to be seen – only faceless numbers, and dehumanising borders to keep out the hordes.

Communities, swarms and the techno-bestiary

The matters of borders and migration foregrounded in Degnbol's work are suggestive not only of how bodies are seen and controlled, but also of how the drone imaginary is transformative in redesigning our human communities. While this book's sections on vision and bodies convey *how* the drone sees and *what* is seen, the chapters on drone communities focus on how drones enter into their surrounding social spheres. Since drone imaginaries are social by default and cannot be reduced to pure fictions or fantasies, they constitute a shared pool of cultural discourses, understandings and images of remote surveillance technology. In doing so, drones and their imaginaries have a constitutive role to play in what is legally and culturally defined as a political community, and even more so in how this definition might change in the future.

In legal and political thought, communities have often been defined as territories of people with a monopoly on the 'legitimate use of violence within a territorial jurisdiction'.[26] In this understanding, the concept of the border is crucial as a defining line that governs the territory of the community. Yet while drones are increasingly deployed as powerful tools for controlling borders and bodies, they can at the same time disrupt the social imagining of human communities as demarcated states and bordered territories. This is not to say, of course, that the occurrence of drones has made political and cultural theorists question the territorial definitions of communities, in the way that Benedict Anderson's notion of imagined communities famously did.[27] But drones nevertheless seem to have the power to disrupt or destroy what has always been the signifier of communities: having something in common, and actively sharing with one another. By means of persistent 24/7 surveillance and big data sorting, drones connect and disconnect people not on the basis of sharing, but according to contingent network principles, machine learning processes and algorithmic operations. The question of whether we are therefore on the threshold of a new era of networked and self-organising drone communities can be contested. But it is certain that a central part of the drone imaginary is about how future generations of drones might potentially create non-human forms of intelligence, cooperation and communication in order to build their own non-human communities, inspired not by fallible, blundering and erratic humans, but by efficient zoological organisational forms such as those of ants or bees.

Although these community scenarios may sound highly futuristic, they were in fact top of the agenda during the post-war conferences on cybernetics and early computing that are often referred to as the Macy Conferences (1946–1953). These post-war seminars synthesised research on animal worlds and technological systems in order to rethink human–machine interaction, communication and control, often inspired for instance by the strange sensorial world of insects. In his chapter, Andreas Immanuel Graae unfolds this historical link between insects and machinic life through the figure of the swarm as it is represented in the novel *The Glass Bees* by the German author and thinker Ernst Jünger. Jünger was an eager entomologist with a keen eye for emerging technologies and their impact on the human, and his story envisions a future community where robotic insects have taken over human jobs. The novel thus reflects a new set of technoscientific imaginaries that flourished in the Cold War period, and which, to a large extent, found inspiration in the zoological world and insect communities. By situating Jünger's novel in this dawning era of computers, networks and automation, Graae argues that it can be read as an early literary work on drone technology, raising questions about how machine autonomy and non-human swarm communities not only challenge human command and control, but also threaten our human integrity and existence.

If Jünger's novel can be seen as an early registration of drone swarming with ever smaller, smarter and smoother forms of automated organisation, Jutta Weber actualises this sinister scenario in her chapter on the ethical implications of self-regulating swarms and killer robots. According to Weber, our current imagining of swarms and artificial intelligence (AI) is heavily coloured by military fantasies of autonomous and self-regulating systems on the one hand, and dystopic images of killer robots such as Skynet from the *Terminator* universe on the other. Weber critically engages with these persistent imaginaries through readings of some of the most widespread cases. In *Slaughterbots*,[28] for instance, a video that went viral on YouTube shortly after its release in November 2017, Weber sees a future scenario quite different from the US military dream of self-healing, intelligent drone swarms. Here, swarms of small, fast and cheap drones are deployed by unknown (and hardly identifiable) protagonists to kill political enemies via AI, facial recognition, machinic vision and shaped charges. In this hybrid between a political statement and a fictionalised near-future scenario, Weber finds that the featured drone swarms are not staged as self-conscious, intelligent organisms that follow their own autonomously determined goals, but rather are preprogrammed to select their targets via social media data analytics according to pregiven criteria. This idea of drone swarming questions the imaginary of self-conscious, intelligent, autonomous machines, in opposition to imaginaries of tomorrow's AI as a collection of smart software programs.

A similar ambition to debunk the myths of drones as monstrous machines that operate perfectly autonomously is also at stake in Claudette Lauzon's careful reading of contemporary drone art. In her chapter, Lauzon draws up a techno-bestiary of drones in order to identify the monsters that populate the Western social imaginary and to question how these monsters come to reshape our consequent fears and desires. In close dialogue with a series of recent artworks, she develops a drone bestiary consisting of three heuristic figures: the swarm, the blob and the living dead. According to Lauzon, these monstrous bodies can help to elucidate an aesthetics of estrangement within the drone imaginary. Her convincing claim is that there exists an uneasy kinship in the form of an 'inoperative community' between drones and humans in which emerging drone technology is at constant risk of turning against its makers. Lauzon finds that it is only by insisting on making the drone strange through the swarm, the blob and the corpse that art is paradoxically capable of cultivating a praxis of solidarity, kinship and change that can reconfigure the drone imaginary and create new human–machine communities.

Art's ability to expose violent power structures and cultivate new communities and possibilities for change is also at play in Caren Kaplan's chapter on the art project *Repellent Fence*. In this project from 2015, the artist collective Postcommodity installed twenty-six 'eyes in the sky' – a term often used for military surveillance drones – in the form of giant scare-eye balloons along the US–Mexico border. As Kaplan shows through her cautious reading of the art project, the twenty-six eyes in the sky connected past, future and present struggles for Indigenous self-determination and open borders, exposing how the atmospheric itself operates as a mode of colonial weaponry. Drawing on the cultural and spiritual traditions and 'complex Indigeneity' of people from the entire region beyond, before, during and after the historical events of bordering, Kaplan argues that the big scare-eye balloons worked as 'aesthetic portals' between worlds to activate an 'Indigenous worldview' and remind us of the violent and unequal histories in such sites. Postcommodity thus reconceived this borderland airspace as both repellent and repelling, reanimating trans-Indigenous presence as ambiently atmospheric as well as territorially grounded.

Drone imaginaries as critical lenses and agents of change

As follows from the above, the aesthetic field of drone imaginaries thus serves a twofold purpose. On the one hand, it provides a unique magnifying glass through which drones can be critically examined; on the other, it also has a more concrete impact on society, as drone artworks become agents of social change and activist intervention. In his coda to the volume, Arthur Holland Michel tracks these various potentials through an extensive catalogue of contemporary drone art, and peeks into the genre's future. According to Holland Michel, the first wave of drone art evolved from about 2010 to 2014, and its main goal was to 'surface' drones in the public sphere, making visible the 'invisible' technologies that were rapidly transforming the conduct of war. The second wave of drone art explores the transition of drone technology from essentially a new way of seeing and killing to the future conundrums of ever smarter and autonomously operating drones. In short, Holland Michels's mapping of contemporary drone artworks reflects some of the key aspects of the drone imaginary – that is, drone vision, bodies and communities – and compiles these different perspectives into a short but vibrant history of drone art.

Using drone art and aesthetics as a critical lens to investigate the diversity of drone technology, its ethical implications, its embodied affects and its impact on social life, we therefore hope that the following chapters will give new insights into the highly vibrant and multifaceted area of drone research. Only through a thorough engagement with past, present and future drone imaginaries can we use aesthetic works as a transformative force to imagine and/or potentially create new collaborations and communities between humans and machines.

Notes

1 M. Smith, '"It's creepy": Unexplained drones are swarming by night over Colorado', *New York Times* (1 January, 2020), www.nytimes.com/2020/01/01/us/drones-FAA-colorado-nebraska.html (accessed 7 January, 2020).
2 Smith, '"It's creepy".
3 Smith, '"It's creepy".
4 C. Kaplan, 'The Drone-o-rama: Troubling the temporal and spatial logics of distance warfare', in L. Parks and C. Kaplan (eds), *Life in the Age of Drone Warfare* (Durham, NC: Duke University Press, 2017), 161–177.
5 I owe this reference to elin o'Hara slavick's art to R. K. Kapadia, *Insurgent Aesthetics: Security and the Queer Life of the Forever War* (Durham, NC: Duke University Press, 2019), 95–101.

6 A. Rothstein, *Drone* (New York: Bloomsbury Academic, 2015), ix.
7 C. Bottici, *Imaginal Politics: Images Beyond Imagination and the Imaginary* (New York: Columbia University Press, 2014), 10.
8 Bottici, *Imaginal Politics*, 6.
9 C. Taylor, *Modern Social Imaginaries* (Durham, NC: Duke University Press, 2004).
10 Taylor, *Modern Social Imaginaries*, 25.
11 *The 9/11 Commission Report: Final Report of the National Commission on Terrorist Attacks Upon the United States* (London: Norton, authorised edn, 2004), 344.
12 The term 'operational images' was originally coined by the artist Harun Farocki to refer to a new visual regime of images that 'do not represent an object but are part of an operation', such as weapons, surveillance cameras, or in the case of drones both at once – in short, images made for machines by machines. H. Farocki, 'Phantom images', *Public*, 29 (2004).
13 See, in particular, J. J. Kaag and S. E. Kreps, *Drone Warfare* (Cambridge: Polity, 2014); H. Gusterson, *Drone: Remote Control Warfare* (London: MIT Press, 2015); P. W. Kahn, 'Imagining warfare', *European Journal of International Law*, 24:1 (2013): 199–226.
14 For more on these legal and political discussions of the asymmetry of drone warfare see, in particular, Kaag and Kreps, *Drone Warfare*; G. Chamayou, *A Theory of the Drone* (New York: The New Press, 2015).
15 Kahn, 'Imagining warfare', 226.
16 I. G. R. Shaw, *Predator Empire: Drone Warfare and Full Spectrum Dominance* (Minneapolis: University of Minnesota Press, 2016).
17 For drones as new media, see for instance N. Franz, 'Targeted killing and pattern-of-life analysis: Weaponised media', *Media, Culture & Society*, 39:1 (2017): 111–121; L. Suchman, 'Situational awareness: Deadly bioconvergence at the boundaries of bodies and machines', *MediaTropes*, 5:1 (2015): 1–24; M. Queisner, '"Looking through a soda straw": Mediated vision in remote warfare'. In K. Maurer and A. I. Graae (eds), 'Tema: Droner og krig', special issue, *Politik*, 20:1 (2017): 45–61.
18 For instance, Yale scholar Inderpal Grewal uses the term 'drone imaginaries' as the title for her chapter on 'the technopolitics of visuality in postcolony and empire', in Park and Kaplan's *Life in the Age of Drone Warfare* – and yet she never really defines or precisely explains what she understands by these 'imaginaries'. I. Grewal 'Drone imaginaries: The technopolitics of visuality in postcolony and empire', in Park and Kaplan (eds), *Life in the Age of Drone Warfare*, 343–365.
19 J. Mieszkowski, *Watching War* (Stanford: Stanford University Press, 2012).
20 P. Virilio, *War and Cinema: The Logistics of Perception* (London: Verso, 1989).
21 For research on the visual empowerment of drones, see for instance D. Gregory, 'From a view to a kill: Drones and late modern war', *Theory, Culture & Society*, 28:7–8 (2011): 188–215; D. Gregory, 'Drone geographies', *Radical Philosophy* 183 (2014): 7–19; P. Adey, M. Whitehead and A. Williams, *From*

Above: War, Violence, and Verticality (New York: Oxford University Press, 2013); C. Kaplan, *Aerial Aftermaths: Wartime from Above* (Durham, NC: Duke University Press, 2018).

22 Gregory, 'From a view to a kill', 193.

23 E. Weizman, *Forensic Architecture: Violence at the Threshold of Detectability* (New York: Zone Books, 2019); L. Parks, 'Vertical mediation and the US drone war in the Horn of Africa', in Parks and Kaplan (eds), *Life in the Age of Drone Warfare*, 134–158; Kapadia, *Insurgent Aesthetics*; A. Bousquet, *The Eye of War: Military Perception from the Telescope to the Drone* (Minneapolis: University of Minnesota Press, 2018).

24 Gregory, 'From a view to a kill', 200.

25 On this topic see S. Braeunert, 'Post-traumatic stress disorder in drone operators relying on uncertainty in Omer Fast's *5,000 Feet is the Best* (2011)', in A. Engberg-Pedersen and K. Maurer (eds), *Visualizing War: Emotions, Technologies, Communities* (New York: Routledge, 2018), 95–109.

26 While as Paul W. Kahn notes, this definition draws on 'centuries of imaginative political framing, beginning with Hobbes' idea of exit from the state of nature', the recent deployment of drones disrupts this imaginative structure. Kahn, 'Imagining warfare', 203.

27 B. Anderson, *Imagined Communities: Reflections on the Origin and Spread of Nationalism* (London: Verso, 1983).

28 *Slaughterbots* (YouTube, November 2017), www.youtube.com/watch?v=HipTO_7mUOw (accessed 5 February, 2021).

Bibliography

The 9/11 Commission Report: Final Report of the National Commission on Terrorist Attacks Upon the United States. London: Norton, authorised edn, 2004.

Adey, P., M. Whitehead and A. Williams. *From Above: War, Violence, and Verticality*. New York: Oxford University Press, 2013.

Anderson, B. *Imagined Communities: Reflections on the Origin and Spread of Nationalism*. London: Verso, 1983.

Bottici, C. *Imaginal Politics: Images Beyond Imagination and the Imaginary*. New York: Columbia University Press, 2014.

Bousquet, A. *The Eye of War: Military Perception from the Telescope to the Drone*. Minneapolis: University of Minnesota Press, 2018.

Braeunert, S. 'Post-traumatic stress disorder in drone operators relying on uncertainty in omer Fast's *5,000 Feet is the Best* (2011)'. In A. Engberg-Pedersen and K. Maurer (eds), *Visualizing War: Emotions, Technologies, Communities*, 95–109. New York: Routledge, 2018.

Chamayou, G. *A Theory of the Drone*. New York: The New Press, 2015.

Farocki, H. 'Phantom images'. *Public* 29 (2004): 12–24.

Franz, N. 'Targeted killing and pattern-of-life analysis: Weaponised media'. *Media, Culture & Society* 39:1 (2017): 111–121.

Gregory, D. 'From a view to a kill: Drones and late modern war'. *Theory, Culture & Society*, 28:7–8 (2011): 188–215.
— 'Drone geographies'. *Radical Philosophy* 183 (2014): 7–19.
Grewal, I. 'Drone imaginaries: The technopolitics of visuality in postcolony and empire'. In L. Park and C. Kaplan (eds), *Life in the Age of Drone Warfare*, 343–365. Durham, NC: Duke University Press, 2017.
Gusterson, H. *Drone: Remote Control Warfare*. London: MIT Press, 2015.
Kaag, J. J., and S. E. Kreps. *Drone Warfare*. Cambridge: Polity, 2014.
Kahn, P. W. 'Imagining warfare'. *European Journal of International Law* 24:1 (2013): 199–226.
Kapadia, R. K. *Insurgent Aesthetics: Security and the Queer Life of the Forever War*. Durham, NC: Duke University Press, 2019.
Kaplan, C. 'The drone-o-rama: Troubling the temporal and spatial logics of distance warfare'. In L. Parks and C. Kaplan (eds), *Life in the Age of Drone* Warfare, 161–177. Durham, NC: Duke University Press, 2017.
Kaplan, C. *Aerial Aftermaths: Wartime from Above*. Durham, NC: Duke University Press, 2018.
Mieszkowski, J. *Watching War*. Stanford: Stanford University Press, 2012.
Parks, L. and C. Kaplan (eds). *Life in the Age of Drone Warfare*. Durham, NC: Duke University Press, 2017.
Queisner, M. '"Looking through a soda straw": Mediated vision in remote warfare'. In K. Maurer and A. I. Graae (eds), 'Tema: Droner og krig', special issue, *Politik*, 20:1 (2017): 45–61.
Rothstein, A. *Drone*. New York: Bloomsbury Academic, 2015.
Shaw, I. G. R. *Predator Empire: Drone Warfare and Full Spectrum Dominance*. Minneapolis: University of Minnesota Press, 2016.
Smith, M. '"It's creepy": Unexplained drones are swarming by night over Colorado'. *New York Times*, 1 January, 2020. www.nytimes.com/2020/01/01/us/drones-FAA-colorado-nebraska.html (accessed 7 January, 2020).
Suchman, L. 'Situational awareness: Deadly bioconvergence at the boundaries of bodies and machines'. *MediaTropes*, 5:1 (2015): 1–24.
Taylor, C. *Modern Social Imaginaries*. Durham, NC: Duke University Press, 2004.
Virilio, P. *War and Cinema: The Logistics of Perception*. London: Verso, 1989.
Weizman, E. *Forensic Architecture: Violence at the Threshold of Detectability*. New York: Zone Books, 2019.

Part I

Visions

1

Flattened vision: nineteenth-century hot air balloons as early drones

Kathrin Maurer

'Sometimes I felt like a God hurling thunderbolts from afar', says a drone pilot of his experience operating drone missions.[1] This God-like, all-encompassing view from the sky is often considered characteristic of military drone vision. Drones, executing a superior and powerful gaze from above, adhere to what has been called a 'scopic regime'. The term was originally developed by scholars of visual studies to express the idea that not only what, but *how* we see is historically conditioned.[2] In research on military drones, it is used to discuss the martial gaze of the drone machine and its human agents. Etymologically speaking, the Greek word *skopos* implies a direct connection between watching and waging war, as *skopos* can simultaneously mean both watcher and target.[3] Drone vision thus instantiates a 'militarised regime of hypervisibility', granting the observer a powerful vertical, synoptic view of the target under surveillance.[4]

The idea that the drone enforces a scopic regime reflects (and in some ways reiterates) a well-established narrative of modern aerial vision: The eye in the sky is sovereign and all-seeing. The drone view, in particular, is often associated with being omniscient, precise, and surgical.[5] But whereas military aerial vision can certainly be scopic, there is much more to be said. Military drone vision is much more complex and heterogenous than the scopic paradigm can describe. In this chapter, I focus on flattened vision as a central aspect of how drones and their agents perceive the world. In contrast to scopic vision, flattened vision is understood as a mode of perception that makes things even and levels them. Instead of a vertical and hierarchical perspective, flattened vision conveys two-dimensionality and the loss of depth. There is neither a central perspective nor a horizon. What remains in a flattened image are surface structures, abstract patterns, and clusters.

To demonstrate the longstanding importance of flattened vision to military sight, this chapter locates the drone's antecedents in early analogue aerial technology. Instead of situating the drone in the context of contemporary digital surveillance technologies, it traces aerial sensing technology to the eighteenth and nineteenth centuries, exploring the vision field of hot air or gas balloons as technologies of visual flattening. The chapter argues that aerial vision cannot be exclusively understood as a scopic vertical mode of perception based on clear hierarchies, binaries, and oppositions. Rather, aerial vision is complex, incorporating many different perspectives, angles, and modes of seeing, with flattening crucial among them.[6] Flattening indicates a specific mode of executing power through vision. No longer is it the vertical form of power exclusively. Rather, the flattened image executes a de-centralised network or grid of power. The flattened view, thus, still executes power and violence, and can be read as a form of dehumanisation, but does so no longer according to vertical hierarchies. Further, this historical comparison of balloons and drones de-fetishises the narrative about drone technology as the newest, game-changing technology. As the chapter demonstrate, drones, like balloons, have a history of unsteerability, unpredictability, and uncertainty; and comparing these technologies makes this evident.

I undertake the comparative approach as an experimental method that, resisting the narrative of scopic vision as *the* aerial perceptive of drones, helps to construct a new narrative of de-fetishisation. In this context, comparison proposes no causal relationship (balloon as cause for drone), nor does it construct a linear temporal connection between balloons and drones. It is better understood as an archaeological effort to find 'family resemblances', digging up the potential ancestors of today's drone family.

The comparison will be effectuated primarily through an exploration of aesthetic works, that is, literary and artistic imaginings of ballooning and military drones. One certainly could have chosen to investigate historical documents, eyewitness accounts of ballooning, or photographs of the balloon view as more 'empirical sources'. But I have chosen to use aesthetic, poetic, and fictional works as my primary source material, precisely for the faculty of aesthetic discourse to highlight the intricate relation between vision, technology, and power. The artificiality of these aesthetic aerial imaginaries should not be viewed as a drawback. Quite the opposite. Aesthetic imaginations highlight the complexity of aerial vision, richly and unpredictably reflecting on its violence and biopolitical effects.

Balloons and drones

At first glance, hot air or gas balloons and drones seem rather different. Balloons are beautiful colourful airships ascending serenely into the sky. Military drones, on the other hand, are noisy flying robots, or remote killing machines. Drones as combat weapons have been developed and utilised mostly in the twenty-first century, while balloons go back to the eighteenth and nineteenth centuries. In addition to drone's digital imaging, the fact that they are remotely controlled could be viewed as another decisive difference between drones and balloons. Balloons are manned airships, and drones, by their very name – 'unmanned aerial vehicles' (UAVs) – fly alone. However, the first balloons were in fact unmanned, entirely without passengers. Later, to test the possibility of human survival at atmospheric heights, animals (sheep and chickens) were sent into the sky. It was only after animals had returned unharmed that humans took to the air. Many of these early manned balloons did not move completely freely, but were tethered to the ground by a rope.

The development from unmanned to 'animal-ed', and tethered to untethered, manned flight, makes one reflect on the notion of 'unmanned-ness' altogether. Considering 'unmanned-ness' in drones from the history of ballooning raises the question of how 'tethering' might be understood. Moreover, drones are never free to fly and float wherever they want to; they remain controlled by human agents on the ground. These agents are not physically present with the drone in the sky, but they are steering and flying it. Just as some balloons are tethered at the end of rope, the drone can be viewed as an extension of the drone operator's joystick. Drone pilots are always connected to a command centre, in which military personnel examine the drone data and give orders to the pilots. Perhaps, in fact, there is nothing such as unmanned flight. Unmanned flight is our wishful fantasy, since we cannot be responsible for something that acts on its own and is totally free of human control.

But let us look at the beginnings of ballooning. On 5 June, 1783, only a few years before the French Revolution, the ancient human dream of flying came true in France when the Montgolfier brothers released their first hot air balloon into the sky. From that day on, engineers, enthusiasts, entrepreneurs, artists, and writers experimented with, improved, developed, and wrote about balloon flying technology. Félix Nadar was the balloonist popstar of the nineteenth century. His spectacular journeys and failures (such as the crash of his balloon Le Géant), as well as his early attempts to shoot aerial photographs from his balloons, still fascinate us today. Similar to what Caren Kaplan calls the drone-o-rama – the media hype around drone technology – balloons triggered a 'balloonomania'.[7] Aside from dramatic shows, hot air balloons also inspired fashion trends, influencing the design of clothing as well as fine china and porcelain figurines. Apart from featuring importantly in popular entertainment culture, balloons, like drones, with their dual usage in leisure and military contexts, were soon identified as potentially strategic tools in war.

As Joseph Montgolfier noted: 'By making the balloon's bag big enough, it will be possible to introduce an entire army, which, borne by the wind, will enter right over the heads of the English.'[8] From their beginnings, balloons were instrumentalised in military battles for aerial reconnaissance, bombing, and transporting goods. For example, the balloon *L'Entreprenant*, owned by the French army in the battle of Fleurus (26 June 1794), was used to get a better view of the coalition army. Although the French won this battle, potentially also due to the balloon's shock and awe effect, the French military's use of balloons was interrupted when, in 1799, Napoleon disbanded the French Aerostatic Corps. French war balloons were in the air again during the Franco-Prussian War of 1870 and the Siege of Paris. Balloons were also used in the Austrian-Venetian war and during the Civil War. Although these examples give proof of the balloon as a strategic weapon, their use never became widespread. They were simply too unpredictable and too unsteerable, and eventually superseded by zeppelins and aeroplanes. Nevertheless, intellectuals, military men, and engineers created powerful imaginaries of balloon weapon technology during the Napoleonic wars.

Take the image shown in Figure 1.1 about a fantastical invasion plan that would not only bring French troops to Britain via tunnel but also through

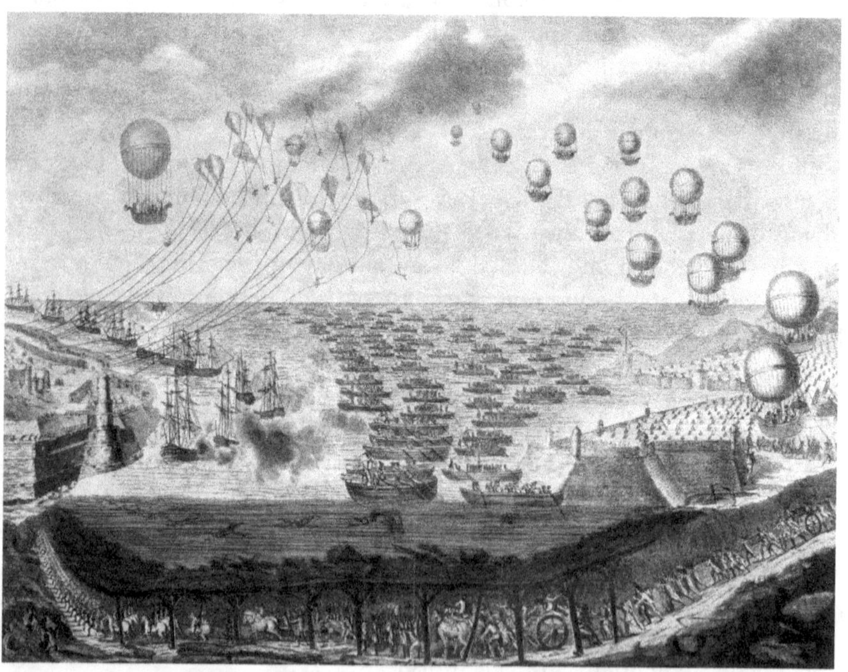

1.1 *Invasion of England*, 1804, French engraving. Imaginary view of Napoleon's invasion of England using ships, balloons and a tunnel under the English Channel.

an armada of aerial balloon warships. These aero-nationalist fantasies certainly express the political tensions of the Napoleonic Wars and embody the desire to conquer the enemy from the air. Balloons are here imagined as a super-weapon that, by delivering a sovereign view of the battlefield, promises victory. Although, in the end, this did not happen for Napoleon, my point is that the balloon's sovereign gaze is, equally, a powerful fantasy. However, aesthetic imaginaries in art and literature of the balloon gaze can demonstrate a very different kind of aerial vision and power relation, which is discussed in the following section.

Flattened vision of balloons

Many late eighteenth- and nineteenth-century literary authors were inspired by balloons. An early German author whose reflections on ballooning were particularly influential was Christoph Martin Wieland. In the journal *Der Teutsche Merkur*, Wieland praised the new flying technology as a product of rational progress, but adopted a sceptical attitude towards its popularisation. He coined the satirical term 'Aeropetomanie' to describe the public's obsession with balloons during his time. Heinrich von Kleist, Arthur Schopenhauer, and Johann Wolfgang von Goethe also wrote diary entries, letters, and essays about ballooning.

Most interesting for a discussion of flattened vision is the work of romantic author Jean Paul in his text *The Diary of the Aeronaut Giannozzo* (1801) [*Des Luftschiffers Giannozzo Seebuch* (1801)], about a balloon journey.[9] This work is the appendix to his novel *Titan* (1800–1803), a 900-page work about the life of the Spanish aristocrat Albano de Cesara. Whereas *Titan* contains some classical elements of the traditional 'Bildungsroman', *The Diary of the Aeronaut* adheres more to Jean Paul's romantic, highly self-reflexive style of writing. *The Diary of the Aeronaut* represents a form of travelogue, with references to actual places (such as small German Dukedoms and cities), historical figures (Frederick II), and historical events. The protagonist Giannozzo is the travelogue's fictive author, while Jean Paul inserts himself as the editorial figure Jean Paul Fr. Richter, commenting on Giannozzo's story from time to time, as well as adding footnotes to the main text. As the protagonist Giannozzo hovers in his balloon over the small dukedoms of Germany, he issues a scathing critique of bourgeois society's narrow-minded view of life, its religious rituals, and its lack of intellectualism. While literary research has often focused on Jean Paul's critique of German bourgeois pre-revolutionary society, I am mostly interested in how *The Diary of the Aeronaut* represents the balloon as a technology of seeing.[10]

In Jean Paul's text, the balloon itself, the so-called envelope, reminds us of an artificial rebuild of a human eye because of its rounded shape. The protagonist notes that the balloon eyeball is covered with a leathery tissue.[11] This tissue is reminiscent of the sclera, the dense skin around the human eye-ball to which are attached the muscles that move the eye. Projected onto the balloon as an artificial eye, these muscles can be represented by the ropes fastened to the balloon's basket. Giannozzo describes the basket as a 'leathery cube, which has windows on all six sides, and also on the floor.'[12] Within the balloon's basket, the windows constitute the multi-faceted lens through with the world can be observed. This lens opens a panoramic view (through the side windows in the balloon's basket) as well as a straight down view (through the window on the floor).

In other words, the balloon reflects the physiological mechanisms of the human eye: the windows as an eye's lens, the basket as the eye's posterior chamber, and the ropes as its optic nerve. Depending on the balloon's position and the surrounding atmospheric conditions, the lens can adjust its visual acuity. Sometimes, the view is crystal clear against the blue sky; at other times, in clouds and fog, visibility is low.[13] Giannozzo, as the balloon's captain, seems to be a part of this balloon eye. The text names him as the black head with green coat.[14] Translating this image into the aesthetics of the artificial balloon eye, this black dot, often described as jumpy and jittery, could itself be a twitching black pupil surrounded by a green iris. The merging of physiological metaphors of sight with the balloon highlights the idea that the balloon embodies a technology of seeing.

Imagining Giannozzo's balloon, one is reminded of Odilon Redon's painting *The Eye Like a Strange Balloon Mounts Towards Infinity* (1882). In Odilon's picture, a balloon is portrayed as one gigantic eye, looking towards the sky. This painting shows the eye dissociated from its physiological situation of seeing and placed into a superhuman context by means of optical technology. Although Redon's eye-balloon is looking upward towards the sky, whereas Jean Paul's balloon-eye is directed downwards, in both cases, the technological construction of the balloon is clearly made into an instrument of seeing.

Jean Paul's balloon-eye machine does not observe the world according to a stable vertical perspective, which in turn could be read as a symbol for social and political superiority. Rather, the balloon-eye perceives the world through flattening. Giannozzo describes the view from the balloon as a 'surface that extended into infinity.'[15] The text notes that Giannozzo 'maps', that is, he measures, and makes cartographic observations.[16] In fact, the topographical flatness of the view from the balloon is beautifully shown in the writings and drawings of Thomas Baldwin's *Airopaidia* (1786). This essay and its coloured illustrations give remarkable insight into early

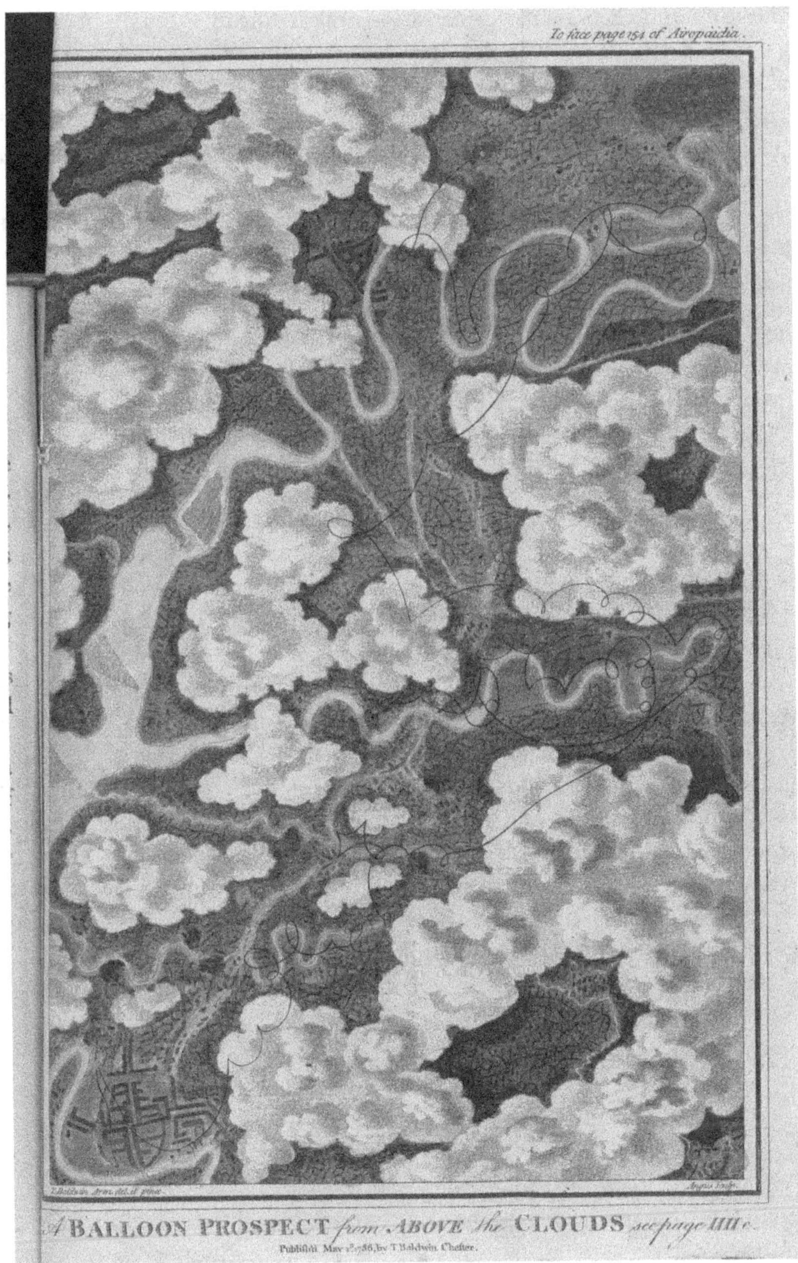

To face page 154 of Airopaidia.
A BALLOON PROSPECT from ABOVE the CLOUDS

1.2 William Angus (1752–1821) after Thomas Baldwin, *A Balloon Prospect from Above the Clouds*, 1786, hand-coloured etching. From *Airopaidia, Containing the Narrative of a Balloon Excursion from Chester, the Eighth of September, 1785*, Chester: J. Fletcher.

ballooning and recount the observations made during one day of ballooning over Chester in the UK. Baldwin describes the balloon view as one that looks down on the earth rather than towards the horizon. The earth seems flattened, and its once striking features, such as hills, cliffs, forests, and villages, form an abstract pattern. The balloon view through the clouds suggests that the ground has lost all spatial depth.

Jean Paul's text, like Baldwin's descriptions and images, suggests the earth as an infinite two-dimensional surface. Note this passage that describes the view from Giannozzo's balloon:

> Four and a half thousand feet deep the wide earth – I thought I floated – ran under me, and its broad plate came towards me, whereupon mountains and woodworks and monasteries [...] were so wildly confused that a reasonable man above had to think that this may only be loose building materials, which you first have to put together into a beautiful park.[17]

The view from the balloon presents the earth as flat. The horizon that ordered the world according to a vanishing point is dissolved, and topographical phenomena are chaotically placed, and seemingly provisional. Giannozzo describes the miniature cities that can be seen from the balloon.[18] Although similar visual experiences could be had from towers, mountains, or through inverted telescopes, the shrinking effect provided by a moving balloon was unprecedented. The minimising vision in Jean Paul's text also has another side: as the miniature landscape takes on new shapes and forms, some objects appear gigantic and out of proportion; their surfaces change and connect in new visual ways. Mountain formations, for example, can look like a giant snake.[19] This shift between micro- and macro perspectives is further enhanced by Giannozzo's telescope, yet another prosthetic that can alter human vision. Thrilled by this new kind of vision, Giannozzo experiences frequent anxiety attacks and episodes of euphoric ecstasy.[20] In sum, the aesthetic representation of Jean Paul's balloon tour highlights flattened vision, which can irritate, and in some way dislocates, the human eye. In a balloon view, the tradition of the central perspective – in which one vanishing point gives the impression of three-dimensional space – is replaced by something else entirely. Rather, through the balloon, the world is expanded into an indefinite and diffused space without clear, fixed boundaries.

What effect does this aerial flattened (non-scopic) perspective have on the subject (the pilot, the human individuals on the ground)? Although Giannozzo is occasionally exuberant about the balloon perspective, his diary of the aerial journey clearly emphasises the destructive side of air travel and its regime of flattened vision. Flattening not only makes individuals on the ground into distorted representations of humankind (Giannozzo ridicules them as 'dwarfs', 'caricatures', and 'travesties'). The flattened view from the balloon also subverts the image of aeronaut as a God-like figure with all-seeing eyes.

The story ends in catastrophe: Giannozzo's balloon is caught between two thunderstorms above the Swiss Alps, and finally crashes into the mountains, causing a terrible inferno. Giannozzo dies not only because his balloon becomes unsteerable, but also because he is gazed upon by two kinds of super-human eyes. In Jean Paul's text, Giannozzo is subject to the deadly and petrifying gaze of a super-human creature, the basilisk.[21] Its deadly gaze is part of the monstrous balloon-eye-machine: 'I opened the air-shafts and buried myself in the steam, in which only the basilisk eye of death blinked.'[22] This mechanical eye annihilates Giannozzo, whose charred corpse is discovered in the mountains. Giannozzo's death by means of the super-human eye symbolises the frailty of an ostensibly sovereign subject. Whereas the balloon view in general is often interpreted as the ascent of bourgeois sovereignty and emancipation, Jean Paul's balloon certainly suggests a critique of such a view.[23] Rather, Giannozzo's blinding and eventual fatal fall from the sky literally dethrones the Enlightenment's autonomous subject. But Jean Paul's depiction of the balloon view does even more than that.

As is well known, Jean Paul, as a romantic author, had a profound interest in images and their representative power.[24] As shown, the balloon's flattening view does not suggest an autonomous seeing subject; rather, the subject is physiologically merged with the balloon to become a conjoined machine of seeing. This balloon-eye-machine no longer sees the world according to realist, symbolic, or iconic aesthetics. Rather, its flattened images – distorted, undecipherable, and abstract – are more or less automatically produced as the uncontrollable balloon hovers above the landscape. I suggest that Jean Paul's balloon eye can also be read as an early representation of the aesthetics of the non-human operative image.

For Sybille Krämer, this aspect of flatness fulfils a criterion of 'operative images'. Such images are no longer three-dimensional but, rather, abstract, topographic, and statistical, connecting non-human systems of knowledge and storage (machines, data processors, scripture).[25] These operative images have a different power relation from panoptic aerial images, which control towards one clear target and are mastered by one subject. Instead, operative images dissolve the boundaries of individuals, subjects, and objects, turning everything into data and information readable by machines; by doing so, they attain 'operative' power. Of course, Jean Paul's text does not emerge from the digital world. However, I argue that his text shows the early entwinements of aerial vision and abstraction, a connection that was later evident in the modernist art of Kazimir Malevich, who, in developing his abstract Suprematist painting style, used varied aerial perspectives.

(For this connection of the aerial view and modernist aesthetics, see Jan Mieszkowski's and Svea Braeunert's chapter in this anthology.) The 'operative' image quality is also, as the following section will show, intrinsic to drone vision.

Drone vision: aerial flattening, the grid, and rasterisation

In the long history of photography and flight, balloons and drones represent the beginning and current point in the development of aerial surveillance technologies. Between these two are many other aerial technologies of seeing, such as zeppelins, aeroplanes, and satellites, which there is not space to discuss here. As mentioned, my rather experimental comparison does not aim to construct a linear narrative. Comparing balloons and drones should, instead, put them into a new constellation, in turn allowing creative insights about remote sensing technology. As the preceding sections have shown, one of these insights is that aerial non-human photography does not first emerge with the twentieth century, but that its imaginaries and practices go way back in history. Further, comparing these balloons and drones also suggests a new narrative about aerial vision: the view from the sky has not always been scopic, panoptic, and transparent, but can also be flattened, oblique, and distorted, as shown in Jean Paul's hyperbolic description of Giannozzo's balloon journey. The complexity of aerial vision is particularly interesting in relation to military drone technology, which is often described as an instrument of surgical warfare. The following discussion demonstrates that contemporary artists who engage with drone technology aim to disrupt and arrest this belief in precision and dismantle it as a myth.

Many contemporary artists who work with drones as an artistic medium, or engage with the topic of military drone strikes in their artworks, are specifically interested in drone vision. James Bridle's work *Dronestagram* (2012–2017), for example, traces drone strikes and their aerial images on an app and social media platform.[26] Omer Fast's short semi-documentary film *5,000 Feet is the Best* (2011), about a drone pilot and his traumata, raises questions about the violence of the aerial view.[27] Below, I discuss the artistic work of Tomas van Houtryve,[28] Trevor Paglen,[29] and elin o'Hara slavick[30] on drones and the aerial, as some of their works exhibit a flatness similar to that of balloon images. The images in Houtryve's video installation *Divided* (2018) are taken by a drone hovering over Baja California, where Mexico and US territory meet, and a steel fence extends the border into the Pacific Ocean. The film begins with a focus on the waves as they crash perpendicularly into the barrier. See this image in Figure 4.2.

The video installation re-enacts the flattened hot air balloon view described in Jean Paul's and Baldwin's work. In the beginning, Houtryve's video shows a fixated bird's eye view of the water. The drone does not move, it hovers above the ocean. There is no central perspective, and the film suggests a topography of abstract material surfaces and clusters. One is no longer sure whether the waves are waves. The white and grey pattern could be an image of a mountain formation shot from a point high in the sky. It could also be, as in Jean Paul's movement between macro- and micro-vison, an enhanced close-up of the surface of an organic structure. Houtryve's installation makes the surface of the distant ground appear close and magnified. Like images made by microscopes, the drone footage highlights texture and materiality.

In the course of Houtryve's film, the still image of the ocean surface eventually becomes a moving one. As in a balloon ride, the landscape glides beneath the aerial eye. A spectator hears only the sound of the waves, and the image stream has an almost hypnotising and mesmerising effect. After a while, the top-down drone camera tilts to capture the shores and mainland. One sees US territory, featuring roads and meadows, and the more inhabited Mexican side, with sports stadium, houses, roads, cars, and trees. Although at the end of the film the perspective is on the horizon, there is still no central focus point. Even when the drone view reaches the horizon line, the horizon seems like an artificial drape as the film whitens and fades out.

How can we interpret this flattened landscape image? On the one hand, the drone's flattening gaze seems to convey an impression of the land's wholeness. Although the waves are divided by a border, they are the same on either side. The drone view fuses together surfaces that have been artificially separated. The drone gaze in *Divided* thus embodies a planetary perspective that suggests the world is one, connected by water, and that the earth belongs to everyone. According to Gayatri Spivak, the term planetary, together with the opposing concepts of the worldly, global, and continental, functions within the ideology of capitalism; each remains imbued with cultural and national essentialism. In contrast, for the 'planetary subjects', alterity is not derivative. In the positioning of human subjects vis-à-vis the planet, the planet erases the conditions of differentiation.[31] In Houtryve's work, the drone hovering over the ocean exudes such a planetary perspective: It highlights the artificiality of political boundaries by flattening them.

However, the utopian imaginary of one-ness in *Divided* is simultaneously destroyed by the border fence. When the drone camera traces the fence (and other structures of ordered space, such as architecture, streets, and buildings), the rationality of border becomes more and more obtrusive. The drone's camera eye organises the earth into a grid – a grid that masters, controls, and rules space.[32]

According to Bernhard Siegert, who has theorised the grid from the perspective of media studies, the aspect of flattening is key to the grid. He sees the grid as a 'cultural technique' that mediates mathematical, geographical, and governmental knowledge and power. The grid 'is an imagining technology that, by means of a given algorithm, enables us to project a three-dimensional world onto a two-dimensional plane.'[33] The grid is a strategy of abstraction, and it can calculate and control individuals in quantitative systems and numbers. Houtryve's film not only shows how the border as a grid controls the public (in this case, immigrants) but also that the drone as technology of seeing operates as a medium of the grid. The drone becomes complicit with the wall, as it divides the people into separate territories. The drone's biopolitical power is no longer scopic and vertical. Rather, it is flattened into a raster image – an aspect that is also decisive in the next example of an artist whose work concerns drone vision.

Trevor Paglen is well-known for his photographs and films about mass surveillance, data mining, and military security technology. For example, his collection and exhibition of official and semi-official military patches worn by American soldiers demonstrate the secret visual codes and clusters of signification within military discourse. He also engaged the topic of military drone operations by making several photographs called *Untitled (Drones)* in 2010. The images show colourful impressions of open sky in which one can only barely make out the almost invisible traces of a reaper drone. Of particular interest is Paglen's film *Drone Vision* (2010), which displays this kind of flattened vision in conjunction with power of the grid. The video exploits a glitch and security flaw in the transfer of images from drones to a US-based pilot via unencrypted satellite uplinks. The source material for this video was intercepted by an amateur hacker from an open channel on a commercial communication satellite over the western hemisphere. The five-minute film mostly shows aerial images from the perspective of the drone, which hovers in the sky, filming mountains, roads, trucks, houses, and clouds.

Paglen's film begins with aerial shots taken by a drone. At first, the images are panoramic, giving views of the sky; first, one sees parts of the aircraft, then the gaze shifts downwards to the ground. Next, the film shows the drone circling around one specific point, then zooming into the landscape (mountains, road with tractor, trees, and cars). All these satellite images exhibit a dimension of flatness; they mainly show land surfaces. There is also no central perspective or vanishing point. The landscape below looks like a map.

These flattened surveillance images do not connect smoothly. They are sometimes disrupted, scattered, or black, or the drone hovers unsteadily.

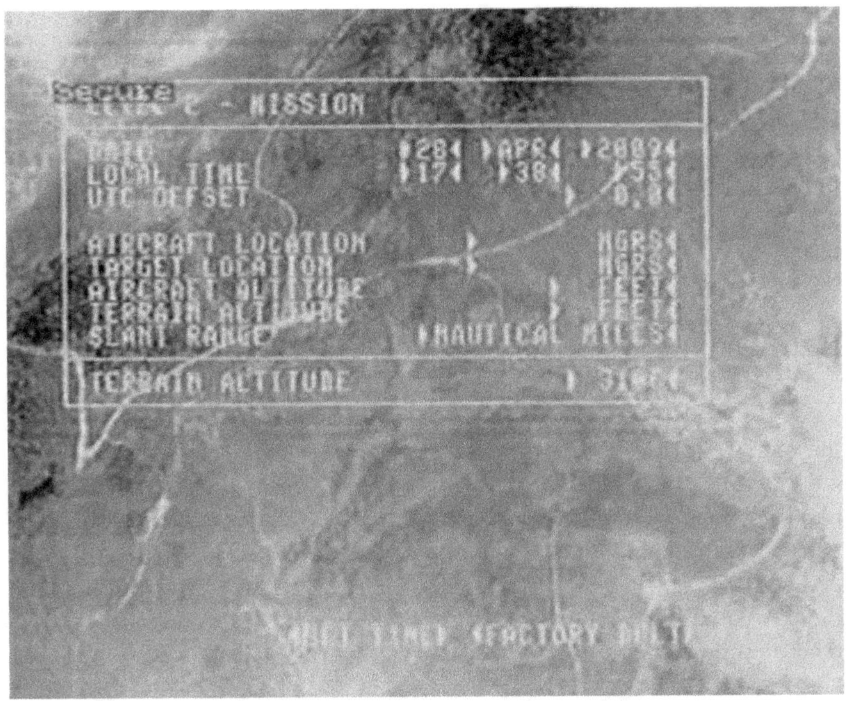

1.3 Trevor Paglen, *Drone Vision* (video still), 2010, archival pigment prints, 16 × 20 inches.

Image quality is rather grainy and often hindered by fog or clouds. Paglen's film certainly does not establish the drone's scopic regime of hypervisibility. Similar to Jean Paul's balloon journey, the art installation temporarily adopts the drone's rhythms of seeing, and the viewer's eye merges with the 'eye' of the drone. In fact, at some moments, the drone seems to be looking under the aeroplane's wings, as if trying to spin around itself. One has the feeling that the drone is not a machine made by humans, but a curious human eye that looks around. This ironic twist hints at the idea that drones are often less precise than assumed, that they also can be disoriented – indeed, that they might have a life of their own. Like Giannozzo's balloon-eye, which goes out of control and crashes, Paglen's drone undermines the idea that drones exercise a reliable and sovereign form of vision.

Furthermore, the flattened images in *Drone Vision* also hint at the grid as a strategy of vision and power. In Paglen's film, the landscape is literally covered with metadata and coordinates, which, in turn, algorithms and data analysts can sort through. At the images' margins can be seen all the technical data about date, location, aircraft, altitude, and mission.

These metadata make this image into a non-human one that speaks more to machines than humans, in the language of the grid. This flattened grid view is non-scopic, but still powerful and effective. Thomas Stubblefield has argued that the drone's visual power has to be understood in de-centred and a-linear modes: 'In articulating hierarchies of repression long binary oppositions, such critiques enact a kind of rhetorical drone hunting, which may not only miss the target, so to speak, but also obscures its dual character.'[34] Paglen's film also dissolves the clear dichotomies between target and observer. The grid dissolves the individual, turning it into dots, patterns, and clusters.

Whereas Paglen's film performs a type of subtle and ironic mimesis towards drones' rasterised vision, elin o'Hara slavick, in her artwork, revolts against the flattened aerial view. Her series of drawings and paintings *Protesting Cartography or Places the United States has Bombed* (1998–2005) is based on flattened aerial images, in particular of places that have been bombed by the US. Using intense colours, her works disrupt the cold, dehumanised, and distanced aesthetics of aerial images.

Whereas o'Hara slavick's paintings and drawings still adhere to a flattened aesthetics, her way of rendering topographical data in ornamental

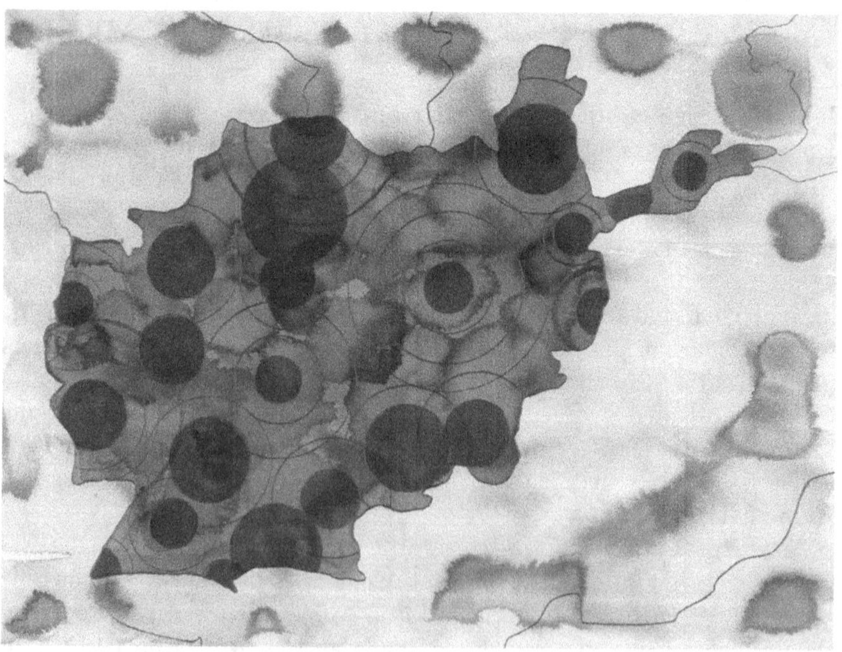

1.4 elin o'Hara slavick, *Afghanistan I, 1979 and Infinite Reach, 1998*, 1999.

lines and beautiful patterns seems to fill these spaces with creativity and imagination. Thereby she does not conceal the violence and trauma that has happened there. Her 'bleeding technique', in which watercolours run down the painting's surfaces, memorises the historical traces of violence. These bleeding flows and colourful patterns arrest the power of the drone.[35]

Conclusion

This chapter has looked at the drone historically and found the balloon to be one of its ancient ancestors. This historisation of the drone, more typological and experimental than previous drone studies, sheds new light on the narratives of drone technology, the aerial perspective, and the relation between power and aerial vision.

Seeing the drone as part of the history of ballooning makes one ponder whether the drone is really the new kid on the block. Being in the same family as the notoriously unstable and unsteerable balloon, the myth of the drone's precision gets tarnished. Digging out balloon history is a gesture against the techno-optimistic narrative that aims to see the drone as a game-changing, unprecedented, and error-free super weapon. It is inherently disposed to uncertainty and fragility.

Bearing a family resemblance to the balloon, the drone shares its flattened vision. Viewing these temporally distant technologies of seeing together rewrites the modern narrative of aerial vision as always scopic, panoptic, and all-seeing. It reveals the aerial as newly complex, displaying forms of vision that are more prone to abstraction, gaps, surfaces, and networks. Thus, an examination of the drone in conjunction with the balloon enacts a critique of ocularcentrism of the kind Donna Haraway has called for. In her feminist critique of science, vision, and technology, Haraway attacks the idea of the eye as a human organ that, together with its technical enhancements, embodies truth, clarity, precision, and control within a rationalist Enlightenment tradition. She puts the relation between vision and technology in this way: 'Vision in this technological feast becomes unregulated gluttony; all seems not just mythically about the god-trick of seeing everything from nowhere, but to have put the myth into ordinary practice. And like the god-trick, this eye fucks the world to make techno-monsters.'[36] Conducting an archaeology of the balloon as the early drone constitutes an intervention in the feast of ocular power and its technologies of seeing.

Flattened vision nevertheless executes violence and power. But it is no longer a scopic form of power based on clear oppositions, binaries, and dichotomies. Rather, flattened vision makes the world operable and connectable to machinic systems, and it can isolate, discretise, and partialise information. This form of pictorial flattening can also be read in conjunction with the process of ethical flattening in modern warfare. The balloon and the drone views illustrate a process of distancing the human within modern warfare by flattening the individual into abstraction, statistics, and clusters. Of course, it is problematic to see distance as the moral gauge for warfare. Remote warfare is not necessarily less ethical than an eye-to-eye confrontation, but certainly the asymmetrical relation between seeing and being seen (visibility and invisibility) raises questions of power and domination. Balloon warfare is a productive starting point to understand the sensing modes of drones' network-centric warfare, and the operative images they produce.

I have illuminated these non-scopic modes of vision by analysing aesthetic imaginaries of aerial vision. Instead of seeing this as a methodological weakness, I maintain that it is precisely the aesthetic realm that has the power to highlight this alliance of flattened vision and power. Literary and visual works of art, spanning from the nineteenth century to the present, are like seismographs, registering this alliance, and its effects on the individual and its social and political environment. In this way, these aesthetic balloon and drone imaginaries can also be seen metaphorically as airships trying to sail against the dominant narrative of drone technology as one that makes us more safe and secure.

Notes

1 Quoted after D. Gregory, 'From a view to a kill: Drones and late modern war', *Theory, Culture & Society*, 28:7–8 (2011): 188–215, 192.
2 C. Metz, *Film Language: A Semiotics of the Cinema* (Chicago: Chicago University Press, 1991); M. Jay, 'Cultural relativism and the visual turn', *Journal of Visual Culture*, 1:3 (2002): 267–278.
3 I owe this insight to A. Bousquet, *The Eye of War: Military Perception from the Telescope to the Drone* (Minneapolis: The University of Minnesota Press, 2018), 10.
4 Gregory, 'From a view to a kill', 193.
5 For the connection of the aerial view and the scopic regime of verticality, see P. Adey, M. Whitehead, and A. J. Williams, 'Introduction: Air-target distance, reach and the politics of verticality', *Theory, Culture & Society*, 28:7–8 (2011): 173–187. For the connection between drone gaze and verticality, see L. Parks, 'Vertical mediation and the U.S. drone war in the Horn of Africa', in L. Parks

and C. Kaplan (eds), *Life in the Age of Drone Warfare* (Durham, NC: Duke University Press, 2017), 134–158; G. Chamayou, *A Theory of the Drone* (New York: The New Press, 2015); B. Noys, 'Drone metaphysics', *Culture Machine*, 16 (2015): 1–15.

6 I draw here on Caren Kaplan's critique of the scopic paradigm in narratives of aerial vision and her attempts to broaden the scope for understanding the view from above also in ways other than as a panoptic, all-seeing, totalised form of perception. In particular, her work on balloons has been important. However, whereas she mostly traces the balloon view in historical sources, my approach focuses mostly on the poetic, aesthetic, and artistic imaginaries of the balloon. See: C. Kaplan, *Aerial Aftermaths: Wartime from Above* (Durham, NC: Duke University Press, 2018).

7 C. Kaplan, 'Drone-o-rama: Troubling the temporal and spatial logics of distance warfare', in L. Parks and C. Kaplan (eds), *Life in the Age of Drone Warfare* (Durham, NC: Duke University Press, 2017), 161–177.

8 Quoted after: J. Christopher, *Balloons at War: Gasbags, Flying Bombs, and Cold War Secrets* (Stroud: Tempus, 2004), 10.

9 Jean Paul, 'Des Luftschiffers Giannozzo Seebuch', in Norbert Miller (ed.), *Jean Paul: Sämtliche Werke*, Vol. 3 (Darmstadt: Wissenschaftliche Buchgesellschaft, 2000), 925–1010. All translations from the German to English are mine. Subsequent references *The Diary of the Aeronaut*.

10 See F. Welle, *Der irdische Blick durch das Fernrohr: Literarische Wahrnehmungsexperimente vom 17. bis zum 20. Jahrhundert* (Würzburg: Königshausen und Neumann, 2009), 123–144.

11 In German: 'mit feinem, aber unbekannten Leder mit Seide überzogen', Jean Paul, *The Diary of the Aeronaut*, 928.

12 In German: 'Lederwürfel, der auf allen sechs Seiten Fenster hat, auch auf dem Fußboden', Jean Paul, *The Diary of the Aeronaut*, 928.

13 In German: 'Ich trat jetzt trübe und wild auf den Brocken hinaus', Jean Paul, *The Diary of the Aeronaut*, 965.

14 In German: 'Schwarzkopf in grünem Mantel', Jean Paul, *The Diary of the Aeronaut*, 928.

15 In German: 'Fläche, die ins Unendliche hinausfloß', Jean Paul, *The Diary of the Aeronaut*, 959.

16 In German: 'mappiert', Jean Paul, *The Diary of the Aeronaut*, 959.

17 In German: 'Vierhalbtausend Fuß tief rannte die weite Erde – ich glaubte festzuschweben – unter mir dahin, und ihr breiter Teller lief mir entgegen, worauf sich Berge und Holzungen und Klöster […] so wild und eng durcheinanderwarfen, dass ein vernünftiger Mann oben denken musste, das seien nur umhergerollte Baumaterialien, die man erst zu einem schönen Park auseinanderziehe', Jean Paul, *The Diary of the Aeronaut*, 959.

18 In German: 'Zwergenstädte', Jean Paul, *The Diary of the Aeronaut*, 927.

19 In German: 'Riesenschlange', Jean Paul, *The Diary of the Aeronaut*, 927.

20 See C. Kaplan on emotions and balloons, and the non-military aspect of balloons. C. Kaplan, 'The balloon prospect: Aerostatic observation and the emergence of

militarized aeromobility', in P. Adey, M. Whitehead, and A. J. Williams (eds), *From Above: War, Violence, and Verticality* (New York: Oxford University Press, 2014), 19–40.

21 In German: 'Basilkenauge des Todes', Jean Paul, *The Diary of the Aeronaut*, 1007.

22 In German: 'Ich riss die Lufthähne auf und vergrub mich in den Dampf, worin nur das Basilkenauge des Todes seine heissen Silberblicke auf und zutat', Jean Paul, *The Diary of the Aeronaut*, 1007.

23 J. Link, 'Literaturanalyse als Interdiskursanalyse: Am Beispiel des Ursprungs literarischer Symbolik in der Kollektivsymbolik', in H. Müller und G. von Graevenitz (eds), *Diskurstheorien und Literaturwissenschaft* (Frankfurt a. M.: Suhrkamp, 1988), 284–307.

24 M. Schmitz-Emans and W. Benda (eds), *Jean Paul und die Bilder: Bildkünstlerische Auseinandersetzungen mit seinem Werk: 1783–2013* (Würzburg: Königshausen & Neumann, 2013).

25 S. Krämer, 'Operative Bildlichkeit. Von der Grammatologie zu einer Diagrammatologie? Reflexionen über erkennenden Sehen', in M. Hessler and D. Mersch (eds), *Logik des Bildlichen: Zur Kritik der ikonischen Vernunft* (Bielefeld: Transcript, 2009), 94–122.

26 J. Bridle, 'Dronestagram' (Instagram, Twitter, Tumblr, 2012–2017), http://dronestagram.tumblr.com/; see also: https://jamesbridle.com/works/dronestagram (accessed 28 January, 2021).

27 O. Fast (dir), *5,000 Feet is the Best* (Denmark: Commonwealth Projects, 2011), 30 min.

28 T. van Houtryve (dir), 'Divided', 2018, single-channel video installation, https://tomasvh.com/works/divided/ (accessed 28 January, 2021).

29 T. Paglen, *Untitled (Drones)*, 2010, http://www.paglen.com/?l=work&s=drones&i=4 (accessed 28 January, 2021).

30 e. o'Hara slavick, *Protesting Cartography or Places the United States has Bombed* (1998–2005).

31 G. C. Spivak, 'Planetarity', in G. C. Spivak, *Death of a Discipline* (New York: Columbia University Press, 2003), 71–102.

32 B. Siegert, '(Not) in place: The grid, or, the cultural techniques of ruling spaces', in *Cultural Techniques: Grids, Filters, Doors, and Other Articulations of the Real* (New York: Fordham University Press, 2015), 97–120.

33 Siegert, '(Not) in place', 98.

34 T. Stubblefield, 'In pursuit of other networks', in C. Kaplan and L. Parks (eds), *Living in the Age of Drone Warfare* (Durham, NC: Duke University Press, 2018), 196.

35 I owe this reference to elin o'Hara's slavick's art to R. K. Kapadia, *Insurgent Aesthetics: Security and the Queer Life of the Forever War* (Durham, NC: Duke University Press, 2019), 95–101.

36 D. Haraway, 'Situated knowledges: The science question in feminism and the privilege of partial perspective', *Feminist Studies*, 14:3 (1988): 575–599, 8.

Bibliography

Adey, P., M. Whitehead, and A. J. Williams. 'Introduction: Air-target distance, reach and the politics of verticality'. *Theory, Culture & Society*, 28:7–8 (2011): 173–187.

Bousquet, A. *The Eye of War: Military Perception from the Telescope to the Drone*. Minneapolis: The University of Minnesota Press, 2018.

Bridle, J. 'Dronestagram'. Instagram, Twitter, Tumblr, 2012–2017. http://dronestagram.tumblr.com/; see also: https://jamesbridle.com/works/dronestagram (accessed 28 January, 2021).

Chamayou, G. *A Theory of the Drone*. New York: The New Press, 2015.

Christopher, J. *Balloons at War: Gasbags, Flying Bombs, and Cold War Secrets*. Stroud: Tempus, 2004.

Fast, O. dir. *5,000 Feet is the Best*. Denmark: Commonwealth Projects, 2011 (30 min.).

Gregory, D. 'From a view to a kill: Drones and late modern war'. *Theory, Culture & Society*, 28:7–8 (2014): 188–215.

Haraway, D. 'Situated knowledges: The science question in feminism and the privilege of partial perspective'. *Feminist Studies*, 14:3 (1988): 575–599.

Houtryve, T.v. dir. 'Divided'. Single-channel video installation. 2018. https://tomasvh.com/works/divided/ (accessed 28 January, 2021).

Jay, M. 'Cultural relativism and the visual turn'. *Journal of Visual Culture*, 1:3 (2002): 267–278.

Kapadia, R. K. *Insurgent Aesthetics: Security and the Queer Life of the Forever War*. Durham, NC: Duke University Press, 2019.

Kaplan, C. 'The balloon prospect: Aerostatic observation and the emergence of militarized aeromobility'. In P. Adey, M. Whitehead, and A. J. Williams (eds), *From Above: War, Violence, and Verticality*, 19–40. New York: Oxford University Press, 2014.

— 'Drone-o-rama: Troubling the temporal and spatial logics of distance warfare'. In L. Parks and C. Kaplan (eds), *Life in the Age of Drone Warfare*, 161–177. Durham, NC: Duke University Press, 2017.

— C. *Aerial Aftermaths: Wartime from Above*. Durham, NC: Duke University Press, 2018.

Krämer, S. 'Operative Bildlichkeit. Von der Grammatologie zu einer Diagrammatologie? Reflexionen über erkennenden Sehen'. In M. Hessler and D. Mersch (eds), *Logik des Bildlichen: Zur Kritik der ikonischen Vernunft*, 94–122. Bielefeld: Transcript, 2009.

Link, J. 'Literaturanalyse als Interdiskursanalyse: Am Beispiel des Ursprungs literarischer Symbolik in der Kollektivsymbolik'. In H. Müller and G. von Graevenitz (eds), *Diskurstheorien und Literaturwissenschaft*, 284–307. Frankfurt a. M.: Suhrkamp, 1988.

Metz, C. *Film Language: A Semiotics of the Cinema*. Chicago: Chicago University Press, 1991.

Noys, B. 'Drone metaphysics'. *Culture Machine* 16 (2015): 1–15.

Paglen, T. *Untitled (Drones)*. 2010. http://www.paglen.com/?l=work&s=drones&i=4 (accessed 28 January, 2021).

Parks, L. 'Vertical mediation and the U.S. drone war in the Horn of Africa'. In

L. Parks and C. Kaplan (eds), *Life in the Age of Drone Warfare*, 134–158. Durham, NC: Duke University Press, 2017.

Paul, Jean. 'Des Luftschiffers Giannozzo Seebuch'. In Norbert Miller (ed.), *Jean Paul: Sämtliche Werke*, 925–1010. Vol. 3. Darmstadt: Wissenschaftliche Buchgesellschaft, 2000.

Schmitz-Emans, M. and W. Benda (eds), *Jean Paul und die Bilder: Bildkünstlerisch Auseinandersetzungen mit seinem Werk: 1783–2013*. Würzburg: Königshausen & Neumann, 2013.

Siegert, B. '(Not) in place: The grid, or, the cultural techniques of ruling spaces'. In *Cultural Techniques: Grids, Filters, Doors, and Other Articulations of the Real*, 97–120. New York: Fordham University Press, 2015.

slavick, e. o'Hara. *Protesting Cartography or Places the United States has Bombed* (1998–2005).

Spivak, G. C. 'Planetarity'. In G. C. Spivak, *Death of a Discipline*, 71–102. New York: Columbia University Press, 2003.

Stubblefield, T. 'In pursuit of other networks'. In C. Kaplan and L. Parks (eds), *Living in the Age of Drone Warfare*, 195–219. Durham, NC: Duke University Press, 2018.

Welle, F. *Der irdische Blick durch das Fernrohr: Literarische Wahrnehmungsexperimente vom 17. bis zum 20. Jahrhundert*. Würzburg: Königshausen und Neumann, 2009.

2

Signature strikes, drone art and world-making

Thomas Stubblefield

On 17 March, 2011, a US drone fired four Hellfire missiles into a public bus depot in Datta Khel, a town in the Waziristan border region of Pakistan. The attack was not prompted by the presence of a suspected terrorist or other member of the kill list. In fact, the identities of the subjects on the ground were unknown to the drone pilots, image analysts and sensor operators of the kill chain that day. Rather, the incident was an example of a signature strike in which targets are identified according to a disposition matrix of behaviours, locations and personal relationships. The general public is perhaps most familiar with this logic via the practice of the so-called double tap in which those who come to the aid of a victim of a drone attack or attend the funeral of a suspected terrorist are themselves targeted by virtue of their presumed connection to the deceased or injured. However, intelligence analysts confirm that signature strikes are more often prompted by relatively inane scenarios such as a typically busy bridge which suddenly empties, a border crossing conducted at night, or possession of a mobile phone that was used to contact a person of interest.[1]

In the case of Datta Khel, the triggering event was a meeting of tribal elders, which was held to solve a local dispute over a chromite mine. Despite informing the Pakistani army of the meeting in advance the event was read as a tactical formation by the US military. As a result, forty-four people died, all of whom are believed to be innocent non-combatants. While the government continues to frame such events as targeted killings, sources report that the majority of drone attacks conducted by the US military are now based on these patterns of life calculations rather than the identification of specific targets.[2]

Officially, such strategies are explained as the necessary correlate to terrorist networks themselves, which tend to be non-hierarchical, loosely defined and dynamic in nature.[3] In response to these ad hoc formations, it would seem only logical that the operations of the Department of Homeland Security prioritise 'the value of the network structure rather than the characteristics of the individual.'[4] However, such assessments not only underestimate the consequences of this intervention, but also mislead the public as to the true nature of these operations. Drone power is not simply a matter of utilising individual actors or events to get at the root causes of terrorism, to work backwards from the singular agent toward the larger social field which produces this violence. Nor can its interventions be understood solely as an acceleration of the familiar operation in which intelligence gathered from a generalised field is used to locate and neutralise a specific actor. Rather, drones seek to actively disconnect identity, places and events from their carriers so as to integrate the ground from which identities are constructed into its operations. This possibility is contingent upon the real time circulation of diagrammatic signs (data from sensors, algorithms and other inorganic assemblages) and more familiar modes of representation (images, verbal and textual descriptions), which together provide the conditions by which targets come into being as such.

As drones migrate from spaces of conflict to the gallery, screen or stage, these relations resurface within everyday media. In the process, these cultural artifacts come to disclose the way in which the sphere of actions that comprise drone power shifts from the symbolic to the ontological so that its intervention becomes primarily one of world-making rather than meaning-making. Most immediately, the former acknowledges the drone's control over an expansive milieu, which extends beyond individual subjects to include land features, material bodies and the host of pre-personal events that are translated into familiar narratives of the global counter-insurgency. However, the term also bears witness to both the exhaustive scale and productive nature of the kill chain's relationship to those external conditions, relations of causality and symbolic systems which necessitate an attack. Collectively, these entanglements push drone power beyond the historical practices of targeting toward a more constructivist relationship to the world it encounters.

This chapter will expand upon these relations of drone power via the introduction of the concepts of tactical animism and simple triggers before turning to readings of Trevor Paglen's appropriated drone video piece entitled *Drone Vision* (2010) and Noor Behram's photographic exhibition *Gaming in Waziristan* (2007–2011). As these works seek to leverage what Bruno Latour refers to as the 'reversibility of foldings' that inhabit the martial networks of drone power, they reveal not only the inner-workings of this unique mode of power, but also the underlying conditions of communities that live underneath drones.[5] Disclosing the specifics of this entanglement renders the extraordinary violence of these systems visible and in so doing begins the process of undermining the relations of asymmetry upon which their operation relies.

Simple triggers and tactical animism

While the dystopian prospect of autonomous killer robots figures prominently in the collective anxiety regarding drones, the dangers of this technology might just as easily be described according to the exact opposite scenario, that is, the all too human nature of drones. In this regard, distinguishing the automated processes of targeting that occur via the martial networks of drone warfare from what is typically considered to be the more thoughtful human modes of sighting is perhaps not as easy as we might like it to be. Not only is the latter always already prosthetic and therefore unisolatable, but so too is the predictive aspect of human vision structurally related to the processes by which the kill chain translates perceptions into force.

Consider Henry James' discussion of identifying and striking targets in his 1890 *Principles of Psychology*:

> A sportsman, while shooting woodcock in cover, sees a bird with the size and color of a woodcock [...] but through the foliage, not having time to see more than that it is a bird of such a size and color, he immediately supplies by inference the other qualities of a woodcock, and is afterwards disgusted to find that he has shot a thrush.[6]

Curiously, the passage omits the firing of the gun as well as the deliberation of the subject from this scenario, shifting instead directly from the misrecognition of the hunter to the corpse of the dead bird. This ellipsis imbues the causality with a productive ambiguity. While one might reasonably assume that the preposition applies to the firing of the gun, semantically speaking, it references the misrecognition of the hunter. As a result, the visual inference of the hunter becomes intertwined with and indistinguishable from the action of the gun. Seeing and striking quite literally coalesce into a single cathartic expression, disclosing the possibility that it is a certain mode of visual apprehension as much as the rifle that has killed this creature.

Only a few years later, Henri Bergson would formalise this relation, arguing in *Matter and Memory* that the perception of objects is largely determined by an impending action.[7] As the eye impregnates the present with this virtual future, a world is brought into being around a latent motor event. We see, says Bergson, in order to act and in so doing configure a world around this impending action. Critical to this model is the fact that the perceiving subject is not the origin of this world. Rather, it is the entanglement of this centre of indetermination with the visual field and its array extended objects that bring into being new worlds. In navigating this field, the subject essentially subtracts from the object those qualities that conform to its intended use ('the size and color of a woodcock' in the case of

James' hunter) and reciprocally fails to apprehend the latent or unrealised possibilities that are irrelevant to this instrumental disposition (those qualities that would identify the bird as a thrush rather than a woodcock). In the instance of automatic recognition and habitual responses, the past is no longer presented to consciousness, despite its having partially structured the action. Instead, the world is experienced as a kind of pure futural medium in which seeing collapses into action.

It is this interpenetration that the inorganic agencies of drone violence seek to reproduce. In fact, one might even say that the function of the kill chain is to escalate the conflation of seeing and striking that plagues James' hunter. This prospect would seem to fly in the face of the drone programme's obsessive intelligence gathering. It is estimated that the average drone collects roughly 20,000 hours of footage each month. The Autonomous Real-Time Ground Ubiquitous Surveillance, or the A.R.G.U.S system, which is featured on select Reaper drones, is capable of capturing eight years' worth of video in one day.[8] In light of the extraordinary amount of information collected by martial networks, one must wonder how it is that the simple possession of a SIM card or travelling in a group at night can transform a subject into a viable target? Would not, in other words, this extensive archive serve precisely to safeguard against such simplistic, kneejerk reactions? The sheer frequency of attacks like the one in Datta Khel suggests that signature strikes not only reject such a logic, but in fact operate upon a reversal of its basic premise. In the case of drone power, the intelligence collected by these networks is directly rather than inversely proportional to the deployment of nonspecific violence. It is, in fact, precisely the contradiction between the insatiable drive to accumulate information and the nonspecific nature of drone violence that allows the signature strike to duplicate these relations of targeting by inorganic means. Put simply, the more drones know, the less beholden they are to a specific, identifiable target. This counterintuitive relation is at the centre of the logic of simple triggers, which appropriates the Bergsonian action-image in order to present a world in which the strike is, in effect, always already present.

This logic of simple triggers is dramatised by the events of 21 February, 2010 when a Predator drone was called in to track three unauthorised vehicles travelling down a dirt road in Khud in the Oruzgan province of Afghanistan. After reviewing video of the passengers, the image analysts identified cylindrical objects that were quickly recast as rifles. One analyst noted cold spots on the subjects' chests and soon became convinced they were concealed firearms. Before long, the group's movements began to appear as tactical manoeuvres. Derek Gregory summarises the systematic translations that the kill chain began to manifest: 'Two SUVs and a pick-up truck became a 'convoy', cylindrical objects 'rifles', adolescents 'military-aged males' and praying a Taliban signifier.'[9] These calculations culminated in an attack on the group of nearly two dozen individuals who, it was immediately discovered, were 'shopkeepers going for supplies, students returning to school, people seeking medical treatment and families with children off to visit relatives.'[10] As this translation of objects and events into strikes relies upon an automation of the symbolic realm, the technological might of the network is disproportionately steered toward the field of virtuality (the building and commandeering of conditions through reconnaissance) relative to the processes of actualisation (the validation and implementation of the strike). This creates a strategic discrepancy between the profusion of data that is mobilised around the attack and the simplified relations of causality which structure the experience of the operators and analysts.

This bottlenecking effect transforms a vast and illegible archive into a coherent operational environment by compressing contingency into simplified 'if [...] then' formations. While the strike itself is the most visible effect of these relations, this process begins at primary computational level. It originates in the ongoing atomisation of data that occurs at the hands of queries and/or metadata creation and is reiterated by an internal movement by which assets are rendered true via the corroboration of new data and/or readers. Commenting upon the Afghan War Diary, a collection of nearly 100,000 classified documents relating to the Afghan War that was released by Wikileaks in July 2010, Graham Harwood describes this evolution:

> A low-ranking larynx fixed by GPS markers that connect by radio wave. The report cascades up a command hierarchy until the SigAct ['Significant Activity'] is [authenticated as] true. Then de-constructed into data-atoms, logical machines compress the contingency of the moment as another higher-ranking larynx calls across another radio wave.[11]

After unearthing a command line MySQL search for smile, Harwood speculates as to how this fragment may have functioned within the kill chain: 'How many children smile with open arms when a solider enters a village can be correlated with the key hostile or friendly at a particular grid reference. Does such calculation lead to a drone strike or a gift of chewing gum or chocolate?'[12]

The crude determinism of simple triggers is made possible by a complementary logic of tactical animism in which the martial network's automation of the symbolic field produces realities that read as the self-revelation of the objects, events and agencies it encounters. In this arrangement, smiles, group formations and cylindrical objects serve not so much as the subject of the drone's eye, but rather as the origin of worlds organised around an impending action. This process relies upon a kind of perverse object-oriented ontology, which prompts the material realm to strategically jettison its passive status in order to materialise the strike as latent presence. Jordan Crandall describes this relation in the following terms:

> As intelligence migrates into unlikely, shared sources, even those spatial and atmospheric, and agency is understood to be distributed and embodied in all manner of organic and inorganic actors, a concept of skill emerges whose source is in negotiation rather than domination: an alliance with material actors rather than an assertion of command over them. Here an actor works with a material rather than against it, cultivating an existing, emergent meaning rather than externally imposing one – a knowingness that is not simply categorical but affective and rhythmic. It transforms objects into situations, their contours not determined in advance but arising within the terms of the encounter.[13]

The mobilisation of data that makes the signature strike possible disconnects intelligence from its humanist base so that rather than offering definitive interpretations of observable phenomena, it prompts the material world to disclose a plurality of discrete realities, which drones and their operators process as action-images. In this way, martial networks detach drone vision from both the realm of representation and the founding questions of surveillance: who is this?; what are they doing? While stopping short of automating the attack itself, these networks nonetheless utilise these dynamics to ensure that the reality in which operators engage their subjects is built around a specific action-image. The strike then becomes a simple matter of acting on the triggers that the network has deposited within the sphere of objects, events and places. Faced with the world's autogenic presentation of itself as a target, the delivery of a Hellfire missile appears as a given, a means of actualising a world which already presents itself as true.

By integrating these complementary logics of simple triggers and tactical animism into its mode of presentation, drone art divulges a pervasive 'hunger', which both structures the interfaces of drone operation and catalyses the enfolded agencies that underlie its power. Exemplary of this dynamic is Trevor Paglen's short video *Drone Vision*, which mobilises the visual iconography of automated war in order to present a mute and expectant world that can only be given meaning by way of the strike.

Post-automation and the hunger of drones

In the grainy videos of automated war that have entered the public sphere in the last several decades, the missile acts as a particularly important narrative device. Like the internal spectator of painting or the voice-over in film, it promises to lead the eye to a point of interest within the otherwise non-differentiated spaces of an elsewhere war, to assemble ungrounded images into a discernible world. This function is so well-established that when the appropriated drone footage of Trevor Paglen's *Drone Vision* conjures this familiar visual language with staticky black-and-white images and ominous crosshairs, its seemingly banal content of empty landscapes and open skies is immediately overpowered by the sense of an impending strike. In fact, the interchangeable cloudscapes and nonspecific desert topographies that populate this appropriated drone footage seem to arrange themselves into a familiar non-place which awaits the arrival of a missile in order to become fully legible as place. The affective presence this latent violence produces cannot be described in terms of simple expectation; nor can the function of this impending attack be adequately conveyed in narratives terms, that is, as a structuring absence. Not only is the Hellfire missile the sole agent capable of bestowing meaning to the metadata that accumulates at the margins of the image, but so is it the only way to bring this image into focus so to speak. While it is commonplace to speak of events needing images in order to come into being, here it is the reverse – the image needs the event if it is to lay claim to a functioning diegesis.

And yet, despite the unsettling sense of anticipation that builds with each replay of this extended video loop, the attack never happens in this video. Targets do not materialise. Narratives do not emerge. Having been disconnected from the networked relations of the kill chain by the artist's act of appropriation (the footage was originally secured by an amateur hacker), the unfulfilled desires of the drone are left to echo and intensify within the frame as an insatiable lack. The experience this creates for the viewer is not unlike the artist Graham Harwood's own encounter with the decontextualised data of the *Afghan War Diaries*:

> You soon find yourself becoming hungry for a device that will sort, join, and create new views out of the 91,000 comma-separated lines. It's as if the image of the parent machine emerges from the potential of the information in front of you. The text blobs scream out to be hung on indexes, laid out on the latitude and longitude of maps, and ordered across the epochs of time.[14]

By removing the unmanned aerial vehicle (UAV) from its native environment of the network, Paglen provokes the drone's eye to divulge a similar 'hunger'. Wandering through environments without an explicit focus or destination, this desiring gaze is oddly subservient to the world it encounters. It marks a specific type of attentiveness, a readiness to translate the generative flow of signifiers which emanate from the world below into violence. It is this 'desire without an object' which penetrates the picturesque clouds and empty landscapes of this footage and which manifests as anticipatory anxiety in the bodies these images leave unrepresented.[15] The act of appropriation allows the work to visualise and reproduce these relations within the confines of the screen, duplicating the powers of the kill chain without explicit condemnation.

The desire that *Drone Vision* discloses is driven by a regime of temporal condensations that operates across both technological and historical registers. As its simulations of the future are fleeting and fluid, made possible by the momentary alignment of real-time data, drone operation fuels a specific mode of urgency that Samuel Weber argues is represented in popular discourse by the phrase 'target of opportunity.'[16] This term was used in the media to describe the alleged hiding place of Saddam Hussein and quickly became representative of a larger logic of the War on Terror. As Weber describes, while the enemy had to be 'identified and localised, named and depicted' in familiar fashion, what is new in the post 9/11 context is the 'mobility, indeterminate structure, and unpredictability of the spatio-temporal medium in which targets had to be sited.'[17] The very singularity of phenomena becomes intertwined with what Weber describes as 'the generality of an established order, scheme, organisation or plan, in respect to which the event defines itself as exceptional [Significant Acts] or extraordinary.'[18] Clearly, responsiveness has always been rewarded in warfare. However, in the case of the signature strike it is not so much that a given event presents an opportunity, but rather that the opportunity is the genesis of the event itself. As a result, the opportunity to strike is incessant, even eternal as each moment contains the possibility of providing the conditions that necessitate a strike. This unique mode of urgency unifies the technical platforms of the kill chain, which in turn collectively produces a pervasive and insistent pull from without.

The capacity of modern drones to satiate this hunger relies upon the elimination of the interval between seeing and striking, a possibility that was gradually realised in response to a series of incidents that took place during the hunt for Osama Bin Laden at the end of the twentieth century. In 1998, then President Clinton ordered a cruise missile attack on a compound in which Bin Laden was residing. In the time between the launch of cruise missiles and the striking of a target (generally, three to seven hours at the time), Bin Laden was tipped off and escaped the compound before the missiles struck.[19] Two years later, a drone flying over an Al Qaeda training camp spotted a man that closely resembled the Taliban leader. Fearing collateral damage, Clinton famously refused to issue the order to strike due to the presence of a swing set on the video feed. In order to create greater precision in targeting and eliminate the delay that had derailed earlier operations, a prototype for the Predator drone was unveiled on 16 February, 2001.[20] For the first time, the surveillance apparatus was merged with the weapon delivery system, materialising a simultaneity of seeing and striking that would structure the modern kill chain.

As Paglen's piece visualises the way in which these historical and technological relations manifest as inorganic desire of contemporary martial networks, the cathartic images of the Gulf War missile camera become important interlocutors for the work. Despite plummeting viewers toward unsuspecting targets with a nihilistic pleasure, the bomb's eye view of these familiar videos nonetheless retained a definitive and active subject position throughout its morbid trajectory. As a result, the nose cone camera issued a paradoxical mode of interpolation which organised the world even as it destroyed it. In comparison, Paglen's work dramatises the ways in which the drone relinquishes this embodiment in favour of an externalised gaze in which the expectation of violence emanates from the material world itself as depersonalised percepts and affects. By prompting viewers to actualise the virtual presences embedded in these images of landscapes and skies at an imaginary level, the work reproduces both the relations of tactical animism that fuel the kill chain's relations of force and the enfolding of human agency that makes this violence possible.

The world as weapon: activated (art) objects

Since 2007, photojournalist Noor Behram has been photographing the devastation of drone attacks in the border region of Pakistan. Exhibited at Beaconsfield Gallery in London under the title *Gaming in Waziristan* the images present the collapsed buildings, charred public spaces and burned out craters left by drone strikes. Alongside these vacant sites, the series also contains horrific images of the dead and severely injured, many of them children. Despite the affective intensity of these images of the deceased and the physical devastation caused by drones, perhaps the most intriguing of the series are the recurring scenes of fathers, husbands and sometimes even children arranged before the camera, holding pieces of twisted metal, broken stone and other debris in front of its lens for inspection. It doesn't take long to realise that in many cases these objects are shards of missiles and other components of a distant killing machine which has caused the scenes of devastation featured in the remaining images of the series.

On the most basic level, these catalogues of partial objects continue the operation of the series as a whole. They offer confirmation of the reality of the event, a rejoinder which cuts through the rhetoric of surgical precision and targeted killings like a knife. However, in their privileging of the object world, these photographs at the same time acknowledge a certain inadequacy of (human) narrative in this system of drone vision. In fact, the unconventional composition of these images can be read as an explicit rejection of the humanist biases of portraiture as it reduces subjects to internal spectators whose personal narratives are subordinated to the object relations they display. On these grounds, Mark Dorrian has suggested that while these images oppose the distance of remote killing with intimacy and closeness, they are simultaneously bound up with a sense of remove from the event. According to Dorrian, this remove is the product of the belatedness that the medium of photography incurs at the hands of the accelerated present of the digital sphere. As such, he regards the work as a 'violent cancellation of the possibility of witnessing [that] positions the photograph – which in its lateness, a lateness made absolute by death, is condemned to remain on the outside, as it were – less as a vestige of an act of witnessing than as a record of its end.'[21]

While Behram's images clearly wrestle with the representability of their subjects, the notion that this emphasis on the inorganic betrays a failure or inability to witness the event assumes a passivity of the objects on display. In fact, when read in relation to the processes of world-making outlined earlier in this chapter, the contradictions that Dorrian identifies seem less about photography's inability to keep pace with networked warfare than its active attempt to reflect back the conditions of drone vision. The spent casing of a Hellfire missile, the broken stones that were once a home, the craters which mark the point of impact – these signs serve as prompts to reverse engineer the logic of the kill chain, to draw out the series of conditions which produced the attack. The corresponding images of shoes, backpacks and other personal belongings of those killed by drone attacks, neatly arranged before the camera as personal shrine, comprise a similarly inverted system of simple triggers which conjure missing victims by interrogating the objects, behaviours, affiliations and locations that conspired against them. Rather than simple overtures to unrepresentability, these strategies allow Behram's images to reproduce the logic of conditions and parameters within the frame. The result is a kind of anti-portrait in which human subjects are not only rendered irretrievable by the image, but forcefully subordinated to the same material relations that have produced the strike. In turn, the strike comes to serve as both the means by which the category of the human is undermined and the force that animates the material world in order to realise its violence.

Conclusion: community and world-making

These works by Paglen and Behram illustrate the fact that drones do not necessarily take over the human functions of targeting, but rather impregnate the material world with a horizontal field of potentialities and triggers from which attacks materialise as inevitabilities. On account of these relations of autogenesis, both human subjects and the inanimate sphere they occupy are shot through with a life giving force which paradoxically necessitates their eradication as the groundlessness of drone power strategically congeals into traditional hierarchies of sovereignty.[22] Reading these processes of world-making in relation to the unique mode of address that drones articulate for those on the ground reveals the way in which these same relations comprise a critical component of the community of drone subjects. However, in order to fully acknowledge the experience of drone subjects, familiar panoptic tropes of invisibility must be read alongside the drone's active pursuit of presence. After all, conventional dynamics of surveillance do not simply co-exist alongside an opposing logic of explicit presence in these relations, but drone power in fact relies upon a strategic oscillation between panoptic modes of invisibility and overt revelation.

In a 2013 issue of *American Quarterly* dedicated to visual culture and the War on Terror, Matt Delmont summarises a familiar refrain when he attributes the 'deadly power' of the drone to its 'twin claims to visual superiority: the ability to see and to resist being seen.'[23] Chamayou similarly attributes the ethical lapses of the drone operation to the ability to 'see [...] without being seen', a scenario he regards as confirming the conclusion of the Milgram experiment that it is 'easier to harm a person when he is unable to observe our actions than when he can see what we are doing.'[24] A similar correlation of drone power with the unseen forms the basis for the title of a 2016 exhibit held at the Kemper Art Museum: 'To See without Being Seen: Contemporary Art and Drone Warfare'. While invisibility comprises a critical component of the UAV's tactics and operations, the ascendancy of this panoptic discourse can easily obscure the gestures of revelation that prove equally critical to its operation.

Field work conducted in Pakistan by the 'Living under drones' project confirms that drones maintain an overt – at times even conspicuous – presence in the lives of their subjects.[25] A young father told interviewers that the drones 'make it difficult to sleep. They are like a mosquito. Even when you don't see them, you can hear them, you know they are there.'[26] Another respondent explained: 'We can't go to the markets. We can't drive cars. When they're hovering over us, we're all scared. One thinks they'll drop it on our house, and another thinks it'll be on our house, so we run out of our houses.'[27] These reports of the everyday presence of drones are echoed by David Rohde, a former *New York Times* journalist, who was held hostage by the Taliban for seven months in Waziristan. He recalls that throughout his captivity:

> American drones were a frequent presence in the skies above North and South Waziristan. Unmanned, propeller-driven aircraft, they sounded like a small plane – a Piper Cub or Cessna-circling overhead. Dark specks in a blue sky, they could be spotted and tracked with the naked eye.[28]

These first-hand accounts confirm that drone power is not only capable of operating outside of imaginary or internalised modes of non-verifiable presence, but in fact regularly traffics in material, embodied and phenomenological presence.[29]

As these repeated performances of presence and absence correlate to the kill chain's internal movement between the actual and possible worlds, these gestures act as the performative equivalent of the relations of tactical animism, which grant the kill chain the ability to interpenetrate manifest reality with the not-yet-present of virtual force. By virtue of this correspondence between the presence of the UAV and the futural vector in which the strike appears as inevitability, the tactical operations of the drone become deeply entangled with the psychic processes of those who live under its shadow. Indeed, these relations play a critical role in the military's pursuit of full spectrum dominance, a strategy which understands the psychological dimensions of combat as inseparable from aerial, nautical, cyber, terrestrial and extraterrestrial fronts.

In *Inhibitions, Symptoms and Anxiety*, Freud distinguishes 'signal anxiety' from its less evolved counterpart, automatic anxiety, on the basis of its anticipatory nature. It is not the loss of the object that produces the former condition, but rather the fear of the impending trauma this loss provokes. As the internal movement of drone networks increasingly manifests as the apprehension of a non-presence that might always assert itself in actual terms, the Pakistani psychiatric community has begun to see the rise of a drone-related condition aptly referred to as anticipatory anxiety. Following Freud, one might break down this anxiety in the following terms: a signal (the drone) announces a danger-situation (its implicit strike) in response to which the subject 'anticipate[s] the trauma and behave[s] as though it had already come' ('anticipatory anxiety').[30] In this case, however, the 'as if' does not require the fantastic mechanism of neurosis (nor the governing power of the ego) in order to attain the status of reality, but rather draws its currency from the inner-workings of drone power itself. After all, this already present nature of possible trauma, which for Freud defines the anxious state, is precisely the logic of the signature strike, which utilises the martial database and its algorithms to organise worlds around violence rather than the reverse. In this regard, the oscillation of the drone between presence and absence does not simply conjure the possibility of violence, but rather reaffirms the presence of an impending world in which such an attack appears inevitable. For those on the ground, its unique mode of address offers confirmation of anxiety's illusion, testifying to the ease with which the 'as if' can pass over into the substrate of the real. It is this prospect that structures both the communities that reside underneath drones and the art which engages their experience.

Notes

1 S. Weinberger, 'How ESPN taught the pentagon to handle a deluge of drone data', *Popular Mechanics* (11 June, 2012), www.popularmechanics.com/technology/military/planes-uavs/how-the-pentagon-will-handle-its-deluge-of-drone-data-9600910 (accessed 16 February, 2021).

2 C. Currier and J. Elliot, 'The drone war doctrine we still know nothing about', *ProPublica* (26 February, 2013), www.propublica.org/article/drone-war-doctrine-we-know-nothing-about (accessed 16 February, 2021). See also: G. Miller, 'Proposal to give federal judges a role in drone strikes faces hurdles', *Washington Post* (8 February, 2013), www.washingtonpost.com/world/national-security/proposal-to-give-federal-judges-a-role-in-drone-strikes-faces-hurdles/2013/02/08/66f53508-721a-11e2-8b8d-e0b59a1b8e2a_story.html (accessed 16 February, 2021).

3 Analysing the organisational structure of the 9/11 terrorists, Valdis Krebs identifies three central components of such networks: incompleteness, fuzzy boundaries and dynamic relations. V. Krebs, 'Mapping networks of terrorist cells', *Connections* 24:3 (2002): 43–52.

4 S. Ressler, 'Social network analysis as an approach to combat terrorism: Past, present, and future research', *Homeland Security Affairs*, 2:8 (July 2006), 2.

5 Cited in U. A. Mejias, *Off the Network: Disrupting the Digital World* (Minneapolis: University of Minnesota Press, 2013), 92.

6 W. James, *Principles of Psychology* [1890] (New York: Dover Publications, 1950), 95–96. The original quote can be found in G. J. Romanes, *Mental Evolution in Animals: With a Posthumous Essay on Instinct by Charles Darwin* (New York: D. Appleton and Company, 1884), 324. See also H. R. Shell, 'The crucial moment of deception', *Cabinet* 33 (Spring 2009), www.cabinetmagazine.org/issues/33/shell.php (accessed 16 February, 2021).

7 H. Bergson, *Matter and Memory* (New York: NY: Zone Books, 1988).

8 In 2008 alone, the US military accumulated 24 years' worth of drone video. Additionally, a massive cache of data leaked by Chelsea Manning and made public by Wikileaks in 2010 suggests that this abundance of visual information may actually be overshadowed by its non-visual counterpart. Referred to as the *Afghan War Diaries*, this archive contains over 90,000 documents which span across an array of fields including: Human Intelligence, Psychological Operations, Engagement, Counter Improvised Explosive Device, Significant Acts, Targeting, and Social and Cultural reports.

9 D. Gregory 'Targeted killings and signature strikes', *Geographical Imaginations* (6 November, 2012), http://geographicalimaginations.com/2012/11/06/targeted-killings-and-signature-strikes/ (accessed 16 February, 2021).

10 D. S. Cloud, 'Anatomy of an Afghan war tragedy', *LA Times* (10 April, 2011), http://articles.latimes.com/2011/apr/10/world/la-fg-afghanistan-drone-20110410 (accessed 16 February, 2021). Such transubstantiation is part of a larger programme of strategic shape shifting, which serves to not only necessitate a future attack but also justify past actions. The latter is confirmed by Airman First Class Brandon Bryant who describes how a child seen on the monitor moments before a drone strike was dismissed as a dog in subsequent reports of the incident. Summarising the fluid nature of these signifiers, interviewer Matthew Power similarly asserts that the alleged rifles carried by the subjects of drone surveillance can just as easily be shepherds' staffs and vice versa. M. Power, 'Confessions of a drone warrior', *GQ* (22 October, 2013), www.gq.com/story/drone-uav-pilot-assassination (accessed 16 February, 2021).

11 G. Harwood, 'Endless war: On the database structure of armed conflict', *Rhizome* (17 March, 2014) https://rhizome.org/editorial/2014/mar/17/endless-war-database-structure-armed-conflict/ (accessed 5 February, 2021).

12 Harwood, 'Endless war'.

13 J. Crandall, 'Un-manned', in *Manifestation & Materialization: UFO Drag Queen: Delirium* (Atlanta, GA: Fort!/Da! Books, 2011), 108.

14 Harwood, 'Endless war'.

15 S. Weil, *Gravity and Grace* (New York: Psychology Press, 2002), 22.

16 S. Weber, *Targets of Opportunity: On the Militarization of Thinking* (New York: Fordham University Press, 2009), 4.

17 Weber, *Targets of Opportunity*, 4.

18 Weber, *Targets of Opportunity*, 5.

19 D. Ensor, 'Drone may have spotted bin Laden in 2000', *CNN* (17 March, 2004) www.cnn.com/2004/WORLD/asiapcf/03/17/predator.video/ (accessed 16 February, 2021).

20 On that day, a prototype for the Predator successfully fired a Hellfire missile at a target at Nellis Air Force base for the first time.

21 M. Dorrian, 'Drone semiosis: Weaponry and witnessing', *Cabinet* 54 (Summer 2014): 55.

22 M. Hill, 'Ecologies of war: Dispatch from the aerial empire', in Tom Cohen (ed.), *Telemorphosis: Theory in the Era of Climate Change*, Vol. 1 (Ann Arbor, MI: Open Humanities Press, 2012), https://quod.lib.umich.edu/o/ohp/10539563.0001.001/1:13/-telemorphosis-theory-in-the-era-of-climate-change-vol-1?rgn=div1;view=fulltext (accessed 16 February, 2021).

23 M. Delmont, 'Drone encounters: Noor Behram, Omer Fast, and visual critiques of drone warfare', *American Quarterly*, 65:1 (March 2013): 193–202.

24 G. Chamayou, *Theory of the Drone* (New York: The New Press, 2015), 118.

25 The study 'Living under drones: Death, injury and trauma to civilians from US drone practices in Pakistan' was conducted by NYU School of Law and Stanford University Law School. Based on the interviews of hundreds of survivors of

drone attacks, the report was published in 2013 and can be found at http://chrgj.org/wp-content/uploads/2012/10/Living-Under-Drones.pdf (accessed 16 February, 2021).

26 'Living under drones'.

27 'Living under drones'.

28 D. Rohde, 'The drone wars', *Reuters Magazine* (26 January, 2012). www.reuters.com/article/us-david-rohde-drone-wars-idUSTRE80P11I20120126 (accessed 16 February, 2021).

29 C. Friedersdorf, 'Every person is afraid of the drones'.

30 S. Freud, 'Inhibitions, symptoms and anxiety', *Standard Edition*. Vol. 20 (1926), 166.

Bibliography

Bergson, H. *Matter and Memory*. New York: NY: Zone Books, 1988.

Chamayou, G. *A Theory of the Drone*. New York: The New Press, 2015.

Cloud, D. S. 'Anatomy of an Afghan war tragedy'. *LA Times*, 10 April, 2011. http://articles.latimes.com/2011/apr/10/world/la-fg-afghanistan-drone-20110410 (accessed 16 February, 2021).

Crandall, J. 'Un-manned'. In *Manifestation & Materialization: UFO Drag Queen: Delirium*. Atlanta, GA: Fort!/Da! Books, 2011.

Currier C. and J. Elliot. 'The drone war doctrine we still know nothing about'. *ProPublica*, 26 February, 2013. www.propublica.org/article/drone-war-doctrine-we-know-nothing-about (accessed 16 February, 2021).

Delmont, M. 'Drone encounters: Noor Behram, Omer Fast, and visual critiques of drone warfare'. *American Quarterly*, 65:1 (March 2013): 193–202.

Dorrian, M. 'Drone semiosis: Weaponry and witnessing'. *Cabinet* 54 (Summer 2014).

Ensor, D. 'Drone may have spotted bin Laden in 2000', *CNN*, 17 March, 2004. www.cnn.com/2004/WORLD/asiapcf/03/17/predator.video/ (accessed 16 February, 2021).

Friedersdorf, C. 'Every person is afraid of the drones: The strikes' effect on life in Pakistan'. *The Atlantic*, 25 September, 2012. www.theatlantic.com/international/archive/2012/09/every-person-is-afraid-of-the-drones-the-strikes-effect-on-life-in-pakistan/262814/ (accessed 16 February, 2021).

Freud, S. 'Inhibitions, symptoms and anxiety'. In *The Standard Edition of the Complete Psychological Works of Sigmund Freud*, Vol. 20, 19125–1926, edited by J. Strachey, 75–175. London: Hogarth Press, 1953.

Gregory, D. 'Targeted killings and signature strikes'. *Geographical Imaginations*, 6 November, 2012. http://geographicalimaginations.com/2012/11/06/targeted-killings-and-signature-strikes/ (accessed 16 February, 2021).

Harwood, G. 'Endless war: On the database structure of armed conflict'. *Rhizome*, March 17, 2014.

Hill, M. 'Ecologies of war: Dispatch from the aerial empire'. In T. Cohen (ed.), *Telemorphosis: Theory in the Era of Climate Change*. Ann Arbor, MI: Open Humanities Press, 2012. https://quod.lib.umich.edu/o/ohp/10539563.0001.001/1:13/-telemorphosis-theory-in-the-era-of-climate-change-vol-1?rgn=div1;view=fulltext (accessed 16 February, 2021).

International Human Rights and Conflict Resolution Clinic at Stanford University Law School and Global Justice Clinic at NYU School of Law. 'Living under drones: Death, injury and trauma to civilians from US drone practices in Pakistan', 2012. https://chrgj.org/wp-content/uploads/2016/09/Living-Under-Drones.pdf (accessed 16 February, 2021).

James, W. *Principles of Psychology* [1890]. New York: Dover Publications, 1950.

Krebs, V. 'Mapping networks of terrorist cells'. *Connections*, 24:3 (2002): 43–52.

Mejias, U. A. *Off the Network: Disrupting the Digital World*. Minneapolis: University of Minnesota Press, 2013.

Miller G. 'Proposal to give federal judges a role in drone strikes faces hurdles'. *Washington Post*, 8 February, 2013. www.washingtonpost.com/world/national-security/proposal-to-give-federal-judges-a-role-in-drone-strikes-faces-hurdles/2013/02/08/66f53508-721a-11e2-8b8d-e0b59a1b8e2a_story.html (accessed 16 February, 2021).

Power, M. 'Confessions of a drone warrior'. *GQ*, 22 October, 2013. www.gq.com/story/drone-uav-pilot-assassination (accessed 16 February, 2021).

Ressler, S. 'Social network analysis as an approach to combat terrorism: Past, present, and future research'. *Homeland Security Affairs*, 2:8 (July 2006).

Rohde, D. 'The drone wars'. *Reuters Magazine*, 26 January, 2012. www.reuters.com/article/us-david-rohde-drone-wars-idUSTRE80P11I20120126 (accessed 16 February, 2021).

Romanes, G. J. *Mental Evolution in Animals: With a Posthumous Essay on Instinct by Charles Darwin*. New York: D. Appleton and Company, 1884.

Shell H. R. 'The crucial moment of deception'. *Cabinet* 33 (2009). www.cabinetmagazine.org/issues/33/shell.php (accessed 16 February, 2021).

Weber, S. *Targets of Opportunity: On the Militarization of Thinking*. New York: Fordham University Press, 2009.

Weil, S. *Gravity and Grace*. New York: Psychology Press, 2002.

Weinberger, S. 'How ESPN taught the pentagon to handle a deluge of drone data'. *Popular Mechanics*, 11 June, 2012. www.popularmechanics.com/technology/military/planes-uavs/how-the-pentagon-will-handle-its-deluge-of-drone-data-9600910 (accessed 16 February, 2021).

3

The drone of data

Jan Mieszkowski

> When I make a photograph, I want it to be an altogether new object, complete and self-contained, whose basic condition is order – (unlike the world of events and actions whose permanent condition is change and disorder).[1]

For all the recent attention that drones have received, there is surprisingly little agreement about whether the burgeoning presence of unmanned aerial vehicles (UAVs) bespeaks genuine ideological and material changes or the persistence of well-established trends. Having been rapidly embraced by businesses, hobbyists, and all branches of government, UAVs strike a nerve in part because they are seen to be symptomatic of a larger transformation taking place in modern society whereby the automation of human labour threatens to alter every aspect of military and civilian life. The aesthetic impact of drones has been similarly formidable. One can scarcely watch a television commercial or documentary clip on YouTube without being confronted with footage that has clearly been shot from a remote-controlled camera in the sky; and whole realms of photography that were once prohibitively expensive for all save the best-funded professionals are now the playgrounds of amateurs.

It nonetheless remains an open question how novel these developments actually are. After all, unmanned aerial devices are far from new, their military uses dating back to the nineteenth century, and it is not hard to show that the cultural shifts they portend may be part of larger patterns. Today's drone craze fits almost too nicely into the familiar story of how modern media technologies have shaped our perceptual faculties and our epistemological practices. Similarly, many of the ostensibly radical claims for the impending automation of human vision echo avant-garde movements of the early twentieth century, where a fascination with the mechanisation of the eye was one facet of a broader preoccupation with a future in which *le corps humain* would be supplanted by the cyborg.[2]

These concerns in mind, this chapter begins by detailing some of the unique features of aerial photography in order to show how the prominence of drones has helped give rise to a new understanding of the digital image, which for many contemporary theorists is less a stable visual phenomenon than an intersection of algorithmically organised data flows. Complicating this familiar story, recent changes in the photographic medium have been paralleled by a growing dependence on data visualisations. Emerging in their modern form more than a century before the invention of photography, these sorts of graphic representations are designed to make even the largest, most complex bodies of information accessible to the lay viewer. The crucial point for my discussion is that the charts and graphs of big data now openly compete for documentary and explanatory authority with photographs. In this context, drone images distinguish themselves by threatening to break the continuity between visibility and readability on which data visualisations rely. If UAVs are the ultimate emblem of omni-surveillance, they may nonetheless help foreground the limits of observation, decoupling the act of visualising and the act of understanding.

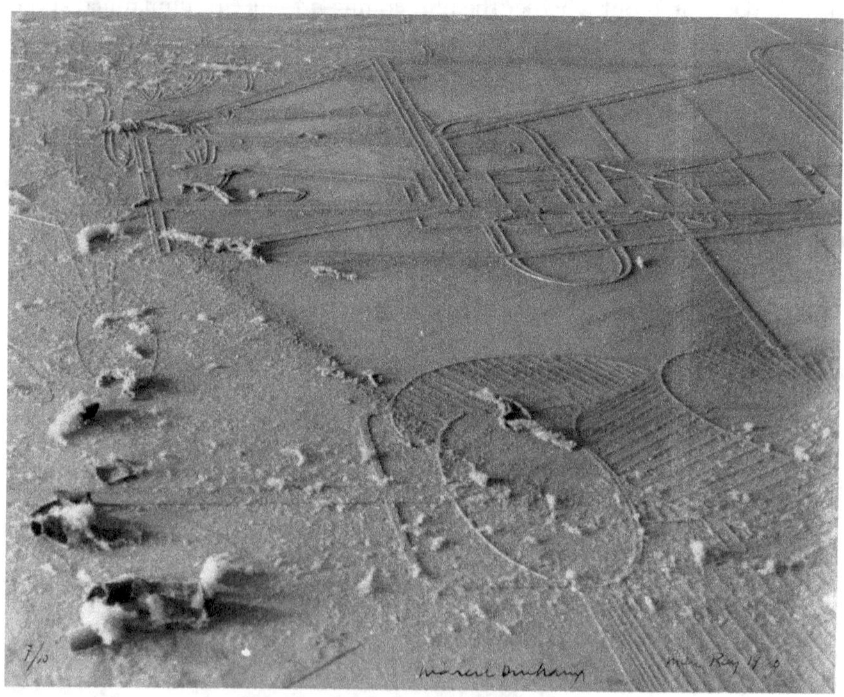

3.1 Man Ray, *Dust Breeding*, 2015.

'Aerial' photography

By definition, drone photography is aerial photography, although what this means in formal terms is far from self-evident. In 1921, a photograph appeared in André Breton's journal *Littérature* with the caption: 'View from an Airplane by Man Ray'. On the face of it, there is nothing remarkable about this fact. Two decades into the twentieth century, pictures taken from the sky were already a celebrated genre, the powers and limits of which had been extensively explored by artists and critics. While the potential for abstraction may exist in every photograph, aerial shots work against the mimetic or indexical pretensions of the medium in a peculiar way, as their perspectival ambiguities can lead the viewer to draw erroneous conclusions about both what is being depicted and the vantage point from which it is being seen. In this regard, Man Ray's photograph is exemplary because it was not made from a plane, a rocket, or a dirigible. Instead, the artist went over to his friend Marcel Duchamp's New York apartment, pointed his camera at a pane of glass covered in dust, and left the shutter open for a long exposure while the two men went out for lunch. Man Ray's image is 'aerial', not because it was shot from above the earth's surface, but because it gives us a sense of having a bird's-eye view of a landscape, although in truth we are looking at an unfinished sculpture in a private studio space. 'Dust Breeding', as it has come to be known, unmoors us from a stable perspectival frame, locating us uncertainly between earth and sky, unsure of our footing and far from confident whether we gain or lose from being in this position.[3]

While aerial images are often celebrated because they capture views that might otherwise never be seen by the human eye, they are no less frequently said to enjoy an unusual independence from what they represent, meaning that their fidelity to the scenes they document can never be taken for granted. The power of the view from above may be as much a creative as a perspectival one. Six years after Man Ray made 'Dust Breeding', Siegfried Kracauer published his well-known essay on the mass ornament, in which he focused on the Tiller Girls, a dance troupe renowned for the perfect synchronisation of its performers as they formed elaborate geometrical patterns with their bodies on stage. Kracauer argued that the mass ornament 'resembles aerial photographs of landscapes and cities, because it does not emerge out of the interior of the given conditions, but rather appears above them'.[4] On this account, aerial photography is necessarily estranged from what it depicts, and under the cartographic reduction effected by its gaze, the surface of the planet starts to look like a field of lines and circles whose interplay is guided by formal principles no less than documentary ones. The resulting images are simultaneously representations of particular physical phenomena and grids of abstract figures. Perhaps most confoundingly, these abstractions can appear to be part of an indecipherable code, as if we were trying to read a map whose key was missing.

Today, Google Maps and Google Earth ensure that a schematic or photographic representation of almost any sector of the planet's surface area is available to anyone with a computer or smart phone, but considerable uncertainty remains about what, if anything, such images impart to the onlooker. Absent an expert to interpret them, one may simply not know what one is seeing, however 'clear' the picture may be. If theorists such as Jean Baudrillard and Paul Virilio have written extensively about these paradoxical logics of modern media ecologies, visual artists have been no less eager to explore these same tensions. The uncertain place of aerial images in the tradition of photographic abstraction was definitely at the forefront of the French photographer Sophie Ristelhueber's concerns when she travelled to the Kuwaiti desert in 1992 to witness the aftermath of the First Gulf War, the conflict that Baudrillard famously said 'did not take place'.[5] Ristelhueber named her resulting series of pictures 'Fait', which in French is

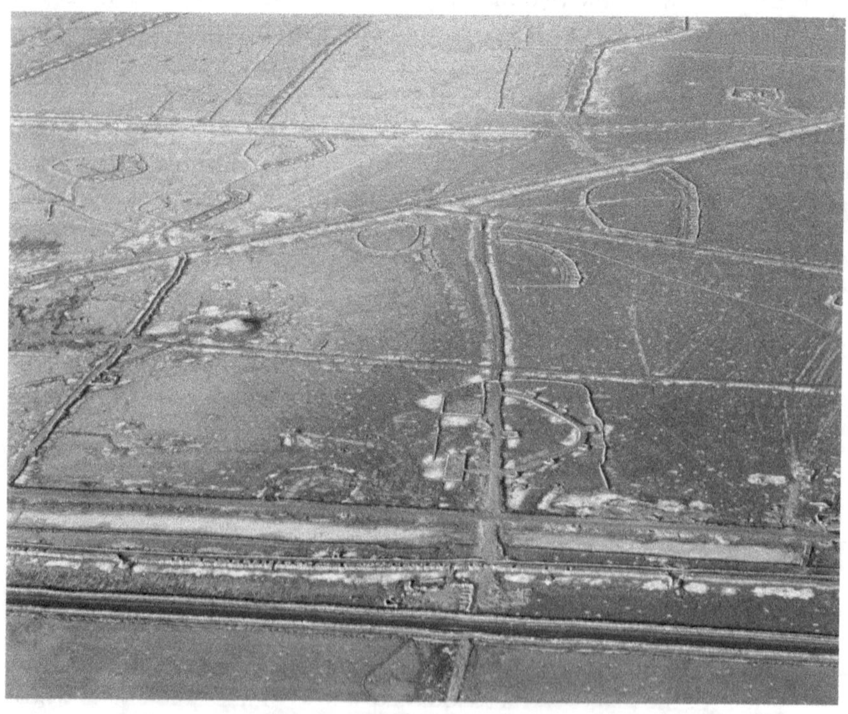

3.2 Sophie Ristelhueber, *A cause de l'élevage de poussière* ('Because of Dust Breeding'), 2019.

both a noun, 'fact', and the past participle of *faire*, 'to do', hence 'done'. In documenting what she called 'traces in the desert' or 'wounds on the earth', she sought to demonstrate that in warfare 'we in a way see nothing'.[6] The distinctive thing about the images Ristelhueber produced is the fact, the *fait*, that 'the viewer [...] doesn't know if [an] image is taken twenty centimetres from the ground or one hundred metres above'; 'that was a point I wanted to work on', she stressed, 'this confusion about what we see: is it big, is it small?'[7]

The assumption that an aerial vantage point is inherently advantageous is belied by the borderline obscurity of the photos in this series, which curator Marc Mayer describes as 'a long catalogue of weirdly parted sands'.[8] Ambiguously close-ups or long shots, each image is as much an example of abstract art as it is a record of a desert scene; together, they constitute a 'book of geometric patterns'.[9] Ristelhueber specifically invoked Man Ray's 'Dust Breeding' as a key influence on her project 'because of the way it plays with scale'; and she even expressed concern that one of her pictures was so derivative of its predecessor that it would likely be dismissed as a mere copy.[10] When the photograph in question was exhibited, she modestly called it 'Because of Dust Breeding'.

In 1990–1991, the US decided to wage war, to *faire la guerre*, in Kuwait; and it is a fact, *un fait*, that this was done (*avait été fait*). The photos in Ristelhueber's *Fait*, however, do not illustrate this fact, offering no perspective on its status as something *fait* ('done'/'fact-ed'). The pictures were prompted by the fact of the conflict, but their status as historical data remains uncertain, since they depict nothing – destroyed tanks or dead bodies – that would allow the viewer to establish an affective relationship to the event's material consequences. As Jacques Rancière has written, Ristelhueber 'effects a displacement of the exhausted affect of indignation to a more discreet affect, an affect of indeterminate effect'.[11] What we see is that we do not see what we expect, and perhaps even desire, to see, e.g., corpses of combatants strewn amongst damaged machinery. Ristelhueber's images are not replications of independently existing scenes. They present something that otherwise could never have been viewed, because what we encounter in them, 'in a way', is 'nothing', and if we were to go to the desert where they were taken, we would see that this onetime 'nothing' has long since faded to less than nothing.

The drone's-eye view

Looking at Man Ray's picture or Ristelhueber's tribute to it, we might well mistake either for a photo taken by a drone camera. As UAVs of all sizes and prices have been welcomed by the military, corporations, and civilian hobbyists, any photo or video that seems to have been shot from more than a few feet off the ground now falls under suspicion of having been made remotely.[12] Aesthetically, the drone-effect is particularly prominent in documentary filmmaking and advertising, where the convenience and relatively low cost of working with UAVs has meant that the distinctive tracking and panning they facilitate has already become something of a visual cliché.[13] No less than with other types of aerial photography, drone images confound the viewer's sense of scale and perspective – pictures taken from 100 metres above the ground often prove to be indistinguishable from those made from five or ten centimetres away.[14] Once again, the narrative of technological triumphalism is tempered by the recognition that no matter how high the resolution of a picture may be, its content may remain completely unknowable unless someone explains what we are being shown. This is especially the case when the camera shoots straight down, something far more easily achieved remotely than from an aeroplane. In such instances, we are offered a cartographic gaze, as if we were looking at the world through the lens of a curated map in which formalisation predominates at the expense of a straightforward correspondence between the image and its object. Indeed, as the collection of geo-spatial data has increasingly been outsourced to drones, the very distinction between a photograph and a diagram has begun to blur, leaving us only a small step from Kracauer's mass ornament, which is always *above* but never *of* its subject matter.

In turning the aesthetic gaze back on the medium of representation and its means of production, drones betray a modernist rather than a postmodernist aesthetic.[15] Crucial in this regard is the foregrounding of the grid, the ultimate modernist schema, which, as Rosalind E. Krauss argues, 'states the autonomy of the realm of art. Flattened, geometricised, ordered, it is antinatural, antimimetic, antireal'.[16] In a tribute to Kracauer's aesthetics or the planar networks of de Stijl, Mondrian, or Malevich, the American news weekly *Time* commemorated its 11 June, 2018 report on the rise of UAVs by using 958 illuminated drones hovering in the sky at dusk to create a 100-metre-tall rendering of the magazine's cover with its iconic typography and red border, a photograph of which was used as that week's cover image. No human being could have managed to coordinate this intricate geometric dance; and naturally, the picture of the computer-directed drone array was taken by yet another drone. The resulting display was clearly a mass ornament, except that it was made up of mechanised apparatuses rather than human bodies, and even on their best day, the Tiller Girls could never have hoped to match the precision with which these appliances interacted in perfect unison in the sky.[17]

In the *Time* cover photo, the points of light effected by the drones make up both the rectangular border around the page and the letters that spell out the magazine's title. What is thereby circumscribed and captioned is a richly coloured but decidedly empty sky, populated neither by flying machines nor people. In this sense, the *Time* image is an emblem of a new visual order, in which the almost unimaginable scale on which digital surveillance and information systems record images ensures that 99 per cent of them will never be reviewed by human eyes. The US military amasses decades' worth of video footage every year, yet even with its immense resources, the Pentagon cannot muster enough analysts to peruse more than a tiny fraction of the material flagged for scrutiny by computer algorithms. In the realm of omni-surveillance, nobody can hope to see how much we are not seeing or to grasp, as Ristelhueber would have it, that what we are seeing is, 'in a way', nothing, which is precisely what fills the rectangular section of the sky framed by the drones in the picture on the front of the magazine.

Like the elaborate two- and three-dimensional maps created by using software to combine thousands of aerial shots, the *Time* cover challenges the distinction between a visual record of an empirical place and time and a visualisation of a more abstract phenomenon – in this case the symbol of a weekly periodical's identity that has no physical analogue and may not even exist independently of the iconographic conventions that give it form. In other words, this photograph of drones made by a drone shows us a world in which there is no simple boundary between what is 'out there' in the sky and what is 'in here' on the page or screen. This raises the question of whether photography in the digital age can still be understood with reference to the model bequeathed to us from the analogue era whereby a human being creates a record of something by allowing an image of it to be projected onto a piece of photosensitive film inside a lightproof chamber. In his three-part *Eye/Image* installation (2000–2003), filmmaker and video artist Harun Farocki announced that today we are increasingly dealing with operative images that 'do not represent an object, but rather are part of an operation'.[18] As artist Trevor Paglen explains, Farocki asked how 'image-making machines and algorithms were poised to inaugurate a new visual realm. Instead of simply representing things in the world, the machines and their images were starting to "do" things in the world. In fields from marketing to warfare, human eyes were becoming anachronistic.'[19]

Farocki's notion of operative images has quickly become a mainstay of contemporary media theory, and with surprisingly little reflection on whether images have always 'done things', it is declared that the human sensorium is being supplanted wholesale. 'What is actually the important part of digital media and digital images', Paglen maintains, 'is that they're fundamentally in the first instance machine readable, and only in the second instance human readable. The digital image is not made for human eyes as much as it is made for different software applications to read.'[20] Echoing this idea, Kate Crawford, co-founder of NYU's AI Now Institute, observes: 'We've moved beyond the era when images were made primarily for human eyes, to vast numbers of images circulating solely within machine-readable networks.'[21] Such pictures are 'not originally intended to be seen by humans'; instead, they are 'supposed to function as an interface in the context of algorithmically controlled guidance processes'.[22]

If the visualisations of the data gathered by digital cameras are in many cases almost indistinguishable from analogue images, this is thanks to 'a gesture of courtesy extended by the machines', and it does not change the fact that such digital phenomena are no longer the end goal of a process – the creation of a photo or video – but intermediary stages in larger programmes of study, surveillance, and even assassination.[23] In this vein, Hal Foster argues that Farocki's work reveals that 'a new "robo eye" is in place, one that, in comparison to the "Kino eye" celebrated by modernists like Dziga Vertov, does not extend the human prosthetically so much as it replaces the human robotically'.[24] The result, as Foster formulates it, is that Walter Benjamin's 'optical unconscious' is being replaced by 'an optical nonconscious', and the vast majority of images are now 'operative' precisely because they are invisible to people.[25]

Once a photograph is understood to be less a discrete, fixed visual phenomenon than an intersection of flows of algorithmically organised data, 'the image as the termination (fixation) of meaning gives way to the image as a network terminal (screen). It is no longer a stable representation of the world, but a programmable view of a database that is updated in real-time'.[26] On this basis, Anthony McCosker has proposed that we should not regard drones simply as 'unruly aerial objects with the capacity for privacy-invasive imaging', but equally as a 'provocation to reconsider wireless networks, visuality and camera-conscious sociality'.[27] By foregrounding the primacy of interface over images and relations over data, drones invite us to go beyond what Joanna Zylinska has termed the 'humanist and human-centric' approaches to photography that treat it primarily as an art form or a socio-cultural practice.[28] Notions of indexicality, memory traces, or even representation as such thereby recede in importance as the photographic medium comes to be understood as a set of dynamic processes that may not involve human beings as agents or addressees.

Whatever authority this new conception of photography enjoys among scholars, it has by no means completely undercut popular loyalty to the traditional understanding of the photograph as a visual document of considerable evidentiary power. Although software technology has made it virtually impossible for even the most sophisticated observer to distinguish between 'genuine' and 'doctored' photos or videos, the demand that such media deliver unadulterated data has never been greater.[29] The more tenuous the claim of any given still or moving image to provide immediate access to an irreducible trace of unmanipulated empirical reality, the louder the call for images to do precisely this. In spite of everything, we hold tight to the conviction that seeing is believing – or at least that it ought to be.

The irony of believing our own eyes in the drone age has been explored by the aforementioned Trevor Paglen, who in a range of projects on military secrecy and the expansion of the modern surveillance state has considered what it would mean to look back at the forces that are potentially always looking at us. In 2010, Paglen used a wide-angle lens to take a series of photographs of the sky at dusk in the vicinity of military installations in the Nevada desert. The colours of the cloud-dappled sunsets he captured are gorgeous; they may even recall Turner paintings. In any case, there is certainly nothing threatening about them.[30] Viewing these images on a gallery wall, one might simply judge them to be pretty pictures and move on, except that each is titled *Untitled*, followed by a parenthetical note consisting of the name of a particular type of military drone. Having read one of the captions, our viewing priorities are quickly upended as we try to ignore 99.99 per cent of what we see in the photograph in an effort to locate what we have apparently 'missed'. With further scrutiny, we eventually come upon a tiny black speck on each picture that could easily be attributed to a printing flaw or a smudge of dirt on the camera lens, but we have no choice but to presume that it is the aerial surveillance and killing machine referenced in the 'title' of the untitled work. The effect is reminiscent of Michelangelo Antonioni's *Blowup*, where it is only after developing some negatives in the darkroom that the protagonist realises that he has photographed the scene of a murder, yet no matter how closely we look at Paglen's pictures, the black speck never becomes more than a black speck. We definitely never see any trace of the people each – alleged – drone may have photographed, or killed, or be about to photograph or kill.

Recasting beautiful skyscapes as a *Where's Waldo?* puzzle, Paglen's *Untitled* series confronts us with the virtual invisibility of UAVs, which have alarmingly little difficulty observing, targeting, and destroying viewers such as ourselves on the ground below. At the same time, there is a reassertion of human agency in these pictures as we look back at the drone rather than simply being observed by it, and we do so, moreover, with considerable aesthetic satisfaction. If Ristelhueber points her camera down to show us traces of past combat that resemble abstract geometric symbols, Paglen points his camera up to show us the traces of potential or future acts of surveillance – or violence. The inversions of scale, perspective, and proportion routinely performed by aerial photographs are thereby turned inside out by images that confirm the power of the specks above us by ensuring that they all but vanish in pleasing swathes of colour. Rather than the ghost in the machine, we see the machine as a ghost.

Considered as a spectacle, each member of Paglen's *Untitled* series may appear to be the antithesis of the mass ornament created by the *Time* cover, although notably all of these images present drones as dots. In Paglen's photos, each black dot cast in relief against a richly coloured sky stands in for a drone, or the spectre thereof, whereas in the *Time* cover, each drone is illuminated red and set into relief against the darkening sky, allowing the aerial vehicle to serve as a representation of a collection of pixels – literally the building blocks of a digital image. What is being mimicked in the *Time* photograph is contemporary graphic design, with the UAVs simulating the look of a printed page or computer screen. In other words, the magazine's illustration for the cover of an issue about drones is made up of the light from drones arranged to look like the cover of the magazine. This suggests that what counts as a powerful visual today is the opposite of what passed for one in the analogue era, since now it is the most mediated rather than the most immediate constructions that arrest the eye. Viewed alongside Paglen's *Untitled* series, the *Time* cover intimates that contemporary consumers of images are not, as is commonly supposed, forever on the verge of being overwhelmed by the endless streams of photos and videos flooding their televisions, laptops, and phones. On the contrary, their visual field is largely empty, as if all they were gazing at were a vacant – albeit pleasing – screensaver or sky. Ironically, the triumph of a surveillance system of unparalleled scope results in a perfect view of, 'in a way', nothing. Even as drone photographs are paying homage to the modernist grid aesthetic, they are frequently challenging the assumption that there is actually anything on display in the representational plane delineated by the intersections of real or imaginary lines.

Big data

Does the superabundance of photos and videos documenting all aspects of contemporary life help us take stock of our political communities and their prospects for change? Or does the glut of visual records cloak the status quo in an air of inevitability, hinting that whatever one may think about current conditions, 'that's just the way it is'? In reflecting on these questions, it is important to remember that if information about the goings and doings of anyone and everyone is being amassed at an unparalleled rate, only a fraction of this data is obtained with cameras. Every gesture of quotidian existence – every tap on a tablet or phone screen, every strike of the keyboard – is now chronicled and becomes an infinitesimally small part of extremely consequential bodies of information and their statistical summaries, the 'results' that will be used to determine a six-year-old child's aptitude for spelling or spatial reasoning, an employee's inclination to focus on one task at a time, or a driver's ability to handle tight corners and thus get a discount on their auto insurance. The selfies we take and delete with impunity or the surveillance tapes made in stores, banks, and restaurants are all surface-level stand-ins for our in-depth profiles, which include medical tests, employment records, credit scores, and of course browser histories. Heralded by some as the solution to society's ills, by others as a sign of the impending collapse of sociability as such, 'big data' has first and foremost come to mean that there is more information at our disposal than we know what to do with.[31] This state of affairs is ideologically controversial, not least because big data's champions see it as the vanguard of a new rationalist order in which the systematic collection and processing of 'the facts' will make ideology itself obsolete as political decisions are replaced by a Fordist managerial calculus that treats human interactions as predictable physical processes.[32]

One consequence of the enthusiasm for data-based reasoning is that the traditional photograph now competes for authority with data visualisations – the charts, graphs, and other diagrams created by abstracting certain features of large bodies of information and schematically illustrating the relationships between them. In a research or diagnostic forum, data visualisations may help identify patterns or unexpected deviations that statistical modelling can miss. In less technical contexts, their aim may simply be to illustrate the complexity of a system, as when we are told that a morass of impossibly convoluted lines is a representation of the network of 10,000 neurons and 30 million connections that make up a single neocortical column in the human brain. In this latter capacity, data visualisations are designed to allow someone with only a passing familiarity with a topic to appreciate something about the wealth of information assembled. In this respect, these charts and graphs are arguably more akin to popular advertisements than to the illustrations in a technical manual.

A data visualisation is an eminently rhetorical medium, employing a variety of strategies for capturing a viewer's attention and persuading them of the truth of its claims about a particular set of relationships. The resulting product can be eye-catching, even beautiful, and may well become reliable clickbait on social media, but it is anything but a mere ornament. A successful depiction of information can prove decisive for a grant application, a sales pitch, or an entire political campaign. Unsurprisingly, there is no consensus about the analytic virtues of such visualisations and their impact on the epistemological assumptions informing various kinds of research.[33] Some argue that the innovative work being done in the presentation of information constitutes the emergence of a genuinely new kind of thinking, while others maintain that it is at best fancy bookkeeping and at worst a very old kind of legerdemain that allows one to cherry-pick results and arrange them into misleading 'proofs'.

The aesthetic experiences peculiar to the processing of data visualisations have received nearly as much attention as their logical and rhetorical features. Given that the name 'big data' foregrounds scale, we might anticipate that the category of sublimity would be invoked, but, in fact, the term 'data sublime' was first used to describe the superabundance of detail in digital photographs rather than in more schematic representations of information. In a widely cited 2007 essay, the art historian Julian Stallabrass proposed that by creating digital pictures of astounding precision, some contemporary photographers 'abandon the viewer in a wilderness of information'.[34] Providing 'the impression and spectacle of a chaotically complex and immensely large configuration of data, these photographs', Stallabrass argued, 'act much as renditions of mountain scenes and stormy seas did on nineteenth-century urban viewers'.[35]

Data visualisations do something quite different. While many of them persuasively make the case that the system of which they offer us a view is almost unthinkably complex, this happens within a stable frame, as a clearly delineated field of coordinates organises a well-defined diagram that fits neatly on the page or screen. Such boundedness is the very antithesis of what Kant and his inheritors understood by the term 'sublime'. As Lev Manovich puts it, 'If Romantic artists thought of certain phenomena and effects as un-representable, as something which goes beyond the limits of human senses and reason, data visualisation artists aim at precisely the opposite: to map such phenomena into a representation whose scale is comparable to the scales of human perception and cognition.'[36] Many datasets presumably are sublime, or would be if we ever confronted them in physical form, for instance as a mountain of printouts. Charts and graphs, however, are expressly designed to head off the sense of shock and awe that such an encounter might inspire. In Kantian terms, they allow us to skip the step of being overwhelmed by the enormity of the external world and take us directly to the reassertion of our mind's powers over the stormy sea of facts. For this reason, scholarship on data visualisations often deems them beautiful rather than sublime, and there are numerous websites that gather examples of data modelling judged to be intensely pleasing – but decidedly not threatening – to the eye.[37]

Even when such graphs are hopelessly complex – there are so many figures, so many coordinates, so many lines – the ostensible precision begins

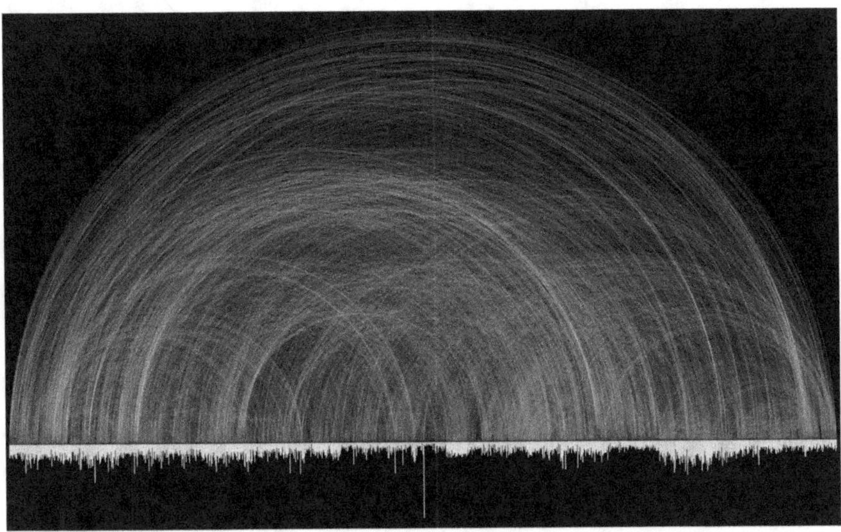

3.3 Chris Harrison, *63,000 Cross References in the Bible.*

to shade into something less than overwhelming, as the wealth of intricate plotting suspends the eye's ability to discern anything with clarity, and we are left with a blob of lines and colours. The proliferation of points or curves within a two-dimensional frame does not precipitate a breakdown in our frame of reference or create a sense that we have somehow transcended the sensory order. Instead, complexity morphs into simplicity, because what we see is an abstract depiction of detail rather than the countless details incarnate; we infer that a stunning amount of information is on display because the morass of shapes and colours is inscrutable and, if we are honest, a mess.

As we nod politely in the face of clever depictions of vast bodies of information, we are tacitly conceding that in the future only computers will be able to do the heavy mental lifting. A 'courtesy' extended to us lest we flounder in the rough sea of evidence, such diagrams demonstrate the folly of the human brain's ambition to process data on this scale. There is no need to look too closely at a data visualisation's serpentine array of lines or curves, because a mere glance suffices to confirm that it would be inutile for us to try to parse the enormous quantities of information on display.

'Who thinks abstractly?' G. W. F. Hegel asked, but today the important question may be: 'Who does *not* see abstractly?'[38] Data visualisations train us to view the world as a set of dynamics whose constitutive forces can be plotted on a Cartesian grid. With this wholesale domestication of existence – 'reality in the aggregate' – we experience not the big data sublime or the big data beautiful, but the big data agreeable, a veneer of the unthreatening that invites us to conclude that the charts and graphs with which we are being confronted are somehow more direct – and therefore more trustworthy – than other discursive formations. As discussed, the photos made by drones have an irreducibly abstract dimension as well, but the crucial difference is that, unlike data visualisations, such pictures lack an explanatory matrix with well-defined units and axes, which is to say that drone photographs are not necessarily 'in-formational' if this means that their subject matter can as a matter of course be slotted into preestablished units or categories. Drone images may push us toward a new conception of media aesthetics – call it posthuman photography or nonhuman vision – but they do not purport to be self-decoding. Irrespective of whether it is humans or computers processing them, these images still have to be read, whereas it is data visualisations, by definition pre-digested, that anticipate a posthuman hermeneutic. Ultimately, then, drone aesthetics is distinguished not by its confirmation of the scope or limits of the visual order, but by its reminder that no matter how much of the world we may be able to document visually, its legibility can never be taken for granted. As all-seeing as our surveillance systems may become, we are not poised to escape Paglen's ghosts or Ristelhueber's depictions of, 'in a way', nothing.

Notes

1 H. H. Smith, Thomas Hess, and Aaron Siskind, *Aaron Siskind: Photographer* (New York: George Eastman House, 1965), 24.

2 This position was famously encapsulated in Dziga Vertov's pronouncement: 'I am kino-eye, I am a mechanical eye. I, a machine, show you the world as only I can see it.' D. Vertov, *Kino-Eye: The Writings of Dziga Vertov*, ed. Annette Michelson (Berkeley: University of California Press, 1984 [1923]), 17.

3 Self-reflexive in the extreme, Man Ray's image illustrates the physical processes peculiar to photography. The visual representation of Duchamp's nascent artwork presents the hidden piece of glass as a field of traces, a surface that can accept the impression of something else, like camera film. In effect, 'Dust Breeding' is an inverted photograph that records what is happening inside the camera rather than what is happening outside of it.

4 S. Kracauer, *The Mass Ornament: Weimar Essays*, trans. T. Y. Levin (Cambridge, MA: Harvard University Press, 1995), 77.

5 See J. Baudrillard, *The Gulf War Did Not Take Place*, trans. P. Patton (Bloomington: Indiana University Press, 1995).

6 S. Ristelhueber, 'Documenting traces of war' (#TateShots Interview), YouTube video, 3:05 (22 January, 2015), www.youtube.com/watch?time_continue=117&v=PBsgm4OBOfE (accessed 3 April, 2019).

7 Ristelhueber, 'Documenting traces of war'. Ristelhueber shot her photos from planes, helicopters, and at ground level. On the production of this series, see J. Ladd, 'Making *Fait*', in S. Ristelhueber, *Fait: Koweit 1991* (New York: errata editions, 2008), n. p. For an excellent analysis of the project, see C. Kaplan, *Aerial Aftermaths: Wartime from Above* (Durham, NC: Duke University Press, 2018), 185–194.

8 M. Mayer, 'Fait', in Ristelhueber, *Fait: Koweit 1991*, n. p.

9 Mayer, 'Fait'.

10 S. Phillips, 'Artist and photographer Sophie Ristelhueber's best shot' (Interview), *The Guardian* (28 April, 2010), www.theguardian.com/artanddesign/2010/apr/28/photography-sophie-ristelhueber-best-shot (accessed 3 April, 2019). As Marc Mayer puts it, 'Man Ray's photograph looks like a mysterious landscape, while [Ristelhueber's] Kuwait desert looks like a Duchamp,' Mayer, 'Fait'.

11 J. Rancière, *The Emancipated Spectator*, trans. G. Elliott (New York: Verso, 2009), 104.

12 Until relatively recently, the costs of aerial photography were prohibitive for hobbyists. The plummeting price of drones and the cameras they can carry has largely removed such financial obstacles, and of the more than 100 million new images uploaded every day to Instagram, a growing number appear under hashtags such as #dronegram, #droneoftheday, or #traveldrone.

13 On the already all-too-familiar kinds of footage facilitated by drones, see B. Ebiri, 'The dronepocalypse is here – in documentary footage, at least', *New York Times* (8 May, 2019), www.nytimes.com/2019/05/08/movies/drones-documentaries.html (accessed 8 May, 2019).

14 Going in the other direction, technological advances are also making it more difficult to know whether one is looking at a picture shot from a drone 100 metres in the air or from a satellite in orbit hundreds of miles above the surface of the earth.

15 Michael Andreas has argued that the archetypal surveillance images taken by military drones are entirely continuous with the visual culture that emerged in Europe around 1910. See M. Andreas, 'Flächen/Rastern. Zur Bildlichkeit der Drohne', *Behemoth: A Journal On Civilisation*, 8:2 (2015): 108–127.

16 R. E. Krauss, *The Originality of the Avant-Garde and Other Modernist Myths* (Cambridge, MA: MIT Press, 1985), 9.

17 The cover can be viewed here: https://time.com/longform/time-drones-behind-cover/. A video about the cover's creation is available here: http://time.com/5294789/time-drone-cover-video/ (accessed 16 April, 2019).

18 H. Farocki, 'Phantom images', *Public* 29 (2004): 17.

19 T. Paglen, 'Operational images', *e-flux journal*, 59 (November, 2014), www.e-flux.com/journal/59/61130/operational-images/ (accessed 14 May, 2019).

20 'A conversation with Trevor Paglen', in Paglen, *Sites Unseen*, 213.

21 'A conversation with Trevor Paglen', in Paglen, *Sites Unseen*, 213.

22 M. Blumenthal-Barby, '"Cinematography of devices": Harun Farocki's Eye/Machine trilogy', *German Studies Review*, 38:2 (May 2015): 329.

23 V. Pantenburg, 'Working images: Harun Farocki and the operational image', in J. Eder and C. Klonk (eds), *Image Operations: Visual Media and Political Conflict* (Manchester: Manchester University Press, 2017), 49.

24 H. Foster, 'The cinema of Harun Farocki', *Artforum*, 43:3 (November 2004): 156–161.

25 Foster, 'The cinema of Harun Farocki', 160.

26 I. Hoelzl and R. Marie, *Softimage: Towards a New Theory of the Digital Image* (Bristol: Intellect, 2015), 3–4. In a similar vein, Edgar Gómez Cruz has argued that 'photography is increasingly being used as an interface, without even involving an image'. E. G. Cruz, 'Photo-genic assemblages: Photography as a connective interface', in E. G. Cruz and A. Lehmuskallio (eds), *Digital Photography and Everyday Life: Empirical Studies on Material Visual Practices* (London: Routledge, 2016), 229.

27 A. McCosker, 'Drone media: Unruly Systems, radical empiricism and camera consciousness', *Culture Machine*, 16 (2015), n. p.

28 J. Zylinska, *Nonhuman Photography* (Cambridge, MA: MIT Press, 2017), 3.

29 As Brian Klaas writes: 'Soon, those with even a rudimentary technical knowledge will be able to fabricate videos that are so true to life that it becomes difficult, if not impossible, to determine whether the video is real.' B. Klaas, 'Deepfakes are coming. We're not ready', *Washington Post* (14 May, 2019), www.washingtonpost.com/opinions/2019/05/14/deepfakes-are-coming-were-not-ready/?utm_term=.c6ffed26ed07 (accessed 14 May, 2019).

30 On Paglen's work during this period, see J. P. Jacob, 'Trevor Paglen: Invisible images and impossible objects', in T. Paglen, *Sites Unseen*, ed. John P. Jacob and Luke Skrebowski (London: Smithsonian American Art Museum in association with D Giles Limited, 2018), 23–85.

31 Billions of gigabytes of data are now recorded every couple of days, arguably as much as was produced in the first 6000 years of human civilisation. For an already somewhat dated effort to quantify these developments and speculate on their ramifications, see V. Mayer-Schönberger and K. Cukier, *Big Data: A Revolution That Will Transform How We Live, Work, and Think* (Boston: Houghton Mifflin Harcourt, 2013). For more recent treatments of the topic, see S. Sarangi and P. Sharma, *Big Data: A Beginner's Introduction* (London: Taylor & Francis Group, 2019), and A. Richterich, *The Big Data Agenda: Data Ethics and Critical Data Studies* (London: University of Westminster Press, 2019).

32 For one such triumphalist narrative, see C. Anderson, 'The end of theory: The data deluge makes the scientific method obsolete', *Wired* (23 June, 2008), www.wired.com/2008/06/pb-theory/ (accessed 6 May, 2019). Some scholars feel that the term 'big data' is overly vague, if not outright misleading insofar as the underlying shifts at issue are less about the scale of information than about how it is being processed and modelled. On these questions, see T. Underwood, 'Against (talking about) "big data"', The Stone and the Shell (blog) (10 May, 2013), https://tedunderwood.com/2013/05/10/ why-it-matters-that-we-dont-know-what-we-mean-by-big-data/ (accessed 16 April, 2019); and d. boyd

and K. Crawford, 'Critical questions for big data: Provocations for a cultural, technological and scholarly phenomenon', *Information, Communication & Society*, 15:5 (2012): esp. 663–664.

33 As Anthony McCosker and Rowan Wilken write, 'Data visualization has ... become an attractive, but contentious tool for social analysis, challenging or extending the methodologies of fields as diverse as digital ethnography, data journalism, digital humanities and computer science. In particular, those working within anthropology recognise the importance of the visual as a way of introducing "significant additions to how anthropologists define their ways of knowing", including rethinking categories of knowledge in relation to science and many technologies of the visual.' A. McCosker and R. Wilken, 'Rethinking "big data" as visual knowledge: The sublime and the diagrammatic in data visualization', *Visual Studies*, 29:2 (April 2014): 155.

34 J. Stallabrass, 'What's in a face? Blankness and significance in contemporary art photography', *October* 122 (Fall 2007): 83. Stallabrass's prime example is the portraiture of the German photographer Thomas Ruff.

35 Stallabrass, 'What's in a face?', 82. The notion that networks are sublime has been important for scholars of postmodern culture as they have worked to characterise the experience of confronting the unimaginable scale and complexity of modern information systems. See, for example, J. Tabbi, *Postmodern Sublime: Technology and American Writing from Mailer to Cyberpunk* (Ithaca: Cornell University Press, 1995), esp. ix; and P. Jagoda, *Network Aesthetics* (Chicago: University of Chicago Press, 2016), esp. 47–49.

36 Lev Manovich, 'Data visualization as new abstraction and as anti-sublime', in B. Hawk, D. M. Rieder, and O. Oviedo (eds), *Small Tech: The Culture of Digital Tools* (Minneapolis: University of Minnesota Press, 2008), 6–7. In a slightly different context, Manovich has argued that data visualisation is the obverse of modernist art, for rather than trying to liberate visual art from its representational function, such visualisations seek to create visible representations of datasets that are by nature invisible. See L. Manovich, 'Forward', in M. Lima (ed.), *Visual Complexity: Mapping Patterns of Information* (New York: Princeton Architectural Press, 2011), esp. 12.

37 See, for instance, Visual Complexity, www.visualcomplexity.com/vc/ (accessed 11 March, 2021). Academic discussions of data visualisations sometimes fail to distinguish between beauty and sublimity. For one example, see McCosker and Wilken, 'Rethinking "big data" as visual knowledge', esp. 157.

38 See G. W. F. Hegel, 'Who thinks abstractly?', in W. Kaufmann (ed.), *Hegel: Texts and Commentary* (Garden City, NY: Anchor Books, 1966), 113–118.

Bibliography

Anderson, C. 'The end of theory: The data deluge makes the scientific method obsolete'. *Wired*, 23 June, 2008. www.wired.com/2008/06/pb-theory/ (accessed 6 May, 2019).

Andreas, M. 'Flächen/Rastern. Zur Bildlichkeit der Drohne'. *Behemoth: A Journal On Civilisation*, 8:2 (2015): 108–127.

Baudrillard, J. *The Gulf War Did Not Take Place*, trans. P. Patton. Bloomington: Indiana University Press, 1995.

Blumenthal-Barby, M. '"Cinematography of devices": Harun Farocki's Eye/Machine trilogy'. *German Studies Review* 38:2 (May 2015): 329.

boyd, d. and K. Crawford. 'Critical questions for big data: Provocations for a cultural, technological and scholarly phenomenon'. *Information, Communication & Society* 15:5 (2012): 662–679.

Cruz, E. G. 'Photo-genic assemblages: Photography as a connective interface'. In E. G. Cruz and A. Lehmuskallio (eds), *Digital Photography and Everyday Life: Empirical Studies on Material Visual Practices.* London: Routledge, 2016.

Ebiri, B. 'The dronepocalypse is here – in documentary footage, at least'. *New York Times.* 8 May, 2019. www.nytimes.com/2019/05/08/movies/drones-documentaries.html (accessed 8 May, 2019).

Farocki, H. 'Phantom images'. *Public* 29 (2004): 12–24.

Foster, H. 'The cinema of Harun Farocki'. *Artforum* 43:3 (November 2004): 156–161.

Hegel, G. W. F. 'Who thinks abstractly?' In W. Kaufmann (ed.), *Hegel: Texts and Commentary*, 113–118. Garden City, NY: Anchor Books, 1966.

Hoelzl, I. and R. Marie. *Softimage: Towards a New Theory of the Digital Image.* Bristol: Intellect, 2015.

Jacob, J. P. 'Trevor Paglen: Invisible images and impossible objects'. In T. Paglen, *Sites Unseen*, ed. John P. Jacob and Luke Skrebowski, 23–85. London: Smithsonian American Art Museum in association with D Giles Limited, 2018.

Jagoda, P. *Network Aesthetics.* Chicago: University of Chicago Press, 2016.

Kaplan, C. *Aerial Aftermaths: Wartime from Above.* Durham, NC: Duke University Press, 2018.

Klaas, B. 'Deepfakes are coming. We're not ready'. *Washington Post*, 14 May, 2019. www.washingtonpost.com/opinions/2019/05/14/deepfakes-are-coming-were-not-ready/?utm_term=.c6ffed26ed07 (accessed 14 May, 2019).

Kracauer, S. *The Mass Ornament: Weimar Essays*, trans. T. Y. Levin. Cambridge, MA: Harvard University Press, 1995.

Krauss, R. E. *The Originality of the Avant-Garde and Other Modernist Myths.* Cambridge, MA: MIT Press, 1985.

Lima, M. *Visual Complexity: Mapping Patterns of Information.* New York: Princeton Architectural Press, 2011.

Manovich, L. 'Data visualization as new abstraction and as anti-sublime'. In B. Hawk, D. M. Rieder, and O. Oviedo (eds), *Small Tech: The Culture of Digital Tools*, 3–9. Minneapolis: University of Minnesota Press, 2008.

Manovich, L. 'Forward'. In M. Lima (ed.), *Visual Complexity: Mapping Patterns of Information*, 11–13. New York: Princeton Architectural Press, 2011.

Mayer, M. 'Fait'. In Ristelhueber, *Fait: Koweit 1991.* New York: errata editions, 2008.

Mayer-Schönberger, V. and K. Cukier. *Big Data: A Revolution That Will Transform How We Live, Work, and Think.* Boston: Houghton Mifflin Harcourt, 2013.

McCosker, A. 'Drone media: Unruly systems, radical empiricism and camera consciousness'. *Culture Machine* 16 (2015): n. p.

McCosker, A. and R. Wilken. 'Rethinking "big data" as visual knowledge: The sublime and the diagrammatic in data visualization'. *Visual Studies* 29:2 (April 2014): 155–164.

Paglen, T. *Sites Unseen*. Edited by J. P. Jacob and L. Skrebowski. London: Smithsonian American Art Museum in association with D Giles Limited, 2018.

— 'Operational images'. *e-flux journal* 59 (November, 2014). www.e-flux.com/journal/59/61130/operational-images/ (accessed 14 May, 2019).

Pantenburg, V. 'Working images: Harun Farocki and the operational image'. In J. Eder and C. Klonk (eds), *Image Operations: Visual Media and Political Conflict*, 49–62. Manchester: Manchester University Press, 2017.

Phillips, S. 'Artist and photographer Sophie Ristelhueber's best shot' (Interview). *The Guardian*, 28 April, 2010. www.theguardian.com/artanddesign/2010/apr/28/photography-sophie-ristelhueber-best-shot (accessed 3 April, 2019).

Rancière, J. *The Emancipated Spectator*, trans. G. Elliott. New York: Verso, 2009.

Richterich, A. *The Big Data Agenda: Data Ethics and Critical Data Studies*. London: University of Westminster Press, 2019.

Ristelhueber, S. *Fait: Koweit 1991*. New York: errata editions, 2008.

— 'Documenting Traces of War' (#TateShots Interview). YouTube video, 3:05, 22 January, 2015. www.youtube.com/watch?time_continue=117&v=PBsgm4OBOfE (accessed 3 April, 2019).

Sarangi, S. and P. Sharma. *Big Data: A Beginner's Introduction*. London: Taylor & Francis Group, 2019.

Smith, H. H., Thomas Hess, and Aaron Siskind. *Aaron Siskind: Photographer*. New York: George Eastman House, 1965.

Stallabrass, J. 'What's in a face? Blankness and significance in contemporary art photography'. *October* 122 (Fall 2007): 71–90.

Tabbi, J. *Postmodern Sublime: Technology and American Writing from Mailer to Cyberpunk*. Ithaca: Cornell University Press, 1995.

Underwood, T. 'Against (talking about) "big data"'. The Stone and the Shell (blog), 10 May, 2013. https://tedunderwood.com/2013/05/10/why-it-matters-that-we-dont-know-what-we-mean-by-big-data/ (accessed 16 April, 2019).

Vertov, D. *Kino-Eye: The Writings of Dziga Vertov*. Edited by Annette Michelson. Berkeley: University of California Press, 1984 [1923].

Zylinska, J. *Nonhuman Photography*. Cambridge, MA: MIT Press, 2017.

4

Empathy and the image under surveillance capitalism: interview with photographer Tomas van Houtryve

Tomas van Houtryve and Svea Braeunert

Tomas van Houtryve is a conceptual artist, photographer and author whose major works interweave investigative journalism, philosophy and metaphor. Van Houtryve makes images using a wide array of processes, ranging from nineteenth-century wet plate collodion to thermal imaging and Augmented Reality. His projects challenge our notions of identity, memory and power, often by highlighting the slippage of wartime structures into everyday life.

His photo series *Blue Sky Days* (2013) was among the first artworks to address drone warfare, reaching a broad audience in- and outside of the artworld. While the photos are striking and beautiful vertical images of American landscapes, the title of the work refers to a statement made by 13-year-old Zubair Rehman at a congressional hearing in 2013. Zubair Rehman's grandmother was killed by a drone strike in Pakistan in 2012, and he was injured by shrapnel. At the hearing in Washington DC, Rehman said: 'I no longer love blue skies. In fact, I now prefer grey skies. The drones do not fly when the skies are grey.'[1]

Calling his series *Blue Sky Days*, van Houtryve integrates Rehman's voice and the experience of Pakistani communities into his work. He hints at the ways in which the constant presence of drones causes major anxiety, traumatises individuals, and disrupts the trust and social rituals binding communities together.[2] Yet, while the political-ethical context of the photos is Pakistan, their spatial-visual context is the US. Using a self-built quadcopter with a camera attached to it, all images were taken there. They offer an American audience a view onto itself, as seen through the eyes of a drone – an effect the photos arrive at not only because of their vertical vantage points but also due to their black-and-white colour scheme, which repeats the black-and-white feed of military drones and thus visually juxtapose the eponymous blue sky of the series' title. Combining Pakistani anxiety with US imagery, *Blue Sky Days* addresses two very different communities, yet asks viewers to establish (imaginary) relations between them, thereby realising photography's civil contract through the act of looking.[3]

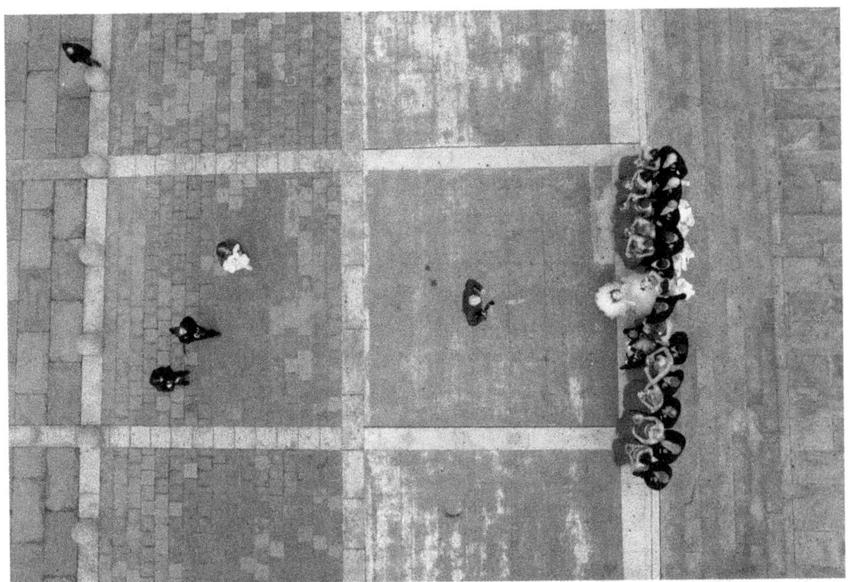

4.1 Tomas van Houtryve, *Wedding*, 2013, gelatin silver print, 100 × 66cm.

Svea Braeunert showed *Blue Sky Days* as part of the exhibition *To See Without Being Seen: Contemporary Art and Drone Warfare*, which she co-curated with Meredith Malone at the Mildred Lane Kemper Art Museum in 2016.[4] Braeunert and van Houtryve have been in conversation about the images and media cultures of drone warfare and surveillance since. In the following, they take up the opportunity to talk about the ideas behind *Blue Sky Days*, what has changed since van Houtryve conceived of the project, and how drones and digital surveillance technology – as they are used in wars, border control and consumer research – are affecting ideas of community and belonging.[5]

Svea Braeunert (SB): Your photo series Blue Sky Days *was one of the first publicly recognised projects dealing with the US engagement of drones in undeclared zones of war and the civilian casualties they cause. An important impetus for the project was that there were hardly any images documenting that war, and this struck you as odd and dangerous, given that war and image-making share a long history and that access to information is a cornerstone of democracy. In order to counter this absence, you decided to create your own set of images, which are large-scale black-and-white photos taken in the US using a high resolution still camera mounted on a self-built quadcopter. The setting for the images was chosen so that they would either mirror social situations in which drone strikes had occurred in*

Pakistan, Yemen and Somalia or show sites in which drones were used by government agencies in the US. Can you tell me a little bit about this dual approach of simultaneously looking here and there? Is there a distinctly relational thrust in these images?

Tomas van Houtryve (TvH): The main aspect of *Blue Sky Days* was to turn things around, so that the people who are usually doing the targeting and surveillance – or their government representatives and agencies – would all of a sudden see themselves from the other point of view: What does it look like? What is it like to be under this gaze of surveillance and targeting rather than being in the comfortable position of paying taxes and voting for politicians that are constructing this infrastructure and projecting it elsewhere? That was the first impetus. I thus came to the project through the actual drone strikes in Pakistan and elsewhere, because that is what initially caught my attention.

It was only while the research was already underway and I had started shooting the mirroring situations that I realised the extent to which drones had spilled over into the domestic space and were being used by government agencies. So that became an addition, as I learned more and more about it. I realised that Customs and Border Protection had their own fleet of Predator drones that they were flying over the Mexican and Canadian borders of the US. These drones were being lent out to other law enforcement agencies, which tried to acquire this new technology as fast as they could and apply it to domestic situations. The domestic implementation of drones really changed fundamental ideas of privacy without there being a debate about it.

The technology really got far ahead of a debate on such fundamental questions as: Should people be under aerial surveillance at all times? What are the settings and situations in which surveillance takes place? Should people expect to be in private when they are on their own land for example? I chose a dual approach for *Blue Sky Days* in order to bring all of these different issues to the fore.

SB: You started working on Blue Sky Days *around 2012, and the work was made public in 2013.*

TvH: Yes, the work started in 2012. First, there was a period of research and grant writing. Then I had to try to get a camera on the drone and the drone up in the air, because what was available for consumers at that point was a bit rudimentary. You couldn't just buy something off the shelf. That took quite a while to manage. However, I was finally able to start shooting in earnest in 2013 and take the kind of photographs that I wanted for the project and publish them.

SB: I asked about the starting date of your project because you stress the domestic application of drones. Clearly, that domestic side has to do with government agencies, but it also has to do with different levels of filmmaking and entertainment, with agriculture and infrastructure. I mean, drones are even used as toys now. So, it seems that quite a lot has happened since 2012. Would you say that the domestic side has become even more important – or at least more visible – since you started your project and has that changed your take on your project or on the way you look at drones?

TvH: Yes, I think there are two major trends going on. Initially I would say it was a slippage of wartime technology into the domestic space, and that mirrors what has happened over the years for many other technologies. There are many things that have been invented on the battlefront and then found applications on the home front – whether it is specific policing gear or something as simple as the trench coat that was made for the First World War and became a fashion accessory around the world. So that is one aspect of it. And then there is another aspect I think is troubling and that you need to keep an eye on. It is something that is not limited to drones but is a much wider trend that has to do with domestic police forces taking up arms traditionally used for counterterrorism such as armoured cars. A police officer in the US used to be a very civil figure who was lightly armed and not wearing any body armour. Over a number of years, that has changed. It is sort of regular now to see people in the kind of full combat gear that you would expect an occupation patrol officer in Iraq to wear. Those same police departments have also acquired drones. And this means that the domestic usage of drones indicates a wider trend of first testing technology on the battlefield and then applying it domestically. The same thing has happened along the US–Mexican border. There has been a militarisation in tactic, in words, in style. It has accompanied an influx of technology first tested on the battlefield and then applied to the border. So that is the one aspect I wanted to point out that has changed over time since I started *Blue Sky Days* in 2012.

The other aspect is the wide adoption of consumer drone technology. It has diverted people's attention from its military and surveillance uses. There are so many consumer applications out there. As you mentioned, drones are used as toys or for filmmaking and agriculture and things like that. Hence, if you pop the word *drone* on somebody these days, their first thought won't be a CIA drone for a targeted strike or even a police drone. The first thing that will come to their mind is probably a toy or a filmmaking tool. As a result, the way the drone is viewed by the wider public has shifted. And some of that shift is not helpful. By making the drone a sort of pedestrian object that can accomplish things that aren't a threat to democracy, the other capabilities of the drone are backgrounded and forgotten a little bit. Yet I think they still pose a threat to democratic institutions and free society, and we need to keep our eye on these military and police capabilities and not just think about the drone's recreational or cultural uses.

SB: I agree with that observation. When I teach classes on the topic, my students usually first think of the kind of drones they use for fun or recreational purposes. When I then go on and tell them what I work on, they are surprised that we are also talking about war. So, the military application of drones is apparently not as present anymore as it used to be. Going with the assumption that a relationship between military and consumer drones exists though, one can make the argument that they affect each other's images and frameworks. What I mean is that the widespread use of drones in the domestic sphere effects a militarisation of that sphere, i.e., that we look at everyday settings with a militaristic and potentially violent gaze. The other side of that relationship is the effect you just mentioned – a domestication of drone technology and a concurrent lack of attention towards its implementation in war.

TvH: Let me add one other aspect. The third issue I was not as aware of at the time and that has become very obvious by now is the massive growth of surveillance capitalism. And the drone is a sort of bridge technology for that. Surveillance used for targeting and political control is one thing, but we also have a new kind of surveillance that is popping up for the psychological targeting of consumers. And I would say that is maybe the area a light needs to be shone on next. It is the middle ground between those two things: the consumer application of the drone and the political-military application of the drone. The drone and its camera not only suck up information for political uses or for fun, but it is also sucking up the information that is added to huge databases which are then turned around and used on populations. It can be used for anything from traffic regulations to figuring out consumer patterns, to stock investment companies like Goldman Sachs using surveillance to predict what quarterly earnings will be before quarterly earnings come out. What I heard about the specific case of Goldman Sachs is that they buy up satellite imagery of places like Wal-Mart parking lots. Over time they can see how many cars showed up during the quarter and predict how many purchases were made before the earning reports come out. What I want to emphasise is the usage of photography as big data and its intricate connection to consumer capitalism.

The drone obviously has a role to play in that dynamic. A perfect scenario to show how this works is Amazon's business model of collecting as much shopping information about you and then serving that back and using it to suggest books or other products you might want to buy. Also, as is very well known, they want to use drones to deliver their products. Yet, if those drones are delivering your Amazon purchases, they can also fly over your house and, in the same way that Wal-Mart parking lots can be photographed for Goldman Sachs, your house can be photographed by Amazon's drones and they can pick up information like: Do you have a swimming pool? Do you have a dog in the backyard? As a result, the data collection as a larger part of capitalism can be carried forward by the drone. When looked at in this way, the drone is basically this sensor that is out there in the world collecting information in ways that we don't expect.

SB: In regard to that topic, I find Grégoire Chamayou's concept of a society of targeting pretty intriguing. His argument is essentially that we have moved from a society of surveillance to a society of control to a society of targeting, and this concept of targeting unites warfare, policing and commercial interests. And I think you are describing some of the latest and very disturbing developments of that.[6]

Also, your answer made me think of two projects that you have done since Blue Sky Days, which was your first project on drones. The first is Packing Heat (2014), for which you photographed New York City with a thermal-imaging camera, thereby using a technology that has originally been used for combat and is now increasingly used for police surveillance. Your interest in the project was to see 'how a technology designed for surveillance rendered the human form'.[7] *The second project I think of is your multi-part engagement with the US–Mexican border in* Lines and Lineage, Divided *(2018) and the photographs you took for* Time Magazine's *special report on* The Drone Age *(2018).*[8] *The central medium of your exploration of the border is photography – and with wet plate photography even a very traditional form of photography. However, you also once again used drones during that project. Can you tell me a little bit more about why you chose these two ways of approaching your topic, i.e. a very traditional form of photography on the one hand and drone images on the other?*

TvH: As a photographer, the project made me aware of the history of photography and the role it plays in shaping perceptions and memory, whether it is how photographs are shown in museums or history books or just in everyday media. And what I noticed is that photography picked up in the US just after the Mexican–American war. Even though photographic technology had been invented, it hadn't made it out to the far West at the time of the US conquest of that land.

The American West is the victim of a triple dose of amnesia. The most obvious one has to do with the fact that the victors write history. It was the Anglo-Americans and not the Hispanics that wrote the history of the war. Number two is that photography which has a particular aptitude to guarding moments in time, saving moments in time, and saving faces from a different past was not available yet. If you want to have a visual memory of the war, you hence have to rely on paintings or tapestries or things like that; they were quite limited. And the third thing is the role of Hollywood, which got really into the idea of the myth of the West. For fifty years, the Western was the dominant genre of Hollywood. It developed into this incredible phenomenon that spread around the world and was adopted by audiences.

Together, the mythical stories created by Hollywood, the history books written in a very ethnocentric way, and the images missing from the other side, form a very ignorant view of Mexican–American relations in the West. Basically, the way it is framed from a Western perspective is that Anglo-Americans are pioneers that were spreading enlightenment, American values of freedom and civil rights and things like that, as the US expanded westward. In fact, it is completely the other way around. Mexico abolished slavery far before the US; it gave voting rights to native people far before the US. So, the US arrival was actually a huge rollback in rights, and the Anglo-Americans are latecomers and spoilers of the nascent civil rights that were coming out of Mexico at the time. I was interested in seeing that photography played a role in this three-part constellation that gave such a misguided view of history that still holds to this day, and that is still being taught to people growing up in that region. This is how I saw photography being wrapped up in the mythology of the history of the US and Mexico and the border. And then I thought I would compare that to how photography plays a role in policing the current US–Mexican border, which is a role of complicity that overlaps greatly with the previous work on *Blue Sky Days*. In fact, I already had a few pictures that I had taken on the US–Mexican border as part of the 2013 to 2015 *Blue Sky Days* work because I knew that Customs and Border Protection was using this fleet of Predator drones along the Southern border.

The debate you have in US administration is not about whether there should be more or less security on the Southern border. The debate is more about the type of security. Under the Bush and the Obama administration, the guiding idea was to build a virtual fence, including things such as ground sensors, agents and aerial drones watching the border and apprehending people using the latest high-tech tools. And now under Trump you have this idea of a physical barrier that is much more symbolic to dissuade people from entering the country. What you don't have is a debate of questions such as: Is the border in the right place? Are its foundations just? Given that you have two cultures that have been cohabiting for centuries, is it really the best way to draw a hard line between them? Is that really the best way to react to economies and cultures that have overlapped over time? But I wanted to highlight that it is not just Trump's wall which is very visible and easily demonised. It is clearly part of a policy of splitting these two people apart in two nations. Instead, I wanted to point to the fact that photography plays an active role in identifying, targeting, and apprehending people that want to cross the border.

SB: You point to the use of different media and technologies that are employed as part of the creation and fortification of the US–Mexican border. In your own work, I have also come to see a widening of your use of media. For although you predominantly work with still images and your main practice is photography, in recent years you have increasingly integrated video into your work. I think, for instance, of Traces of Exile *(2016–2017), a single-channel video installation that follows the paths of migration from North Africa and the Middle East to Europe by collecting Instagram posts by refugees and mapping them onto slow-moving images of different sites. Another example is* Divided, *a video you shot with a drone of the seaside at the US–Mexican border. To me, the video is interesting and evocative on the one hand because of the way in which it shows the arbitrariness of borders when seen through the lens of landscapes, traditions, and communities. As you mentioned in regard to* Lines and Lineage, *the people living along the US–Mexican border share a common culture and*

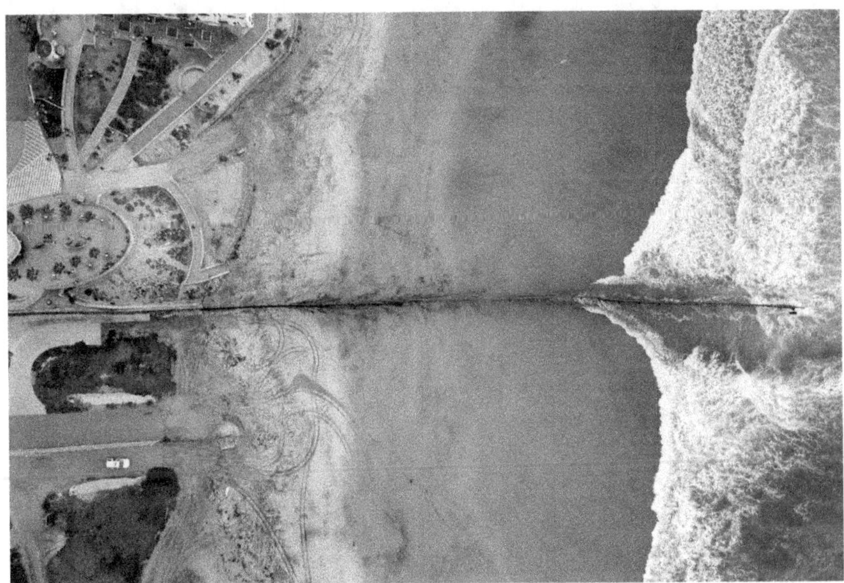

4.2 Tomas van Houtryve, *Divided*, 2018, single-channel video installation.

landscape that is artificially and violently divided by that border. In its slow progression from water onto land, your video shows both the aspect of belonging and the aspect of a forceful division through the material realities of water, walls, and land.

On the other hand, I find it interesting to see how the video for Divided *came out of your photographic exploration for* Lines and Lineage. *Looking at these two examples, what would you say is the relationship between still and moving images nowadays? And what role does video play in your artistic practice?*

TvH: Part of my move to video is technology-driven, because still photography is now more linked to its moving counterpart than it used to be. Previously, the devices that recorded still photography and film and video were completely separate. Today, however, even your average mobile phone records a second before and after taking a picture. The result is a slightly moving picture. Or just think of the popularity of gifs and things like that which are just a series of still photos played in a loop. What is happening is that the purely still image is fading off and is barely around. It is becoming backgrounded into a still image with a little bit of life to it. And that is a separate thing from what cinema has been doing over a long, long time, right?

When I am out shooting, the difference between me and somebody with a real motion background is often the formal approach. The way filmmaking is taught in film school is often more akin to theatre. It is more about narrative than capturing moving imagery. That is the background a lot of filmmakers come from, while my background is still photography. Still photography is about seizing a moment in time. But now you can see a little bit before or a little bit after that moment, or maybe the photo can even magically come to life. There is an overlap between still and moving images.

Also, the intriguing thing about working with video is that there are certain messages, stories or ideas that a purely still photo can't carry very well. But all of a sudden if you add a little bit of sound or a little bit of motion, you can bring across that idea. And the way of conveying this idea can still be less narrative-driven and more ambiguous than traditional filmmaking, which is about telling a story in motion, time, and sound that has its roots much more in theatre.

SB: That is a very interesting way of putting it, because it makes me think about the debates regarding the ways in which categories and understandings of images are changing in digital culture. One way to talk about that change is the operative image of machine vision and the increasing invisibility and action-driven dimension of these images. Taking your comment into account, it seems to me that we need to add the erosion of a difference between still and moving images to that and understand images in digital culture as always already moving and as always already being more than one. You have said to me in an earlier conversation that you think of your videos as photographs with a little bit of motion, and I think that is a beautiful way of putting it. But it is also an evocative way of looking at the ways in which categories of the visual are currently shifting.

Another pairing that shows us this shifting – at least to me – is the relationship between figure and ground/landscape. In regard to your work on the US–Mexican border but also in regard to you work on the US drone war in Pakistan, I find it very interesting how you navigate that relationship. It is very obvious in the case of Lines and Lineage, *for which you actually took portraits of people. However, with the aerial view, the landscape also comes into view. And in the case of* Blue Sky Days, *you often have both: landscape and human figure. Would you say that the ways in which these works and images navigate human figure and landscape is another defining feature of these new types of images and vision machine such as drones? And what role do these two dimensions of figure and ground play in your work?*

TvH: They absolutely do. The drone dehumanises from its point of view. Seeing from a drone's point of view, we see the earth as a bird or a satellite would see the earth rather than this frontal view that we would see in portraiture. And that frontal view of portraiture is about mimicking the feeling that we are able to look into somebody's eyes. And the advantage of that in the case of photography is that you could look into the eyes of somebody whose neighbourhood you might never enter, or who is from a culture you might never go to; or there could be all kinds of social, racial, economic barriers between you. Looking into the eyes of that person, portraiture allows you to contemplate that. Drone photography is pretty much as far from that as you can possibly get. I feel it offers you the viewpoint of the bomb-door. It is the point of view as if you were flying a bomber plane and looking straight down on somebody. It's the top of their head that you can see. That is the sort of view that the drones can give you. Yet it also gives you these incredible sweeping landscapes that are much harder to capture in portraiture where you are tied to keeping the horizon perfectly flat. You can get a very cartographic view of the world instead.

The fact that these two types of images are so visually different also mimics the difference in how different organs of control and policing view people. It is different to have people come through a port of entry or meet them on a face-to-face basis and see them. What you get out of the human experience from that is different from seeing them through drones, through heat sensors and other things that are turning people into something that is closer to data or statistics than to a human figure that is capable of bringing out emotion or empathy or that establishes the sort of connection that you get by looking someone in the eye. There is a very wide gap between those two kinds of photography and what they elicit in human viewers.

SB: There are a number of photographs in Blue Sky Days *where the human bodies cast large shadows. A good example is* Signature Behavior *(2013), a photo taken in a public square with people passing through. Their physical bodies are mere schematic dots that are barely discernible as bodies, but their virtual bodies loom large in the form of their shadows. These shadows show gestures and movements; a whole shadow play reminiscent of Weimar era photography such as Umbo's* Mystery of the Street *(1928). It is only through these shadows that we can encounter the people in the image as human; and it is – at least on the level of the photograph – only in their shadows that the people can encounter each other. Given that* Signature Behavior *is just one among many instances, why was it important to you to photograph the scenes in this way where the human figure is doubled by its shadow?*

TvH: Well, I think that you get a hint of empathy by seeing a human form, but the human form is often distorted and it becomes two-dimensional. Some people have compared it to a silhouette that you would see in a shooting range. When you have a target in a shooting range, it is usually a black silhouette. People's shadows are cast on the ground with a very similar texture as these figures in the shooting range. But the distortion also has to do with the sun and with other objects on the ground. If the sun is higher or lower in the sky, then the shadow won't be a perfect reproduction of a human. It will be longer or shorter. Also, whatever is on the ground can distort the shadow. Gravel or rocks or other things can all change the shape of it a little bit.

I think that this is a fitting metaphor for what is going on when we are judged based on metadata. Metadata and other information collected through sensors and surveillance don't show a very true picture of us. They show a distorted picture of us. It is a little bit circumstantial, it is dependent on the light, it is dependent on who is looking at it and what their built-in biases are. Once I noticed that a drone allowed you to capture people's shadows in a way that flattened and distorted them, I found that to be a very fitting analogy to putting somebody under surveillance and using all their data points to judge their behaviour. After all, that is also a sort of distorted and flat way to understand a person. And let's be honest about this.

Once they use that data, they are using it for very important decisions in the case of drone strikes. It is life-and-death data. Whether somebody lives or dies or not is based on data points. Or in the case of the US–Mexico border, whether somebody will be apprehended or deported or not, is based on that. It is very, very important how you appear to the surveillance machinery, even though there are so many inaccuracies built into it.

SB: Yes, I think that is a very important point that we need to stress and remember time and again. And it is one that you want to bring across to your viewers through empathy – or so it seems to me. You have mentioned empathy several times in our conversation, suggesting that it is an important concept to you. What do you hope to achieve with empathy? Or what role does it play for your work and for the message you want to send?

TvH: There is a long tradition of empathy in photography, and there are specific case studies that you could point to where two people separated by conflict or tribal or economic differences occasionally can bridge their differences with a photo that generates empathy. I think that is one of the skills that photography has. Photography can do all kinds of things, just like the written language; but evoking empathy is one particularly useful skill of photography.

I don't think it should be used unquestioningly though, because it is often overused to the point that it becomes trite and useless. The classic example would be charity campaigns that will use a crying or starving child on the cover to solicit donations. I would say that this is the most vulgar and easily tired use of it, bordering on emotional manipulation. But there are a lot of cases in-between. If you have never imagined yourself – and why would you – in the shoes of somebody that is at risk of being in a drone strike, maybe seeing a wedding from a drone's eye point-of-view will suddenly make you be able to see that point of view, to put yourself in their shoes and imagine the vulnerability that arises from that situation and the arbitrariness of justice that can come out of that drone strike. In that case, the empathy can be quite useful. It can show how everyday life can be rendered in a way that seems unfair and distorted, and it can show how people in another place can be treated in a way that is dehumanising or objectifying. I think empathy is the sort of the thing that breaks those spells.

SB: I agree, and you just mentioned another word that I find very important in that regard. And that is imagination. Because on the one hand you need to have very strong images, but on the other hand these very same images also need to leave you some room to invest your imagination and invest yourself in the image. I think it is only through that engagement and investment that it becomes a truly powerful image. Could you talk a little bit more about what ambiguity means to you and your work? Or to put it differently: would you describe your mode of presentation as one in which you do not present a picture that is so saturated and complete that it does not leave room for the viewers to invest themselves any longer?

TvH: Yes, I completely agree with that, and I think part of the reason why my work has become more abstract over time is to give the viewer more space to contemplate, to question, and to break down easy categorisations of what they are seeing in images. I think that is essential. In fact, in a lot of my work I will try to throw people for an initial loop or put them in a situation where they try to make an easy categorisation that then quickly disintegrates; and then they have to do some deep thinking of what they are actually thinking; they have to engage their full brain.

I mean, in this day and age, we see so many images. Most of those result in a snap judgment. The way that mobile telephones are used now – whether it is online dating or Instagram or watching your friends' vacation photos – is based on fast-read imagery, snap judgments and easy categorisations. And I think ambiguity, which can be driven by abstraction or just by leaving a little bit of information out of the picture, can slow that process down and hopefully invite engagement rather than snap judgement.

SB: That brings us back to the beginning of our conversation when we talked about the fact that although drone technology has become ever more ubiquitous and we are surrounded by it, we still don't really know what we're dealing with. And we still don't really know what we're looking at most of the times, although certainly these extreme vertical views have become not necessarily more familiar, but we do get to see them more often.

TvH: Your average television ad showing a car or something like that will almost always have a breakaway shot of the drone's eye-view of the car driving. People see that about 80 times a day, so it has become much more familiar. I have wondered if this work on *Blue Sky Days* would stand the test of time, now that we are used to the bird's eye point of view and that it has become so accessible that it seems just like one more way of seeing things. I think what saves the project, and keeps people wondering about it, is actually the abstraction that you don't have in most advertising or drone photography. In most of the commercial drone images, even if you have a purely vertical shot, the camera usually switches to the horizon or a ground shot. And so a transition is made from a shot that can create a feeling of vertigo or that is quite graphic to a more human perspective of looking at things. This way, people can get their bearings, and if you cut back-and-forth between these sorts of images, nobody gets lost. But I think it is important for people to stay a little bit disoriented, to keep that ambiguity alive and nurture it long enough for people to have a conversation or at least put in doubt some of their snap judgments and preconceptions.

Notes

1 A. Abad-Santos, 'This 13-year-old is scared when the sky is blue because of our drones', *The Atlantic* (29 October, 2013), www.theatlantic.com/politics/archive/2013/10/saddest-words-congresss-briefing-drone-strikes/354548/ (accessed 22 October, 2019).
2 International Human Rights and Conflict Resolution Clinic at Stanford Law School, Global Justice Clinic at NYU School of Law, 'Living under drones: Death, injury, and trauma to civilians from US drone practices in Pakistan' (2012), https://chrgj.org/wp-content/uploads/2016/09/Living-Under-Drones.pdf (accessed 16 February, 2021).
3 A. Azoulay, *The Civil Contract of Photography* (New York: Zone Books, 2008).
4 S. Braeunert and M. Malone (eds), *To See Without Being Seen: Contemporary Art and Drone Warfare* (Chicago: University of Chicago Press, 2016).
5 The conversation took place via Skype in April 2019. It was gently edited to make for a better reading experience.
6 G. Chamayou, 'Patterns of life: A very short history of schematic bodies', *The Funambulist Papers* 57 (4 December, 2014), http://thefunambulist.net/2014/12/04/the-funambulist-papers-57-schematic-bodies-notes-on-a-patterns-genealogy-by-gregoire-chamayou/ (accessed 8 December, 2019).
7 Tomas van Houtryve, *Packing Heat* (2014), https://tomasvh.com/works/packing-heat/ (accessed 22 Ocotber, 2019).
8 Tomas van Houtryve, *Lines and Lineage* (Santa Fe: Radius Books, 2019); *Time Magazine*, *The Drone Age* (31 May, 2018), https://time.com/collection/drones/ (accessed 22 February, 2021).

Bibliography

Abad-Santos, A. 'This 13-year-old is scared when the sky is blue because of our drones'. *The Atlantic*, 29 October 2013. www.theatlantic.com/politics/archive/2013/10/saddest-words-congresss-briefing-drone-strikes/354548/ (accessed 22 October, 2019).

Azoulay, A. *The Civil Contract of Photography*. New York: Zone Books, 2008.

Bräunert, S. and M. Malone (eds). *To See Without Being Seen: Contemporary Art and Drone Warfare*. Chicago: University of Chicago Press, 2016.

Chamayou, G. 'Patterns of life: A very short history of schematic bodies'. *The Funambulist Papers*, 57, 4 December, 2014. http://thefunambulist.net/2014/12/04/the-funambulist-papers-57-schematic-bodies-notes-on-a-patterns-genealogy-by-gregoire-chamayou/ (accessed 8 December, 2019).

International Human Rights and Conflict Resolution Clinic at Stanford Law School, Global Justice Clinic at NYU School of Law. 'Living under drones: Death, injury, and trauma to civilians from US drone practices in Pakistan', 2012. https://chrgj.org/wp-content/uploads/2016/09/Living-Under-Drones.pdf (accessed 16 February, 2021).

Time Magazine. *The Drone Age*, 31 May, 2018. https://time.com/collection/drones/ (accessed 22 Ocotber, 2019).

van Houtryve T. *Packing Heat*, 2014. https://tomasvh.com/works/packing-heat/ (accessed 22 Ocotber, 2019).

van Houtryve, T. *Lines and Lineage*. Santa Fe: Radius Books, 2019.

Part II

Bodies

5

Disappearing, appearing, and reappearing: imaging the human body in drone warfare

Svea Braeunert

Drone warfare is about the human figure.[1]
The whole point of the figure/ground image is appearance and disappearance.[2]

'Drone warfare is about the human figure.' The figure is the schematised human body, and, as such, it is the prime entity of a targeted, individualised killing programme pushed forward by drones. Given that drones are supposed to track and target people at the level of the single body, it is remarkable that the drones' cameras are ill-equipped to do so. Although operators' testimonies vary, a significant number of reports attest to the fact that the drone's view makes it difficult to discern individual features and to recognise a body as human.[3] Instead, the drone offers a narrow focus on the land, which shares key characteristics with vertical views in general, including a high level of abstraction and a flattening of the landscape into an image that has map-like qualities. Within these abstracted, flattened landscapes, human bodies come to look like figures. Depending on the settings on the image feed, they take on the shape of black or white blotches; and they are present – but not necessarily visible – as data-sets. Because they are visually stripped of their humanity, the drone's framework turns bodies into targets. They are targets precisely because they are hard to see and recognise. Hence, the precarious state of the body as a potential target is met by the precarious state of the image as something that is hard to decipher. Visual and physical precariousness thus go hand in hand when it comes to the framing of the human body as a non-human figure in drone warfare.

In the following, I want to look at the connection between physical and visual precariousness by tracing the ways in which the human body is treated as a precarious image in three projects perched on the line between art and activism: British, Athens-based artist James Bridle's record of satellite images connected to the sites of drone strikes on his *Dronestagram* (2012–2015); the online campaign *#NotaBugSplat* (2014) initiated by the Pakistani Foundation for Fundamental Rights and the British organisation Reprieve to give civilian victims of drone attacks a face; and Palestinian,

New York-based artist Seth Price's photo series *Danny, Mila, Hannah, Ariana, Bob, Brad* (2015), which uses satellite software to create landscape views of the human body. While the first two projects are directly related to drone warfare, Price's work does not have such an immediate link to the topic. Due to its imaging of the human body through the unconventional means of satellite software, it nevertheless gives meaningful insights into the question of how the view of digital technologies and machines such as satellites and drones render the human body into an uncertain image that disappears, appears, and reappears.

None of the projects discussed employ actual drone footage, but all of them can be read as comments on what the drone does or does not allow one to see. Both Bridle and Price work with satellite views, which, due to their verticality, abstraction, map-like quality, and uncertainty can be understood as an escalation of the drone's point of view. Satellite images present us with an even more extreme view than drone images. They emphasise the fact that these are non-human views; the machines – be they drones or satellites – see differently from 'us'; and as such, they do not just see things differently, but certain things may not come into view at all, as is the case with the human body. When viewed through the non-embodied lens of the machine, the human body disappears from sight. The images under scrutiny are thus disembodied in more than one way: Cast by disembodied machines, they also visually disembody the image by masking the fact that a body is/was there. In its place, landscape takes over, making up the content of the image. This can be seen in a number of artworks addressing drone warfare, which treat the topic through politically charged views of the land. Bridle's *Dronestagram* and Price's *Danny, Mila, Hannah, Ariana, Bob, Brad* are two such examples, while *#NotaBugSplat* aims to counter the disappearance of the human body by focusing on a single face instead.

Looking at the concepts and modes of depiction informing the three projects and reading them in light of the drone's mission and reality, landscape and body suggest themselves as central categories to analyse the drone's visual framework. Another way of talking about landscape and body are ground and figure: the two fundamental principles organising human perception and artistic representation. Tilted images are based on the interplay of figure and ground; one can look at them to reflect on the working of the two and analyse guiding principles informing perception and representation. Therefore, tilted images will serve as an essential background to the thoughts I develop in the following. In a tilted image, two images are present but only one can be seen at a time. Canonical examples include the picture of a duck and a rabbit, a young and an old woman, a vase and two faces in profile. In an attempt to see each of them, the eye switches back and forth; the brain knows that two figures are there, but the eye can only see one of them. It is a mechanism I find intriguing when thinking about the appearance and disappearance of the human figure because, similar to the drone's imaging, the tilted image combines physical presence with perceptual absence.

Commenting on the functioning of these images, visual culture scholar W. J. T. Mitchell writes: 'The whole point of the figure/ground image [i.e. the tilted image] is appearance and disappearance.'[4] The quote stands as an epigraph at the beginning of the chapter next to the quote by critic and architect Eyal Weizman stating that 'drone warfare is about the human figure' because my aim is to read the two together in order to make sense of the imaging of the human body in drone warfare. For on the one hand, landscape (ground) appears when the body (figure) disappears, effecting an increase in landscape representations in contemporary art dealing with drones and war. On the other hand, one can take the dynamic between figure and ground in order to think about the process of appearance and disappearance and treat drone warfare as a tilted image that asks viewers to constantly switch back and forth, focusing on that very blink in-between figure and ground that suggests the idea of an image existing beyond representation. My argument is set up as such a blink, as it moves back and forth, tracing the ways in which the human body disappears, appears, and reappears in contemporary products reflecting on the imaging of drone warfare.

Disappearing: satellite images in James Bridle's *Dronestagram*

The artist-scholar-research group Forensic Architecture conducted a number of studies on drone attacks in the Federally Administered Tribal Areas (FATA) in the border region between Pakistan and Afghanistan. When undertaking their research, they were challenged by the fact that access to FATA was extremely limited. The solution to getting a view into the secluded area from the outside was found in commercially available satellite images. Yet the resolution of these images was such that it masked the human body and made it disappear. As the director and one of the principal investigators of Forensic Architecture Eyal Weizman explains: 'Throughout the height of the drone campaign and for the entire duration of the investigation, the resolution at which satellite images were made publicly available was legally kept at 0.5 meters per pixel, with each pixel representing half a meter by half a meter of ground's surface.'[5] The reason this resolution was chosen was 'because it is aligned with the dimension of the human body. [...] Half a meter square is the frame within which the human body fits when seen from above.'[6] The satellite view was calibrated to protect people's privacy; yet, the result of this protective measure was that humans could not be seen although they were there. Satellite images hence let the human body disappear, while the surrounding ground appears and makes up the content of the image.

Turning to satellite images to build their case and overcome government secrecy, Forensic Architecture follows a strand of human rights investigations that architect and media artist Laura Kurgan has described as a counter-hegemonic strategy of appropriating a technology once owned by the state into a visual strategy owned by the people. What she calls 'civic satellite surveillance' and 'satellite imagery activism'[7] was made possible by President Bill Clinton's declassification of Cold War-era satellite imagery in 1995, the privatisation of commercial high-resolution satellites later in the 1990s, and the launch of Google Earth in 2005.[8] Employing satellite images as witnesses, 'activists were granted the clarity of vision to be able to identify burned villages in Darfur, nuclear sites in Iran, prison camps in North Korea, or the ruins of Grozny in Chechnya.'[9]

Works straddling the line between art and activism make use of satellite views for similar reasons when trying to come to terms with the drone campaign. They include James Bridle's social media site *Dronestagram* (2012–2015) and his digital photo series *Watching the Watchers* (since 2013), as well as Josh Begley's iPhone App *Metadata* (since 2012) and his interactive map *Empire.is* (2014). What these works have in common is their aim to counter secrecy by revealing the hidden structures of the US military and its clandestine wars, which find their material footprints in the sites of drone attacks, drone ports, landing strips, and other military installations. Their practice adheres to artist Trevor Paglen's observation 'that all human undertakings, including secret programs, are spatial. In other words, even though classified programs are organised in such a way as to maximise their own invisibility, they have to happen somewhere.'[10] Artists employing satellite images give this somewhere an image by locating it on a map and placing that map in a digital media environment.

The images one can find on Bridle's *Dronestagram* are vertical views depicting the land. They were chosen based on data of US drone strikes compiled by non-governmental organisations such as the British Bureau of Investigative Journalism. Each of the images refers to the coordinates of a specific site were a drone attack had taken place; the attack is represented in a single Instagram post, combining a satellite image from Google Earth or Bing Maps and a text listing the information available for the specific incident. The images have a surface-orientation that makes them look map-like. A lot of them are almost monochrome, fashioning the ochre, brown, and sandy-red colours of the desert and steppe. There are some but not too many mountains, also the greenery of trees and fields. For the most part, one sees the rectangular shapes of houses, most of which are part of small village-like structures. There are streets; in a couple of instances one can see a car but no people. Although they must have been there, hanging laundry in the courtyard, working in the field, walking the streets, they are not to be seen. The satellite's resolution has masked their figure from appearing in the image. They have blended in with the surrounding land, thus effecting an exchange of ground for figure that is indicative of the overall increase in landscape representations in artists' dealings with drone warfare.[11]

The pictures in Bridle's *Dronestagram* correspond to an aesthetic of mapping that art historian Svetlana Alpers has described as the transformation of 'the surface of the earth [...] onto a flat, two-dimensional surface. It does not suppose a located viewer.' Also, it 'can virtually be said to be without people.'[12] Looking at Dutch art of the seventeenth century, Alpers establishes a connection between mapping and imaging that allows us to look at maps as if they were pictures. Summarising what commonly differentiates the two forms of representation, she writes:

> In the study of images we are used to treating maps as one kind of a thing and pictures as something else. [...] We can always tell maps and landscapes apart by their look. Maps give us the measure of a place and the relationship between places, quantifiable data, while landscape pictures are evocative, and aim rather to give us some quality of a place or of the viewer's sense of it. One is closer to science, the other is art.[13]

While maps stand for information, pictures or landscapes stand for sensation; the one is remote, the other embodied. Yet, as Alpers argues, the distinction makes little sense in regard to Dutch painting that is both map and picture, using mapping as a technique of picturing and vice versa.

I believe that a similar framework of considering maps as pictures is instructive when looking at Bridle's *Dronestagram*. Bridle's images taken from Google Earth and Bing Maps are vertical views; they are abstractions that favour shapes and colours and are devoid of people. In that, they follow an aesthetic of mapping and are indicative of a contemporary increase in map-like representations. Nevertheless, the addition of text to these images assists viewers in filling the gap and thinking of the people who were there, although they are not to be seen. Their presence is marked in the form of short descriptions added to the images. Depending on how much information was available, these texts tell the victims' names, numbers, and the circumstances of their deaths. From these stories, the eye can wander to the images and try to find the human factor in them. It can look at the maps as pictures in a non-expert, empathetic way that is open to the imagination. It can imagine the people and their presence by way of the sites of their deaths.

Commenting on the satellite images that were taken of the site of the World Trade Center attack, Kurgan suggests something similar when noticing, 'what is missing are the missing [...] Beneath or beyond the limits of visibility, of data, are the dead. And yet they remain in the image, in the ruin of the image, and demand a certain care or respect.'[14] The same holds true for the sites of the drone attacks that Bridle pictures via Google Earth. The images mark a spot – something that, according to Kurgan, is needed to mourn the dead. 'Graves simply need markers, and more than anything else, that's what the image did for me: it did not reveal a lot, it did not fill us with awe, it just marked the spot, one of the spots, where something happened.'[15]

The images on Bridle's *Dronestagram* function as such markers. They are 'digital memorial[s]'[16] that mark a site to mourn the dead. In that, the project is engaged in making visible what has little representation: the human side of the drone war. In a paradoxical yet consequential move, Bridle has decided to represent that human side through map-like, vertical landscapes, in which the human figure itself is not to be seen. By doing so, he drives home the point that the victims of the drone campaign are mostly invisible to public perception. He uses their perceptual invisibility, caused by the resolution of the satellite image, to 'show' their structural invisibility. Or, to put it differently: Bridle attempts to make the unseen visible, but he does not do so through direct representation. Instead, he opts to show human bodies through landscapes, thus offering an indirect image that corresponds to the look of the drone's imaging. It favours spaces over bodies, thus letting the human body disappear.

Appearing: social media in *#NotABugSplat*

Landscape and body are fill-ins for the general dynamic of figure and ground that lies at the heart of the tilted image. In *Dronestagram*, the ground dominates; it takes the place of the figure. Yet the human is also there, albeit as a mental image. Similar to the tilted image, we are asked to switch back and forth between what we see (landscape) and what we know of and can imagine (body). The switching back and forth between figure and ground corresponds to a switching back and forth between proximity and distance that Bridle effects by attempting to bring the distant war close(r). The media he relies on to achieve this effect are the remote sensing technology of satellites and social media platforms. They approximate images of far-away places and represent them in familiar digital frameworks, such as Google Earth, Instagram, Tumblr, and Twitter. Relying on these well-known modes of representation, *Dronestagram* can be regarded as a contemporary update of seventeenth-century cartographer Willem Blaeu's conviction that 'maps enable us to contemplate at home and right before our eyes things that are farthest away'.[17]

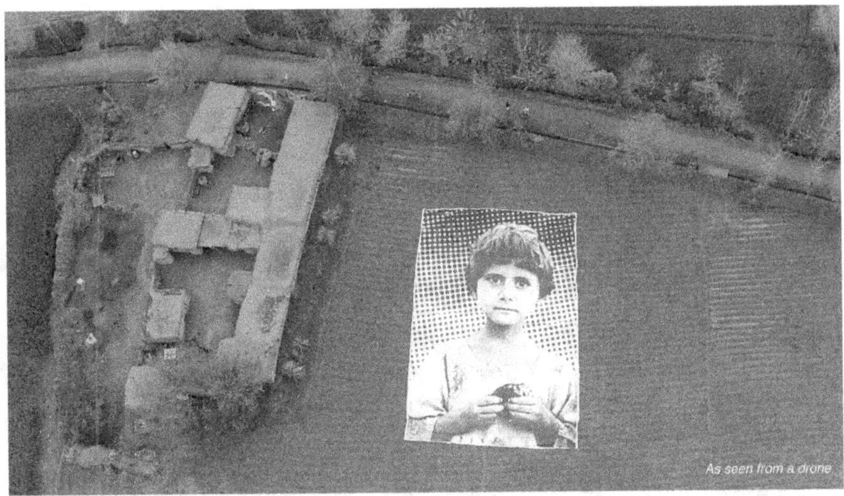

5.1 Ali Rez, Saks Afridi, AssamKhalid, Akash Goel, Insiya Syed, Noor Behram, Jamil Akhtar, *#NotABugSplat*, 2014.

In its attempt to overcome distance, to give visibility to those who are underrepresented, and to spread their images and stories through social media, Bridle's *Dronestagram* shares features with another project that was designed to counter the disappearance of the human body. The campaign *#NotABugSplat* was initiated by the Foundation for Fundamental Rights and Reprieve in FATA to focus attention on the civilian victims of drone attacks. Following one of human rights campaigns' preferred strategies to zoom in on individual faces and stories, it consists of blown-up photographs of children affected by drone attacks that are large enough to turn anonymous dots on a screen into individual faces. The project is part of French street artist JR's campaign *Inside Out* (since 2011), which set out to give 'everyone the opportunity to share their portrait and make a statement for what they stand for. It is a global platform for people to share their untold stories and transform messages of personal identity into works of public art.'[18] The photos of the children come from Pakistani activist and journalist Noor Behram, who has documented the drone war in FATA for many years, taking photos of the site of drone attacks and the victims and survivors of these attacks, while also collecting shrapnel from the drones' missiles that bear the mark of US manufacturers.[19]

The photo that circulates online shows a young girl looking into the camera. She is depicted in half chest, her hands holding an object. The photo is black-and-white with benday dots in the background, thereby mimicking the drone's optics of abstraction. Yet her picture is sharp, and her gaze goes straight into the camera. She casts a glance where no one is supposed to look, where no gaze is supposed to be returned. Showing faces of those who suffer is an established strategy of human rights campaigns seeking people's attention and wanting to make them care about suffering that is not their own and may be geographically and culturally far removed. It draws on the peculiar function of the face as a medium of interpersonal communication, mediating between individual and collective, inside and outside. Literary scholar Sigrid Weigel stresses the political importance of the face, which derives from its liminal and mediating function:

> On the edge between the inside, the non-visible and impenetrable of a human being, and its outside that is turned toward their environment, the face regulates the border traffic between the self and social space, between the intimate and the public: the face as an outpost of the self in a community. For that reason, the face does not solely function as the representation and placeholder of a person, but – as an interactive medium – it is also the bodily precondition to participate in and shape social and political conventions.[20]

Being part of the public sphere, participating in social life and partaking in shaping a political community is also what is at stake in the portrait of the young girl in *#NotABugSplat*.

Although the face is a marker of personal identity, used to identify me (or you), we do not know the name of the girl in the picture. As the text on the project page states: 'The child featured in the poster is nameless, but according to FFR [Foundation for Fundamental Rights], lost both her parents and two young siblings in a drone attack.'[21] The portrait is about her and her story; it is about recognising her, but not necessarily as *herself* but as *human*. This becomes clear when looking at another picture on the project's homepage. It shows a still image of a drone camera in which human bodies appear as white dots on a plane surface that looks like a valley. The caption explains: 'Humans appear as disposable bugs when viewed through a traditional drone camera. We changed this. Now, a drone will see an actual face of a child, creating dialogue and, possibly, empathy.'[22]

Taking the photo of a survivor from FATA, enlarging it and placing it on site, *#NotABugSplat* is grounded in the material realities of local communities affected by drone warfare. That fact notwithstanding, the project would not be complete – or it would be a different one – without another community: the globally dispersed, politically engaged community online that is supposed to look at the image and recognise the girl in her humanity. Both *#NotABugSplat* and *Dronestagram* use social media to promote their case, thereby making clear that a significant number of political action today takes place online. Online activism takes advantage of social media's ability to reach a lot of people instantaneously who are bound together by shared concerns and interests. They build imagined communities on the internet, thereby updating political scientist Benedict Anderson's concept for the twenty-first century.[23] Yet, while Anderson developed his concept of imagined communities in regard to the rise of the nation-state in the nineteenth century, emphasising the enabling effect of print capitalism and a shared national print language, imagined communities today are formed on the backdrop of surveillance capitalism operating on a global scale through the digital environments of social media. The prime medium building and connecting these communities is no longer one language but a globalised visual culture that allows communication through images.

While in the nineteenth century, communities were formed by reading the same texts, today they are bound together by looking at the same images. Sharing images on social media functions akin to a (potentially universal) language that can (but does not have to) be understood across linguistic divides. Or as media critic Nathan Jurgenson writes: 'Today, a global flow of image-speak among those who do not write in the same language allows for new possibilities in visual communication.'[24] For Jurgenson, photography on social media is social photography, for its imperative is not representation but communication:

> Photos now exist much more fluidly as communication – a form of visibility more discursive than formally artistic. As such, social photography should be understood not as something removed from the moment but as something deeply immersed in social life. More than documenting moments to archive and preserve them behind glass, social photography often attempts to communicate being.[25]

Understood as social objects that are part of and engender communication, images build communities around them and the issues they stand for. In the case of *Dronestagram* and *#NotABugSplat*, images are implemented to tackle one of the long-time blind spots of mainstream media: the fact that a drone war is taking place outside of officially declared war zones where it is affecting local communities and costing human lives, including the lives of civilians. The two projects find different modes of representation to do so: the portrait of a girl in *#NotABugSplat* and map-like landscapes in *Dronestagram*. Taken together, they stand for two dominant modes of representation in regard to drone warfare: the human body and landscape. Although only one is visible in each case, both need to be considered when trying to understand not only the drone's visual regime but also art's address of that regime. On a conceptual level, the two projects hence complement each other, one making visible what the other hides. They function as tilted images for each other, asking viewers to switch back and forth between landscape (ground) and the human body (figure).

Reappearing: the body as landscape in Seth Price's *Danny, Mila, Hannah, Ariana, Bob, Brad*

While *Dronestagram* and *#NotABugSplat* are divided between landscape and body, a series of photographs by artist Seth Price presents viewers with yet another option: to view the body itself as a landscape. Price's photos with names such as *Danny, Mila, Hannah, Ariana, Bob, Brad* (2015) are large-scale, state-of-the-art digital prints that are hung vertically in lightboxes, which illuminate the flimsy fabric from behind, giving it a translucent glow.[26] Their colours vary from ochre to greyish-white to light-pink shot through with red lines. Interspersed are landmarks: brown hills, charred ground, red canals, grasses on the plains. They look like lunar landscapes or aerial views of the desert and steppe. Some of them fill up the entire frame; others have jagged edges, revealing that they were stitched together from several images, which makes them look like contemporary renditions of the aerial composites shot by reconnaissance planes in the First World War.

In his interpretation, art critic and new media curator Ed Halter follows this line when seeing in them 'topographically rich textures that resemble

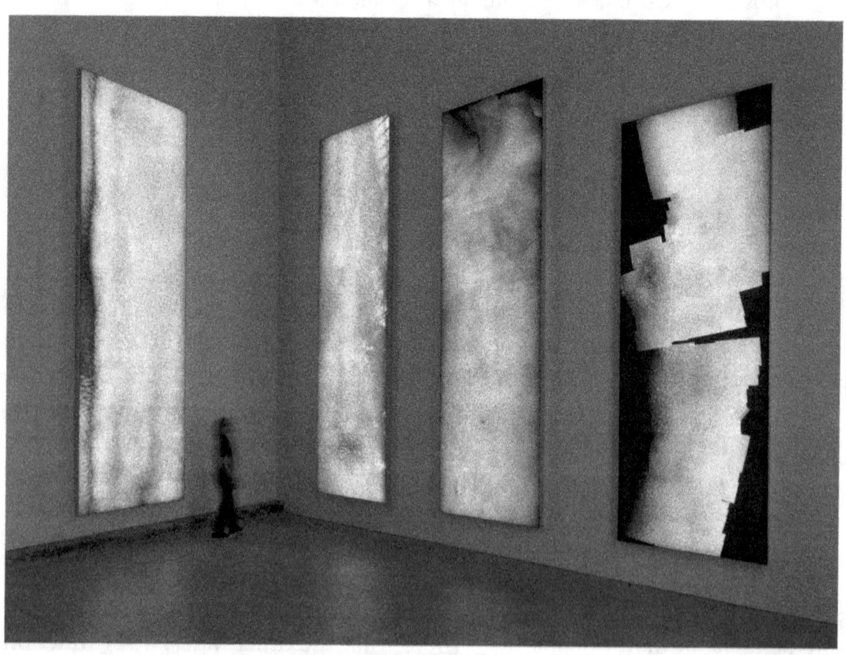

5.2 Seth Price, *Danny, Mila, Hannah, Ariana, Bob, Brad*, 2018. Installation view, MoMA PS1, New York.

photographs of desert expanses shot by aerial drones, or algorithmically generated versions of the same'.[27] They also have a likeness to the satellite images one can find on Bridle's *Dronestagram*: deserted landscapes hovering on the edge of abstraction.

And indeed, they are satellite images, but satellite images of the human skin. The photos are the result of a multi-step process involving several imaging technologies, rendering software, and retouching. As the didactic at MoMA PS1, where *Danny, Mila, Hannah, Ariana, Bob, Brad* was shown in 2018, explains:

> Using a robotic camera typically deployed for scientific research or forensic study, Price captured thousands of high-definition images in a single sitting, focusing on a specific area such as the arm or leg. The resulting images were subsequently stitched together using satellite-imaging software, run through a 3D graphics program, and adjusted by a fashion retoucher.[28]

The images coming out of this process are microscopic and macroscopic at the same time. They are extreme close-ups of human skin that look like satellite images of distant landscapes. In that, they attest to literary scholar Jan Mieszkowski's observation that close-up and distant (often aerial) shots have come to look conspicuously alike.[29]

Yet, although it is almost impossible to decide whether one sees a distant landscape or a detailed shot of the human body, what most readily presents itself as an interpretation varies depending on the physical distance one has to the images. When looked at from afar, the pictures unfold their appeal as landscapes. The installation at MoMA PS1 furthered this impression by allowing viewers to see the whole arrangement from an elevated landing. When one looks at the images from up-close, however, their skin comes into view. One sees the lines of the epidermis; one discerns the texture of a black mole; and one sees the root of a single hair coming out of the skin. One sees pores and the pattern of skin. Yet one can just as easily reverse this statement. For the resolution of the images is so high that they can equally be perceived as abstractions – a quality often accredited to the distant, vertical view. For Halter, the pictures exemplify 'a confusion common to our age, when photographs have become malleable and, at the same time, computer-generated images have become hyperrealistic'.[30] In the case of Price, the question of hyperrealism and malleability is taken up in the way he aligns skin and image, using the skin as an image and the image as skin in order to meditate on the relationship between the material and the virtual in digital culture.

In his artist novel *Fuck Seth Price* (2015), Price suggests that through 'flat printing, image became skin'.[31] Likening the image to skin turns it from a virtual into a material property – a transformation that is contained in the differentiation between the words and concepts of 'image' and 'picture' peculiar to the English language. Mitchell explains the distinction between the two in the following way:

> I like to start from the vernacular, listening to the English language, in a distinction that is untranslatable into German and French: 'You can hang a picture, but you can't hang an image.' The picture is a material object, a thing you can burn or break or tear. An image is what appears in a picture, and what survives its destruction – in memory, in narrative, in copies and traces in other media. [...] The picture, then, is the image as it appears in a material support or a specific place.[32]

Once printed, the image is turned into a picture. It takes on a material dimension that Price likens to skin, thereby bringing the haptic dimension of the human body into play. To push the metaphor further, one could say that the picture is the image become body. It is an embodied image – a notion that is rather evocative given Price's subject matter. For not only does photographing people's skin alert viewers to the role of the haptic in digital culture, where 'moving images [are] consumed largely by individuals, who [...] [lay] hands on their machines to set private pictures in motion'.[33] But the material property of a picture depicting the digital rendering of a human body also speaks to the ways in which physical and virtual, body and image intersect in Price's work and in contemporary digital culture in general.

In Price's case, that intersection finds expression in his improper use of satellite technology. As shown in the beginning, satellite images make for sweeping overviews of the land and can produce stunningly abstract landscape views; what they mask, however, is the human body. By employing satellite-imaging software to stitch together thousands of high-definition close-ups of the human skin, Price not only treats the body as if it was a landscape; he also uses the software for the one thing it is not meant for: to create an image of an individual human body. The individuality is comprised in the title of each work that gives the name of the sitter. Also, the epidermis is individual to each person, as the finger print makes clear. These features notwithstanding, Price's pictures remain rather unusual portraits. Similar to the strategy employed in *#NotABugSplat*, their main goal is not the individuality of each body but what that individual body stands for when put into a digital framework. Showing the physical materiality of skin in the form of the physical materiality of a picture, the photographs insist on the importance and maybe also the obstinate force of the human body in digital culture; at the same time, however, they also point to the rather ambivalent status the body takes on in the digital realm. For when we speak of bodies in the digital realm in general, and in drone warfare in particular, these bodies are defined by material as well as by virtual properties. In Price's case, these virtual properties are not only contained in the processing of the pictures, that is, in their digital rendering through satellite software, but are also apparent in their surface-orientation and in the pictures' reliance upon light to shine and become visible as part of their light-box installation.

Beyond representation: physical presence and perceptual absence

I have thus far written about the body as if it was solely a fleshy and material entity; yet, the body targeted in drone warfare is actually more often than not a schematic body.[34] Its appearance is defined by data, which turns the human into a figure and potential target. Media artist and critic Josh Begley emphasises the importance of metadata in targeting decisions when pointing out that 'hellfire missiles – the explosives fired from drones – are not always fired at people. In fact, most drone strikes are aimed at phones. The SIM card provides a person's location – when turned on, a phone can become a deadly proxy for the individual being hunted.'[35] Former director of the NSA and CIA Michael Hayden put this into the infamous phrasing: 'We kill people based on metadata.'[36] The human figure that is of interest in targeting decisions is thus the human as it figures against its data-sets. As such, it becomes visible but its shape is not that of a human body. Instead, its matter is immaterialised. It is digitally rendered so to speak.

This transformation of a physical entity into a data-set is of central importance when thinking about the state of the human body in drone warfare and the way it appears, disappears, and reappears when processed by the different technologies, including drones and satellites. The examples I have looked at, ranging from Bridle's *Dronestagram* and *#NotABugSplat* to Price's *Danny, Mila, Hannah, Ariana, Bob, Brad* employ these technologies to create images of landscapes and bodies that, taken together, suggest that the digital is intricately interwoven with material realities. The distinction between 'image' and 'picture' that Mitchell makes can provide a conceptual framework to think through this interweaving of the material and the digital. For I believe that 'image' and 'picture' need to be thought together as 'image-pictures' in order to do justice to the ways in which the drone combines virtual and material properties that, in turn, let the human body appear and disappear in its imaging. The image that is the ultimate image-picture is the tilted image, as it combines absence and presence, visibility and invisibility, digital and material, appearance and disappearance.

One of the canonical instances of the tilted image is the Rubin's vase, where one has to switch between figure and ground in order to see either a vase or two faces in profile looking at each other. Although the picture itself never changes, one's perception of it does, depending on what one decides to focus on. Hence, although vase and faces are both there all the time, only one of them can be seen at once. The other remains present but invisible. One can only see it by neglecting the other. In the case of art and activism dealing with drone warfare, this switching back and forth takes place between landscape and body. They are stand-ins for ground and figure that make-up the two elements of the tilted image; as such, landscape and body are exposed to the same dynamic of appearance and disappearance that Mitchell attests to the tilted image, i.e. one can only see one (body) or the other (landscape), although both are there. In my reading, I have used this constellation to trace the appearances and disappearances of the human body in the imaging of the drone; and I have found that due to its combination of physical presence and perceptual absence, the drone image too can be treated as a tilted image. It stands in for the interweaving of the material and the virtual that reminds viewers that contained in the visible, material picture lurks another invisible, immaterial image that needs to be thought.

It is this co-presence of a manifest picture and a mental image that, following Kurgan, has allowed me to 'see' people in Bridle's satellite images where no people are to be seen, including the survivor whose portrait is shown and globally disseminated as part of the *#NotABugSplat* campaign. Also, it has allowed me to make a connection between Price's photographs and drone warfare, although the works themselves are not directly related to the topic. Nevertheless, they are useful for thinking about the state of the human body in drone warfare, because they too expose the body to a satellite view that makes landscape take over. Just in this case, it is the body itself that makes up the landscape. *Danny, Mila, Hannah, Ariana, Bob, Brad* thus return a bodily element to the supposedly disembodied satellite view. As a result, they remind me that on the ground of each image rendered by a drone or a satellite, I may find a body. The tilted image lets me think (of) it, because it is both image and picture, providing me with a picture that contains an image, which is not to be seen.

Due to its combination of physical presence and perceptual absence, the tilted image can be regarded as making visible a suffering of those who are not seen, but not as a straight-forward representation. Instead, it exists as an image beyond representation. This image may not be an appropriate medium for news reports and human rights campaigns; regardless, I would like to suggest that it is an appropriate medium for a more conceptual way of thinking about the precarious state of the human body in drone warfare.

For the image that exists beyond representation is exactly the image that – through empathy and imagination – can attempt to make up for that what is missing. It gives me (and you) something to contemplate without covering up the absence. It is a precarious image and thus the most appropriate form of 'representation' for the precarious state of the human body in drone warfare.

In my reading of *Dronestagram, #NotABugSplat*, and *Danny, Mila, Hannah, Ariana, Bob, Brad*, I have traced the human body as it disappears (*Dronestagram*), appears (*#NotABugSplat*), and reappears (*Danny, Mila, Hannah, Ariana, Bob, Brad*) in different visual frameworks. As it has become clear in the course of my argument, neither the images nor their connected bodies are stable. They are marked by a precariousness that puts them beyond representation. Although this could be seen as a political shortcoming, I would instead like to draw on philosopher Judith Butler's notion of precariousness as a mode for community-building across established boundaries and identities. According to Butler, 'precarity cuts across identity categories as well as multicultural maps, thus forming the basis for an alliance focused on opposition to state violence and its capacity to produce, exploit, and distribute precarity for the purposes of profit and territorial defense.'[37] Precariousness thus contains the political potential to build communities where there was no common ground before. In the case of the works I have looked at in this chapter, one can see this attempt at community-building through the use of social media that is meant to bring the distant war close and make some of its images more familiar. Quite fittingly to the notion of precariousness though, the images employed in this communicative process are less stable than they appear at first. They are precarious images that hide or display precarious bodies. Due to their different calibrations, they are best viewed together. For only if I look at them together, both body and landscape come into view. And if I treat them as tilted images for each other, they even let body and landscape silhouette against each other in a constant play of appearance, disappearance, and reappearance that lets me recognise that it is neither figure nor ground that matter but the fleeting and quite precarious mental image in-between when neither or both are visible to the human eye. It is here that an image exists beyond representation that can give justice to the demand to be seen and recognised by (one) another.

Notes

1 E. Weizman, 'Introduction, part II: Matter against memory', in S. Sheikh, *Forensis: The Architecture of Public Truth* (Berlin: Sternberg Press, 2014), 372.

2 W. J. T. Mitchell, 'Foundational sites and occupied spaces', in: W. J. T. Mitchell, *Image Science: Iconology, Visual Culture, and Media Aesthetics* (Chicago: University of Chicago Press, 2015), 160.

3 For a selection of operators' testimonies see B. Bryant, 'Letter from a sensor operator', in L. Parks and C. Kaplan (eds), *Life in the Age of Drone Warfare* (Durham, NC, London: Duke University Press, 2017), 315–323; H. Linebaugh, 'I worked on the US Drone Program: The public should know what really goes on', *Guardian* (29 December, 2013); C. Woods, *Sudden Justice: America's Secret Drone Wars* (London: Hurst & Company, 2015).

4 W. J. T. Mitchell, *Image Science: Iconology, Visual Culture, and Media Aesthetics* (Chicago, London: University of Chicago Press, 2015), 160.

5 E. Weizman, *Forensic Architecture: Violence at the Threshold of Detectability* (New York: Zone Books, 2017), 28.

6 Weizman, 'Introduction, part II', 371. In June 2014, that resolution was changed 'to 31 centimeters per pixel after an appeal from a commercial satellite company to the US Department of Commerce convinced them that a person could still not be recognised at this resolution – a change that, again, applied in all places but Israel.' Weizman, *Forensic Architecture*, 29.

7 L. Kurgan, *Close Up at a Distance: Mapping, Technology and Politics* (New York: Zone Books, 2013), 113.

8 Kurgan, *Close Up*, 14.

9 Kurgan, *Close Up*, 113.

10 T. Paglen, 'Sources and methods', in N. van Tomme (ed.), *Visibility Machines: Harun Farocki and Trevor Paglen* (Baltimore: Center for Art, Design and Visual Culture, 2014), 145.

11 Examples of this trend towards landscape representations include works by Basma Alsharif, Edward Burtynsky, and Trevor Paglen, among others.

12 S. Alpers, *The Art of Describing: Dutch Art in the Seventeenth Century* (Chicago: University of Chicago Press, 1984), 141.

13 Alpers, *The Art of Describing*, 124.

14 Kurgan, *Close Up*, 132–133.

15 Kurgan, *Close Up*, 130.

16 Kurgan, *Close* Up, 120.

17 Johan Blaeu, *Le Grand Atlas* (Amsterdam, 1663), quoted by Alpers, *The Art of Describing*, 159.

18 'About the Inside Out Project', (n.d.), http://insideoutproject.net/en/about (accessed 8 December, 2019).

19 See, for instance, S. Ackerman, 'Rare Photographs show Ground Zero of the drone war', *Wired* (12 December, 2011), http://wired.com/2011/12/photos-pakistan-drone-war/ (accessed 8 December, 2019).

20 'Als Schwelle zwischen dem Inneren, Nichtsichtbaren und Unzugänglichen eines Menschen und seiner Außenseite, die er der Umgebung zuwendet, regelt das Gesicht gleichsam den Grenzverkehr zwischen dem Selbst und dem sozialen Raum, zwischen Intimität und Öffentlichkeit: das Gesicht als Vorposten des Selbst in der Gemeinschaft. Insofern ist das Gesicht nicht nur Stellvertreter und

Inbegriff der Persönlichkeit, sondern, als Medium der Interaktion, auch leibhaftige Voraussetzung zur (Mit-)Gestaltung sozialer und politischer Konventionen.' S. Weigel, 'Das Angesicht: Von verschwundenen, bewegten und mechanischen Gesichtern', in S. Weigel, *Das Gesicht: Bilder, Medien, Formate* (Göttingen: Wallstein, 2017), 18. Translation from German into English by S. Braeunert.

21 *#NotABugSplat*, http://notabugsplat.com (accessed 8 December, 2019).

22 *#NotABugSplat.*

23 B. Anderson, *Imagined Communities: Reflections on the Origin and Spread of Nationalism* (London: Verso, 1983).

24 N. Jurgenson, *The Social Photo: On Photography and Social Media* (New York, London: Verso, 2019), 14.

25 Jurgenson, *Social Photo*, 84.

26 Michelle Kuo explains the printing process in the following way: 'At the time he [Price] began conceiving of the pictures, he learned of a new printing technology from a production specialist with whom he had been working for eight years. The technology had been commissioned by a 'special client' – which turned out to be Apple – for its store displays. The process employed a new type of fabric that is able to receive a dye-sublimation transfer – an extremely high-resolution print that uses heat to transfer the ink – and resist wrinkling. The image was then stretched onto a light box. Price persuaded the consultant to let him use the technology, and they started doing tests in the studio. The finished works were dye sub printed onto the textile at 300 dpi (standard printing resolution) and fitted onto light boxes, illuminated from behind.' M. Kuo, 'Creative suite', in B. Ruf and A. Hochdörfer (eds), *Seth Price: Social Synthetic* (Cologne: Walther König, 2017), 362.

27 E. Halter, 'Seth Price: A new suite of works from the "Uncanny Valley"', *4 Columns* (8 June, 2018), http://4columns.org/halter-ed/seth-price (accessed 8 December, 2019).

28 Didactic on the occasion of the exhibition *Seth Price: Danny, Mila, Hannah, Ariana, Bob, Brad*, MoMA PS1 (3 June–3 September, 2018), www.moma.org/calendar/exhibitions/4981 (accessed 8 December, 2019). A detailed description of the production process can be found in M. Kuo, *Creative Suites*.

29 J. Mieszkowski made this point during his presentation 'Drones and the big data sublime' at the symposium 'Drone imaginaries and society' at the University of Southern Denmark in Odense, 5–6 June, 2018. See also his contribution to this volume based on the symposium in chapter 3 above.

30 Halter, 'Seth Price'.

31 S. Price, *Fuck Seth Price: A Memoir* (New York: Leopard, 2015), 49.

32 Mitchell, *Image Science*, 16.

33 Price, *Fuck Seth Price*, 58–59.

34 For a definition of the schematic body perched between the individual and the dividual, see G. Chamayou, 'Patterns of life: A very short history of schematic bodies', *The Funambulist Papers* 57 (4 December, 2014), http://thefunambulist.net/history/the-funambulist-papers-57-schematic-bodies-notes-on-a-patterns-genealogy-by-gregoire-chamayou (accessed 8 December, 2019).

35 J. Begley, 'A visual glossary: Decoding the language of covert warfare', *The Intercept*, *The Drone Papers* (15 October, 2015), http://theintercept.com/drone-papers/a-visual-glossary/ (accessed 8 December, 2019).

36 M. Hayden quoted by D. Cole, 'We kill people based on metadata', *The New York Review of Books* (10 May, 2014), http://nybooks.com/daily/2014/05/10/we-kill-people-based-metadata/ (accessed 8 December, 2019).

37 J. Butler, *Frames of War: When is Life Grievable?* (London, New York: Verso, 2010), 32.

Bibliography

Ackerman, S. 'Rare photographs show Ground Zero of the drone war'. *Wired*, 12 December, 2011. www.wired.com/2011/12/photos-pakistan-drone-war/ (accessed 8 December, 2019).

Alpers, *The Art of Describing: Dutch Art in the Seventeenth Century*. Chicago: University of Chicago Press, 1984.

Anderson, B. *Imagined Communities: Reflections on the Origin and Spread of Nationalism*. London: Verso, 1983.

Anonymous. 'About the Inside Out Project'. (n.d.) www.insideoutproject.net/en/about (accessed 8 December, 2019).

Anonymous. *#NotABugSplat*. 2014. https://notabugsplat.com (accessed 8 December, 2019).

Anonymous. *Seth Price: Danny, Mila, Hannah, Ariana, Bob, Brad*. MoMA PS1, 3 June–3 September, 2018. www.moma.org/calendar/exhibitions/4981 (accessed 8 December, 2019).

Begley, J. 'A visual glossary: Decoding the language of covert warfare'. In *The Intercept*, *The Drone Papers*, 15 October, 2015. https://theintercept.com/drone-papers/a-visual-glossary/ (accessed 8 December, 2019).

Bryant, B. 'Letter from a sensor operator'. In L. Parks and C. Kaplan (eds), *Life in the Age of Drone Warfare*, 315–323. Durham, NC, London: Duke University Press, 2017.

Butler, J. 'Introduction: Precarious life, grievable life'. In J. Butler, *Frames of War: When is Life Grievable?* 1–32. London, New York: Verso, 2010.

Chamayou, G. 'Patterns of life: A very short history of schematic bodies'. *The Funambulist Papers*, 57, 4 December, 2014. https://thefunambulist.net/history/the-funambulist-papers-57-schematic-bodies-notes-on-a-patterns-genealogy-by-gregoire-chamayou (accessed 8 December, 2019).

Cole, D. 'We kill people based on metadata'. *The New York Review of Books*, 10 May, 2014. www.nybooks.com/daily/2014/05/10/we-kill-people-based-metadata/ (accessed 8 December, 2019).

Halter, E. 'Seth Price: A new suite of works from the "Uncanny Valley"'. *4 Columns*, 8 June, 2018. www.4columns.org/halter-ed/seth-price (accessed 8 December, 2019).

Jurgenson, N. *The Social Photo: On Photography and Social Media*. New York, London: Verso, 2019.

Kuo, M. 'Creative suite'. In B. Ruf and A. Hochdörfer (eds), *Seth Price: Social Synthetic*, 356–365. Cologne: Walther König, 2017.

Kurgan, L. *Close Up at a Distance: Mapping, Technology and Politics*. New York: Zone Books, 2013.

Linebaugh, H. 'I worked on the US Drone Program: The public should know what really goes on'. *Guardian*, 29 December, 2013.

Mitchell, W. J. T. *Image Science: Iconology, Visual Culture, and Media Aesthetics*. Chicago, London: University of Chicago Press, 2015.

Paglen, T. 'Sources and methods'. In N. van Tomme (ed.), *Visibility Machines: Harun Farocki and Trevor Paglen*, 121–126. Baltimore: Center for Art, Design and Visual Culture, 2014.

Price, S. *Fuck Seth Price: A Memoir*. New York: Leopard, 2015.

Weigel, S. 'Das Angesicht: Von verschwundenen, bewegten und mechanischen Gesichtern'. In S. Weigel, *Das Gesicht: Bilder, Medien, Formate*, 8–21. Göttingen: Wallstein, 2017.

Weizman, E. *Forensic Architecture: Violence at the Threshold of Detectability*. New York: Zone Books, 2017.

Weizman, E. 'Introduction, part II: Matter against memory'. In Sheila Sheikh (eds), *Forensis: The Architecture of Public Truth*, 361–380. Berlin: Sternberg Press, 2014.

Woods, C. *Sudden Justice: America's Secret Drone Wars*. London: Hurst & Company, 2015.

6

The gender politics of the drone

Lauren Wilcox

> Once again, the drone upsets the available categories, to the point of rendering them inapplicable.[1]
>
> Drones have opened up an unusual moment of vertigo in the gender-war matrix.[2]

The phenomenon of 'the drone' has been the target of a great deal of recent critical enquiry, much of which has focused on the ways the use of this particular technological apparatus of surveillance and violence appears to disrupt and change the calculus of war, including the categories of foreign and domestic, distance and proximity, and human and machine. The imbrication of the human body with technology is not a new development in war, but the spectre of 'the drone', in particular, has led to some 'gender trouble', as the use of drones appears to challenge some of the ways in which feminists have theorised war as an institution that makes use of, and reproduces, violent forms of masculinities (and femininities), and ultimately serves to uphold patriarchal gender relations. The problem of the 'drone' opens up, to cite Cara Daggett's words, an 'unusual moment of vertigo in the gender-war matrix',[3] because drones complicate the relationship between power, embodiment, and technology in ways that push us to consider what 'gender' means and does in war.

This chapter argues that the question of gender and drones requires unpacking to understand the historical linkages between technology, gender, race, and war. War has been considered one of the most 'gendered' of all human practices because of how pervasive and stable the 'war-fighter' role has been for men, as well as the ways in which war serves as an arena for rationalising male and masculine dominance throughout society at large.[4] Megan MacKenzie argues, for example, that certain military roles have excluded women so as to exalt men, remaining exclusive to maintain the cultural hegemony, or at least potency, of militaries and war as institutions.[5] Whether war can still be seen as a practice of masculine domination in the era of drone warfare, or whether war has become 'feminised', or 'unmanned' by the use of drones, has been the subject of debate among feminist scholars. Most work on gender and drones focuses on the lived experiences of pilots and the effect of life in drone warfare for those subject to its violence, and reproduces a 'social constructivist' model of gender in which power circulates to reproduce patriarchal power but does not touch upon sexed bodies themselves. Some argue the 'cyborgs', or combined human-technology hybrid forms of drone warfare, are not removing gender from the battlefield but rather are allied with hegemonic, high-tech, aggressive militarised masculinity, enabling soldiers to become 'super-soldiers'.[6] Others have argued that technology serves as protector of 'the feminine' not only of the (deserving) women and children back at home, but also the bodies of the soldier on foot patrol, transformed from heroic, aggressive bodies into fragile bodies in need of oversight and protection.[7] Lorraine Bayard de Volo similarly notes how drones are used to assert patriarchal masculine protection in war but also that – because piloting drones is considered to be 'low status', not as prestigious or requiring as much skill or training in the military compared to piloting combat aircraft – 'drone warfare is less effective than previous warfare in conferring traditionally venerated forms of masculinity, and thus unsettles the cross-referential nature of military-masculinity that refers to and derives meaning from these traits.'[8] Drones have also been described as 'queer', that is, challenging the stability of the gender binary by embodying aspects of masculinity and femininity at once. In Daggett's argument, drones are both masculine in technological achievement and emasculating as they remove the body of the US soldier from direct peril. The 'queerness' of drone warfare also lies in the disruption of the gendered time/space of war, blurring distinctions between the femininised 'home' and masculinised 'battlefield' as well as feminised 'everyday life' and masculinised 'war' in the experience of drone operators.[9]

These works on gender and the drone rely upon an understanding of gender as a kind of characteristic or possession of certain bodies, as well as gender as a system of meaning and hierarchies of power. In particular, Daggett usefully sets up the separation between gendered bodies and gender as a cultural system designating proximity to power, and notes, as others have, that 'queerness' cannot, per se, stand for that which is excluded from the mechanisms of the state's violent apparatuses. Drone warfare, as a specific iteration of state violence in late liberalism, partakes in the liberal discourse of 'equal opportunities', promoting the idea that 'we' are the bearers of equal opportunity for men and women, 'we' are the forces of equality and freedom against an illiberal, patriarchal, homophobic, uncivilised foe.[10] Queer people and certain forms of queer life do not necessarily stand outside or opposed to projects of nationalism and militarism but rather can be selectively incorporated into the community of lives to be preserved at the expense of racialised populations marked for exclusion and elimination.[11]

To carry on this work about the relationship between gender, technology, and violence in late liberal warfare, the chapter investigates how the question of the 'gender' of drone warfare opens up space for investigating the deeper connections between the work that the concept of 'gender' does and how this concept can be seen as epistemologically and historically intertwined in the military and post-war technologies and scientific practices that brought us the drone. This is not to say, of course, that 'gender' as a concept, field, mode of analysis, or signifier of power relations should be thought of as complicit or supportive of the drone as an apparatus of surveillance, policing, war, and assassination. Rather, the argument here is that our understanding of the more radical possibilities of 'gender', such as questioning the inevitability of certain forms of lives and being from certain bodily enactments, can also be tied to visions of embodiment that underpin the drone as human/machine assemblage. In particular, the chapter argues that 'posthuman' visions of the separability and malleability of bodies, technologies, and cultures can enable radical visions of gender and sexual freedom, but also can be used in violent, exclusionary practices. Therefore, the 'posthuman' subject of the drone complicates the question of gender and warfare considerably. This is because the question of 'gender' becomes even more complicated when we cannot assume an individual, humanist body as our grounds for politics, as theorists of media and technology in the digital age make clear. Anne Balsamo presciently illustrated this problem of gender and the posthuman subject when she queried over two decades ago: 'When the human body is fractured into organs, fluids, and genetic codes, what happens to gender identity? When gender can no long be mapped onto a sexed body in a humanistic model of individuality and autonomy, what are we to make of gender as a category of analysis?'[12]

The works on gender and drone warfare mentioned above provide important insights into the ways in which gender is encoded in drone warfare, but gender is implicitly understood as a kind of ideology that is mapped onto an already-sexed body, that is, a body that is figured as 'naturally' either male or female, and then subjected to the cultural and ideological forces of gender in terms of structuring all aspects of social and political life, including war. In these accounts, the distinction between a sexed body (the male or female drone pilots and presence of 'military-aged men' in the 'kill zone') is taken for granted. If we were not to take this 'sexed body' for granted – if, rather, we were to enquire as to precisely what marks the distinction between the 'natural' sexed body and the 'cultural' gendered body and its signification – this distinction would fall apart and we would find ourselves with a more complicated story about sex, gender, technology, and violence.

First, gender theorists such as Judith Butler and many others argued that the distinction between 'sex' as a biological imperative, as contrasted to social and institutional concepts of 'gender', mistakenly relegates 'sex' and 'the body' to the status of an apolitical material ground for politics as opposed to a wider consideration of how norms, including those of scientific and clinical practices, constitute intelligible bodies in and through discourses of sex and gender in the first place.[13]

These problems of bodies, technologies, information, norms and more are amply illustrated in the case of 'the drone'. Derek Gregory, Alison Williams, Ian Shaw, and Majed Akhter, among others,[14] have demonstrated at length that it is a mistake to think of 'the drone' as a kind of disembodied substitute for the bodies of soldiers, that is to say, as a kind of 'other-than-human' but humanoid monstrous body as it is often portrayed in both popular media and some academic literature. While this image resonates fears surrounding drone warfare, particularly the fear that 'killer robots' may take on the powers of targeting and killing for themselves outside of human control, this image mistakes the most prominent mechanical aircraft component for the complex assemblages of bodies and technologies that make up the multi-layered embodied geographies of the drone. This has implications for how we might think of the relevance of 'gender' for our diagnosis of the drone as a tool of violence. What we think of as 'the drone' in terms of a singular machinic body entails global apparatuses and capacities involved in the researching, finding, targeting, and killing individualised targets, with dozens of analysts, sensor operators, and other layers of functionaries and nodes along a communications, command, and control system. The complex assemblage of humans, surveillance technologies, and weapons systems in a hierarchical system of command and control that also incorporates actors involved in more traditional forms of counter-insurgency operations points to precisely the opening that the question of 'gender' in the drone provides.

On this understanding of embodiment, the question becomes less whether or not drone warfare is as 'masculine' as other types of political violence. Rather it is about the status of 'gender' in a kind of posthuman ontology in which the biological, individual body is no longer – if it ever was – a stable referent for a coherent gender identity. To explore this, we need to open up the concept of 'gender' to enquire into the mutual history of the development of the concept of 'gender' and the capitalist and militarist apparatuses that drones are a part of. In short, we need to see the mutual influence and the co-constitution of the concept of 'gender' in the kind of technological and racialising practices that the 'drone' both partakes in and brings to light. Rather than attempting to understand gender analysis as something that can be applied to drone as a kind of external critique, this chapter tells a story about how our concepts, subjectivities, and ways of inhabiting bodies and worlds that are implied by the term 'gender' are part of similar and related processes that also brought us drones. There is no such thing as a 'gender analysis' apart from the development of 'the drone' because the two are mutually imbricated in the politics of bodies, sexuality, technology, race, and violence. None of this is to say that the critical knowledges and perspectives that feminist and queer views on war and technology are necessarily complicit with this form of violence; rather, the point is to contend with the genealogies of bodies, technology, and power that haunt both 'gender' and 'the drone'.

Gender and/as technology

Just as we only tend to learn about drone strikes when something has gone wrong, that is, when the drone assemblage fails to hit the 'right' targets – as in a 2019 US drone strike killing 30 Afghan farmers[15] or the 2010 massacre in Uruzgan, Afghanistan[16] that has been the centrepiece of so many theorisations of drone warfare – 'gender' also shows up in various 'failures'. 'Gender' as a concept becomes visible in various kinds of 'failures' in one's psychological, sexual, or cultural disinclinations to conform to expectations of certain sexed bodies. In her genealogical analysis of the concept of gender, Jemima Repo notes, 'gender belongs to the twentieth century like a fish to water – it could not have emerged anywhere else'.[17] 'Gender', a concept that is now the basis of entire fields of discourse, debate, and activism about the nature of power, identity, bodies, and difference, has a crucial moment in its development in post-Second World War psychiatry. John Money and his colleagues' controversial work serves as an important site to think through the relationship between post-war techno-scientific and clinical practices and 'gender'. Money's work in paediatric endocrinology is synonymous with the view that 'biological sex' and gender roles and identities should be considered separate categories. His work led to protocols developed to 'correct' bodies of infants born with ambiguous genitalia (who we might describe today as intersex) in order to better approximate social gender norms. This insight, now usually thought of as the basis for challenging societal norms and expectations for certain bodies, was at the time used to discipline and 'fix' bodies into prescribed roles based on anatomical inspection. As Judith Butler writes, 'Gender named a problem, an errancy or deviation, a failure to actualise the developmental norm in time.'[18] In this 'problem' of gender, science in terms of medical interventions and clinical practices were to be the solution to eliminate any such deviations.

Here we might notice similarities between the technologies of the drone that enable military and security professionals to collate intelligence, including metadata and 'pattern of life' analysis as well as visual imagery to locate, track, target, and ultimately use violence against bodies deemed to be 'out of place.'[19] Gender is thus made feasible by the possibilities and actualities of incongruence between the visual signs of 'sex' in an infant's genitals and of an internal, perhaps psychic, 'gender' as a complex product of psychology, physiology, and cultural interactions. This distinction itself is the product of techno-scientific discourses, and was used to intervene, in ways often physical and psychically violent, to 'fix' bodies of infants to better approximate gender and sexual norms. In her reading of Money's work and that of related mid-century scientists and medical professionals, Repo concludes, 'Gender was therefore invented as a mechanism for normalising, disciplining, and governing sex.'[20]

This genealogy of 'gender' not only suggests its origin in twentieth-century scientific practices, but also suggests that our sexed and gendered bodies are, as Haraway has famously written, 'thoroughly denaturalized as sign, context, and time.'[21] The idea of a naturally 'sexed' body is challenged not only by postmodern feminists, but arguably by the techno-scientific practices that attempt to fix bodies: here, I mean 'fix' both in the sense of 'correct' but also 'fix' in the sense of to track, to locate, and to make knowable. In Haraway's figuration of the cyborg, we 'might consider more seriously the partial, fluid, sometimes aspect of sex and sexual embodiment.'[22] What then, is the 'use' of gender, what does gender 'do', when it can no longer be thought of as a characteristic or possession of an individualised body? For, as Haraway reminds us, 'bodies as subject of knowledge are material-semiotic generative modes, their boundaries materialize in social interaction; "objects" like bodies do not pre-exist as such.'[23] Drones appear as such bodies, operating on the basis of humans, visual and metadata surveillance, networks and algorithms, engines and weapons, images and affects and much more to derive their lethal potential.

Cybernetic bodies

In following this story of the blurred boundaries between subjects and objects, bodies and technologies involved in the concept of 'gender', we find that, as J. Halberstam writes in an early essay, 'the very legacy of cybernetics, automated machines, in fact, provide new ground upon which to argue that gender and its representations are technological productions.'[24] The history of cybernetics points to the ways in which the 'gendered body' is based upon a 'cybernetic' model of embodiment. The role of hormones as 'gendering' bodies demonstrates this idea. Paul Preciado's provocative declaration that invention of the 'hormone' is a decisive break in the epistemology of gender provides an opening to rethink epistemologies of gender, science, and technology.[25] The 'hormone' here signals a shift in the early twentieth century away from sex difference being determined by a 'visual inspection' of the genitals and towards an internalisation and even molecularisation in this category of the 'hormone'. This model of embodiment was widely influential in the twentieth and twenty-first centuries, especially in terms of the availability of synthesised hormones to influence reproduction and to enable transgender people to transition by altering their bodies and voices with hormones. The 'hormone' as a key determinant of gender leads to a way of thinking through gender as 'technology' in terms of the techno-scientific practices, of which hormones, their synthesis, and their use to modulate gendered bodily attributes, are but one part. We can, then, put means of embodying 'gender', practised by cis and trans people alike, as means of 'signalling' and embodying gender, such as make-up, clothing, hairstyles, cosmetic surgeries, gestures and postures, language and more, which become part of the broader post-war culture and technological practices.

One can see the influence of 'the hormone' as both a sign of the 'truth' of gender and the ultimate inadequacy of any such test in the famous example of track athlete Caster Semenya from South Africa, whose body is reported to produce an amount of testosterone that is above the level deemed acceptable for women, and who was forced out of international track competitions because she would have been required to undergo medical interventions to lower this level in order to compete internationally in women's track events.[26] This hormone model of embodiment also influenced the development of artificial intelligence in the early stages of cybernetics, thus showing how the development of 'gender' and drones are intertwined. Quite famously, for example, the so-called 'Father of Cybernetics', Norbert Wiener, imagined the body of artificial intelligence in the twentieth-century age of communication and control to be based on 'the accurate reproduction of signal'.[27] This new way of looking at the human body as essentially an information-processing machine was an influential outgrowth of the post-war Macy Conferences on Cybernetics.[28] This model not only enables the development of cybernetic technologies and the development of computing and artificial intelligence that underpin drone technologies but also give us the dominant model for understanding gendered embodiment in the early twenty-first century. The relationship of embodiment to technology operates here not in terms of 'identity': rather, the late twentieth-century militarised and capitalist formations have produced a body that is, in Haraway's terms, a cyborg, whose embodiment collapses the distinction between nature and technology.[29] Building on this work, Preciado provocatively builds a theory of embodiment, regulation and control through the 'microprosthetics' of molecules, chemicals, and digital bits. In this kind of 'posthuman' form of embodiment that 'the drone' exemplifies, we see that 'gender', understood as cultural interpretations of the sexed bodies of men and women is increasingly irrelevant, as traits linked to militarised masculinity, such as physical strength and courage, are similarly less relevant. 'Human' bodies are but one node in complex network of visual surveillance, algorithmic detections of movements and networks, information processing, and military/militarised command and control hierarchies. A key point here is that the visual order of 'gender' based on institutional control of bodies in space is currently being supplanted or at least complemented by this 'microprosthetics' of the body. This microprosthetic model might well describe drone bodies as they are less about 'fixing' the gender of bodies that make up the human/technological assemblage of the drone, a mode of embodiment that then enables the 'fixing' of bodies to be targeted for violent exclusion through warfare and policing.

For Preciado, 'gender' is no longer about the difference between a culturally shaped psychology and sexed embodiment, it is about a position within the global political economy of being a penetrator or penetrated. While Preciado's work doesn't fully address the necropolitical regimes living and dying of which drone assemblages are a key component, his work on gender shows 'gender is a biotech industrial artifact',[30] one that transforms the question of gender away from a model of identities and towards an 'assemblage' model of affects, technologies, bodies, signals, and more that are connected and modulated in the global economy. Preciado's formulation of 'gender' as penetrator/penetrated in the global economy is overstated in its scope, yet can point us to perceiving a crucial way in which drone warfare is gendered, as drone warfare 'works' precisely by making only one side penetrated and penetrable. It prevents the bodies of one side from being penetrated and injured or killed while making vast swaths of the world into penetrable bodies; the 'visual' or at least external sensory mode of apprehending bodies is the dominant mode here still. The much-noted 'voyeuristic intimacy'[31] of the drone in the field of the visual (and we can also note, the visual interaction with the algorithmic, metadata collections of social networks and relations) is meant to see into spaces coded as 'feminine' – the home and other intimate spaces. This one-sided gaze, seeing without being seen and all its intendant pleasures is linked to masculinist and colonialist politics of power and domination, and the production of gendered subjectivity.

Preciado's work consciously blurs the line between the visual and sexual/violent in theorising gendered subjectivity in the penetrator/penetrated relationship, transcending the model of unitary sexed embodiment from this equation. Emphasising the pornographic image's capacity to activate the body of the spectator, Preciado, following Williams, defined pornography as 'embodied image': an images that captures the body in an 'encounter with an eroticised technological apparatus.'[32] One might consider the intimacy of the visual images of drone warfare as pornographic, particularly as a kind of 'extra' taboo imagery of death: the snuff film. Alex Danchev reports on the connections between sex and violence in the watching of drone strikes in real-time: 'The drone strike is the ultimate snuff movie. The plot is as simple and satisfying as the original single-reelers of the silent era.'[33] In the drive and desire to reveal what has been hidden and then to penetrate it, resulting in a climax of violence – a 'money shot' – followed by the surveillance of the aftermath to count bodies, we can see the narrative of drone war replicating this structure. As the use of drones for surveillance and targeting of individuals is dependent upon having air dominance (drones are relatively easy to counter and shoot down) drone warfare's visualising and violent capabilities render large swaths of the world into penetrable bodies by those bodies constituted as impenetrable. What this exploration of gender and/as technology shows is the radical potential opened up by the concept of 'gender', and its constitutive excesses and failures are rooted in similar political imaginaries of technologies in which the flexibility, enhancement, and 'cyborgification' of drone bodies enables the fixing, targeting, and violent intervention of those bodies deemed dangerous to the existing order.

Gender as a racialising apparatus

While the visual order of 'anatomy' in gender has been overturned in the posthuman, cybernetic age into a more complex order in which gender functions not as 'identity' or a characteristic of certain bodies, this is not a universal or global outcome of the drone. In fact, while the assemblage of bodies, technologies, affects, information and code that make up 'the drone' belongs to the register of 'gender' (as already a technological apparatus of regulating the capabilities of certain bodies), the 'drone assemblage' is also of course inseparable from its current use in counterinsurgency and pacification operations. Such operations are often predicated upon 'fixing' certain kinds of sexual and gender relations. These operations in counterinsurgency practices are just as technological and 'artificial' as any other bodily formation. However, this kind analysis of gender politics does not necessarily take into consideration how both gender and 'the drone' are bound up in the politics of race and racialisation, which I turn to now.

Building on the insights of Butler, Puar, and others[34] who argue that imperialist power in the War on Terror works through racialised configurations of sexuality and sexual difference as enacted through violence, I suggest that drone warfare draws upon, and reproduces, sexual difference as a means towards racialisation. If we don't take the drone as a *sui generis* technology of surveillance and death-dealing, nor other technological forms of detection, tracking, and targeting as purely late twentieth- and early twenty-first-century phenomenon, we can recognise precursors from the early modern and particularly the colonial era as well.[35] Simone Browne's recent work, for example, addresses the development of surveillance capacities as something not inaugurated by new technologies such as facial recognition or drones, but as sustaining technologies of racism and anti-blackness.[36] Chamayou's work on the 'man-hunt', as a mode of asymmetrical violence representing the precursor to the 'drone' in terms of technologies of surveillance, lethal use of force, and racial hierarchy is another such example.[37]

While historicising the precursors to drones in terms of visualising, tracking and targeting technologies that have similarly enabled the violent reproduction of imperialist and white supremacist forms of state violence, the very concept of 'gender' can be traced to epistemologies of racial differences and hierarchy as well. Black and other women of colour feminist and queer scholars such as Hortense Spillers and Sarah Haley have taught that gender normativity coagulates through biopolitical control of reproduction, civilisational discourses, and racial hierarchies, through which the status of 'woman' has included white women only.[38] The science and politics of sexual difference has been based upon presumed differences in anatomies of racialised black women. Popular and scientific accounts of black anatomy – such as in the famous nineteenth-century example of the 'Hottentot Venus'[39] – formed the basis of racial distinctions and hierarchies made in and through accounts of gender and sexuality. Likewise, the formulation of knowledge governing the 'truth' of sexuality was also made through the production of racial differences. As Siobhan Somerville documents, 'the formation of notions of heterosexuality and homosexuality emerged in the US through (and not merely parallel to) a discourse saturated with assumptions about the racialisation of bodies.'[40]

The capacity of drone assemblages and drone bodies to 'queer' war – that is, to participate in a politics of undermining the (seemingly) monolithic masculinism of war through a kind of reassembly of bodies and their parts, technologies, and cultures into something more flexible and fluid – is thus entwined with histories of racialisation. Given this history of gender, and of the uses to which technological apparatuses such as drones are and have been put, we can say, along with Puar, that 'the potential for gender differentiation in the first instance is already the potential – indeed the capacitation – of whiteness; the capacity to lean into gender 'undecidability', the province of that same whiteness.'[41] Drone assemblages, in a mode that both *resembles* the politics of gender and also *makes use of* gender, take part in the production of a capacity to 'fix' certain bodies and identities so various war machines might be able to 'tell the difference' to mark certain bodies as subject to death.

In drone warfare, and in warfare more generally, gender (or more properly, the signs of sexual difference) is also a technology that serves to classify people based on perceptions of gender as civilians or combatants.[42] If we focus on the most prominent use of drones in counterinsurgency operations, we can see how drone bodily assemblages play a role in racialising populations in and through 'gender'. Famously, the perception of 'military-aged men' within a designated zone in Afghanistan is taken to indicate the presence of combatants, and thus, killable persons.[43] The drone apparatus uses not only the visual and algorithmic – both means of knowledge production that are linked to certain regimes of gendering bodies – but also the affective as well, based on felt senses of resemblance.[44] As Laleh Khalili notes: 'The practice of counterinsurgency itself is predicated on 'telling' (combatants from civilians, hostiles from friendlies, etc.), invading, organising, fighting, detaining, transforming, and destroying on the basis of gender (cross-hatched with class and race).'[45]

Scholars of counterinsurgency practices note how patriarchal notions of gender are assumed and reproduced throughout various strategies and tactics, reproducing racial differences between the 'target populations' and the 'practitioners' of counterinsurgency. Patricia Owens, for example, has described the 'armed social work' strategy in Afghanistan in terms of the assumptions undermining strategic doctrine that women's lives were closer to biological realities and thus depended more on stable social organisation. The goal of strengthening patriarchal families has had the effect of forcing women back into their homes, which has in term increased their daily burdens.[46] Synne Laastad Dyvik likewise notes that the perception of women as heterosexual reproduces women as 'targets' of counterinsurgency practice, in which family life has come to stand for the social itself. 'Population-centric counterinsurgency needs to concern itself with the most intimate parts of life, the lessons taught to children and the conversations had with husbands.'[47] Dyvik has even noted a distinction in the language of counterinsurgency: 'women' is used to describe women in 'traditional societies' as mainly socio-economic beings, defined by their relation to their families, communities, and culture, while 'female counterinsurgents' carry no such essentialist baggage, allowing them freedom and the ability to bridge the divide from 'traditional women' and their own, 'normal' societies.[48] Such efforts are not only part of the 'rush to the intimate' in terms of knowing and 'fixing' the population in order to more effectively govern,[49] but also rely upon the 'gender mutability' or 'undecidability' of drone bodies and female counterinsurgency forces alike in order to do so.

Conclusion

The 'drone' and its operation are part of a broader constellation of surveillance, tracking, targeting, violence and confinement that opens up deep connections between the work that 'gender' does and the violent practices of drone warfare. While 'gender' has opened up many avenues of cultural and political critique that have enabled movements for gender and sexual freedom, 'gender' is also derived from a particular historical, geopolitical, and technological moment. Apprehending how certain formulations of 'gender' are woven into the very technologies and world-views that made up our 'drone worlds' not only leads us to a better understanding of how gender politics enables the drone and its racialising, lethal surveillance but also to better view the 'drone' as part of a wider matrix of violence and subjugation.

The focus on the drone as the monstrous humanoid synecdoche for a broader assemblage of bodies, organs, codes, information, prostheses, infrastructures, and affective currents is related to the focus on 'drone' as a singular technological body. Because of this, drone theorists, myself included, have tended to overemphasise war fighting and counterinsurgency uses of drones and perhaps underemphasised their role in domestic policing, in which the link to racist, and particularly anti-black, violence is even clearer.[50] Likewise, the feminist emphasis on militaries and militarisation in the politics of the drone similarly often reproduces the international/domestic boundaries of our conceptual language surrounding violence to the detriment of a fuller appreciation of the uses of different forms of political violence to uphold white supremacy.[51] While the use of drones as instruments of targeted killing became prominent in the War on Terror, notwithstanding their earlier usage by Israel against the Palestinian people, increasingly varying forms of drones and other technological forms of identifying, tracking, apprehending, and applying violence are being used by the militarised police forces in the US, especially on its borders. From a broader consideration of modalities of violence in late liberalism, we can insist that the conditions of permanent war and mass incarceration are not exceptional but the increasingly routine means of organising and governing/abandoning surplus populations. We can place drone warfare on a continuum of violence that serve as a 'network of cultural, legal, and politico-economic apparatuses [which] were inaugurated to (re) criminalise blackness and ensnare black subjects within intensified forms of punishment, confinement and expropriation.'[52] While there is certainly more work to be done to think through the uniqueness of 'the drone' and its imbrication in wider circuits of violence and carcerality, understanding how the drone is but one element of a wider practice of fixing and governing populations in and through gender opens important pathways for further analysis.

Notes

1 G. Chamayou, *A Theory of the Drone*, trans. J. Lloyd (New York: The New Press, 2015), 111.

2 C. Daggett, 'Drone disorientations: How "unmanned" weapons queer the experience of killing in war', *International Feminist Journal of Politics*, 17:3 (2015): 375.

3 Daggett, 'Drone Disorientations', 375.

4 J. S. Goldstein, *War and Gender: How Gender Shapes the War System and Vice Versa* (Cambridge: Cambridge University Press, 2003).

5 M. H. MacKenzie, *Beyond the Band of Brothers: The US Military and the Myth That Women Can't Fight* (Cambridge: Cambridge University Press, 2015).

6 M. Manjikian, 'Becoming unmanned: The gendering of lethal autonomous warfare technology', *International Feminist Journal of Politics*, 16:1 (2014): 48–65.

7 L. Wilcox, *Bodies of Violence: Theorizing Embodied Subjects in International Relations* (New York: Oxford University Press, 2015); C. Masters, 'Bodies of technology: Cyborg soldiers and militarized masculinities', *International Feminist Journal of Politics*, 7:1 (March 2005): 112–132; L. Nicholas and C. Agius, 'Drones and the politics of protection', in L. Nicholas and C. Agius (eds), *The Persistence of Global Masculinism: Discourse, Gender and Neo-Colonial Re-Articulations of Violence* (Cham: Springer International Publishing, 2018), 115–140.

8 L. Bayard de Volo, 'Unmanned? Gender recalibrations and the rise of drone warfare', *Politics & Gender*, 12:1 (March 2016), 50–77.

9 Daggett, 'Drone disorientations'.

10 See, for example, J. K. Puar, *Terrorist Assemblages: Homonationalism in Queer Times* (Durham, NC: Duke University Press, 2007); S. R. Farris, *In the Name of Women's Rights: The Rise of Femonationalism* (Durham, NC: Duke University Press, 2017).

11 See, for example, J. Haritaworn, A. Kuntsman, and S. Posocco (eds), *Queer Necropolitics* (Abingdon: Routledge, 2014); L. Wilcox, 'Drones, swarms and becoming-insect: Feminist utopias and posthuman politics', *Feminist Review*,

116:1 (July 2017): 25–45; N. Manchanda, 'Queering the Pashtun: Afghan sexuality in the homo-nationalist imaginary', *Third World Quarterly*, 36:1 (2015): 130–146.

12 A. Balsamo, *Technologies of the Gendered Body: Reading Cyborg Women* (Durham, NC: Duke University Press, 1996), 6.

13 J. Butler, *Gender Trouble: Feminism and the Subversion of Identity* (New York: Routledge, 1990); J. Butler, *Bodies That Matter: On the Discursive Limits of 'Sex'* (New York: Routledge, 1993).

14 D. Gregory, 'From a view to a kill: Drones and late modern war', *Theory, Culture & Society*, 28:7–8 (2011): 188–215; A. J. Williams, 'Enabling persistent presence? Performing the embodied geopolitics of the unmanned aerial vehicle assemblage', *Political Geography*, 30:7 (2011): 381–390; I. G. R. Shaw and M. Akhter, 'The unbearable humanness of drone warfare in FATA, Pakistan', *Antipode*, 44:4 (2012): 1490–1509; L. Wilcox, 'Drone warfare and the making of bodies out of place', *Critical Studies on Security*, 3:1 (2015): 127–131; L. Wilcox, 'Embodying algorithmic war: Gender, race, and the posthuman in drone warfare', *Security Dialogue*, 48:1 (2017): 11–28.

15 'U.S. drone strike kills 30 pine nut farm workers in Afghanistan', *Reuters*, 20 September, 2019. https://uk.reuters.com/article/uk-afghanistan-attack-drones-idUKKBN1W40O9 (accessed 23 February, 2021).

16 See, for example, the many analyses of this massacre in the academic literature, including Wilcox, 'Embodying algorithmic war', J. Allinson, 'The necropolitics of drones', *International Political Sociology*, 9:2 (June 2015): 113–127; D. Gregory, 'Eyes in the sky – bodies on the ground', *Critical Studies on Security*, 6:3 (2018): 347–358; Chamayou, *A Theory of the Drone*; L. Suchman, 'Situational awareness: Deadly bioconvergence at the boundaries of bodies and machines', *MediaTropes*, 5:1 (2015): 1–24; C. Wilke, 'Seeing and unmaking civilians in Afghanistan: Visual technologies and contested professional visions', *Science, Technology, & Human Values*, 42:6 (2017): 1031–1060; S. Ahmed, 'From threat to walking corpse: Spatial disruption and the phenomenology of "living under drones"', *Theory & Event*, 21:2 (2018): 382–410.

17 J. Repo, *The Biopolitics of Gender* (New York: Oxford University Press, 2016), 2.

18 J. Butler, 'Gender in translation: Beyond monolingualism', *PhiloSOPHIA*, 9:1 (2019), 13.

19 See also Wilcox, 'Drone warfare and the making of bodies out of place'.

20 Repo, *Biopolitics of Gender*, 2. For more on Money's work and its implications for gender theory, see K. Karkazis, *Fixing Sex: Intersex, Medical Authority, and Lived Experience* (Durham, NC: Duke University Press, 2008).

21 D. Haraway, 'The biopolitics of postmodern bodies', in *Simians, Cyborgs and Women* (New York: Routledge, 1991), 208.

22 D. Haraway, 'A cyborg manifesto: Science, technology, and socialist-feminisms in the late twentieth century', in *Simians, Cyborgs and Women* (New York: Routledge, 1991), 180.

23 D. Haraway, 'Situated knowledges: The science question in feminism and the privilege of partial perspective', *Feminist Studies*, 14:3 (1988): 575–599.

24 J. Halberstam, 'Automating gender: Postmodern feminism in the age of intelligent machine', *Feminist Studies*, 17:3 (1991): 439.

25 P. B. Preciado, *Testo Junkie: Sex, Drugs, and Biopolitics in the Pharmacopornographic Era* (New York: The Feminist Press at the City University of New York, 2013).

26 Caster Semenya has been subjected to 'gender verification' tests since her victory in the 2009 World Championships in the 800m race. Believed to have an intersex condition, Semenya has always defended her identity as a woman and her right to participate in sport as such. In May 2019, the Court of Arbitration for Sport rejected her challenge to IAAF (International Association of Athletics Federation) rules that would force her to take medications to lower her testosterone levels. These rules are based on theories that women with testosterone above certain arbitrary levels are in not possession of the kind of unique physical gifts that grace many world-class athletes, but rather have an unfair advantage due to their proximity to male-ness. Semenya's blackness and gayness (she married her partner in 2015) also point to the interplay of racism and gender normativity in the decade-long scrutiny of her body and the 'truth' of her gender that has been questioned on the international stage. While appealing the rulings, including to the European Court of Human Rights, in order to be able to compete in the next Olympics, Semenya has joined a women's football team in South Africa.

27 N. Wiener, *Cybernetics, or Control and Communication in the Animal and the Machine* (Cambridge, MA: MIT Press, 1961 [1948]).

28 See also N. K. Hayles, *How We Became Posthuman: Virtual Bodies in Cybernetics, Literature, and Informatics* (Chicago: University of Chicago Press, 1999).

29 Haraway, 'A cyborg manifesto'.

30 Preciado, *Testo Junkie*, 101.

31 M. Power, 'Confessions of a drone warrior', *GQ* (October 13, 2013), www.gq.com/news-politics/big-issues/201311/drone-uav-pilot-assassination (accessed 16 February, 2021). This 'voyeuristic intimacy' can be considered one of the unique hallmarks of the drone assemblage that differs from other forms of aerial surveillance and bombing, in that drone operators can often see the targets of surveillance without being observed themselves.

32 Preciado, *Testo Junkie*, 265, citing L. Williams 'Porn studies. Proliferating pornographies on/scene: An introduction', in L. Williams (ed.), *Porn Studies* (Durham, NC: Duke University Press 2004), 7.

33 A. Danchev, 'Bug splat: The art of the drone', *International Affairs*, 92:3 (2016): 704.

34 J. Butler, *Frames of War: When is Life Grievable?* (London: Verso, 2009); Puar, *Terrorist Assemblages*, C. Reddy, *Freedom with Violence: Race, Sexuality, and the US State* (Durham, NC: Duke University Press, 2011); M. Richter-Montpetit, 'Beyond the erotics of orientalism: Lawfare, torture and the racial-sexual grammars of legitimate suffering', *Security Dialogue*, 45:1 (2014): 43–62.

35 Some recent works that draw on longer histories of aerial surveillance, cartography, and the like for martial and imperialist politics include: A. Bousquet, *The Eye of War: Military Perception from the Telescope to the Drone* (Minneapolis: University of Minnesota Press, 2018); C. Kaplan, *Aerial Aftermaths: Wartime from Above* (Durham, NC: Duke University Press, 2018); K. H. Kindervater, 'The emergence of lethal surveillance: Watching and killing in the history of drone technology', *Security Dialogue*, 47:3 (2016): 223–238; P. Satia, 'Drones: A history from the British Middle East', *Humanity: An International Journal of Human Rights, Humanitarianism, and Development*, 5:1 (2014): 1–31.

36 S. Browne, *Dark Matters: On the Surveillance of Blackness* (Durham, NC: Duke University Press, 2015), 8.

37 G. Chamayou, *Manhunts: A Philosophical History* (Princeton: Princeton University Press, 2012).

38 H. J. Spillers, 'Mama's baby, Papa's maybe: An American grammar book', *Diacritics*, 17:2 (1987): 65–81; Sarah Haley, *No Mercy Here: Gender, Punishment and the Making of Jim Crow Modernity* (Chapel Hill: The University of North Carolina Press, 2016); Robyn Wiegman, *American Anatomies: Theorizing Race and Gender* (Durham, NC: Duke University Press, 1995).

39 Wiegman, *American Anatomies*, 55–64.

40 S. B. Somerville, *Queering the Color Line: Race and the Invention of Homosexuality in American Culture* (Durham, NC: Duke University Press, 2000).

41 J. K. Puar, *The Right to Maim: Debility, Capacity, Disability* (Durham, NC: Duke University Press, 2017), 40.

42 H. Kinsella, 'Securing the civilian: Sex and gender in the laws of war', in Michael Barnett and Raymond Duvall (eds), *Power and Global Governance*, 249–272 (Cambridge: Cambridge University Press, 2005); and Helen Kinsella, *The Image before the Weapon: A Critical History of the Distinction between Combatant and Civilian* (Ithaca: Cornell University Press, 2011).

43 J. Becker and S. Shane, 'Secret "kill list" proves a test of Obama's principles and will', *New York Times*, 29 May, 2012.

44 Wilcox, 'Embodying algorithmic war'.

45 L. Khalili, 'Gendered practices of counterinsurgency', *Review of International Studies*, 37:4 (2011): 1473.

46 P. Owens, *Economy of Force: Counterinsurgency and the Historical Rise of the Social* (Cambridge, Cambridge University Press, 2015), 270.

47 S. Laastad Dyvik, 'Women as "practitioners" and "targets": Gender and counterinsurgency in Afghanistan', *International Feminist Journal of Politics*, 16:3 (2014): 422.

48 Dyvik, 'Women as "practitioners" and "targets"', 422.

49 D. Gregory, '"The rush to the intimate": Counterinsurgency and the cultural turn', *Radical Philosophy*, 150 (July/Aug 2008), https://www.radicalphilosophy.com/article/the-rush-to-the-intimate (accessed 23 February, 2021).

50 O. Davis, 'Theorizing the advent of weaponized drones as techniques of domestic paramilitary policing', *Security Dialogue*, 50:4 (2019): 344–360. For

example, US security forces used drones and other aerial vehicles as surveillance over many protests that followed the killing of George Floyd by police officers in Minneapolis in May 2020. See Zolan Kanno-Youngs, 'U.S. Watched George Floyd protests in 15 cities using aerial surveillance'. *The New York Times*, 19 June, 2020, www.nytimes.com/2020/06/19/us/politics/george-floyd-protests-surveillance.html (accessed 23 February, 2021).

51 For a trenchant critique, see A. Howell, 'Forget "militarization": Race, disability and the "martial politics" of the police and of the university', *International Feminist Journal of Politics*, 20:2 (2018): 117–136.

52 A. M. Agathangelou, M. D. Bassichis, and T. L. Spira, 'Intimate investments: Homonormativity, global lockdown, and the seductions of Empire', *Radical History Review*, 100 (2008): 120–143.

Bibliography

Agathangelou, A. M., M. D. Bassichis, and T. L. Spira. 'Intimate investments: Homonormativity, global lockdown, and the seductions of empire'. *Radical History Review*, 100 (2008): 120–143.

Ahmed, S. 'From threat to walking corpse: Spatial disruption and the phenomenology of living under drones'. *Theory & Event*, 21:2 (2018): 382–410.

Balsamo, A. *Technologies of the Gendered Body: Reading Cyborg Women*. Durham, NC: Duke University Press, 1996.

Bayard de Volo, L. 'Unmanned? Gender recalibrations and the rise of drone warfare'. *Politics & Gender*, 12:1 (March 2016): 50–77.

Bousquet, A. *The Eye of War: Military Perception from the Telescope to the Drone*. Minneapolis: University of Minnesota Press, 2018.

Browne, S. *Dark Matters: On the Surveillance of Blackness*. Durham, NC: Duke University Press, 2015.

Butler, J. *Gender Trouble: Feminism and the Subversion of Identity*. New York: Routledge, 1990.

— *Bodies That Matter: On the Discursive Limits of 'Sex'*. New York: Routledge, 1993.

— *Frames of War: When is Life Grievable?* London: Verso, 2009.

— 'Gender in translation: Beyond monolingualism'. *PhiloSOPHIA*, 9:1 (2019): 1–25.

Chamayou, G. *Manhunts: A Philosophical History*. Princeton: Princeton University Press, 2012.

— *A Theory of the Drone*, trans. Janet Lloyd. New York: The New Press, 2015.

Daggett, D. 'Drone disorientations: How "unmanned" weapons queer the experience of killing in war'. *International Feminist Journal of Politics*, 17:3 (2015): 361–379.

Danchev, A. 'Bug splat: The art of the drone'. *International Affairs*, 92:3 (2016): 703–713.

Davis, O. 'Theorizing the advent of weaponized drones as techniques of domestic paramilitary policing'. *Security Dialogue*, online first 14 May, 2019.

Farris, S. R. *In the Name of Women's Rights: The Rise of Femonationalism*. Durham, NC: Duke University Press, 2017.

Goldstein, J. S. *War and Gender: How Gender Shapes the War System and Vice Versa*. Cambridge: Cambridge University Press, 2003.

Gregory, D. 'From a view to a kill: Drones and late modern war'. *Theory, Culture & Society*, 28:7–8 (2011): 188–215.

— '"The rush to the intimate": Counterinsurgency and the cultural turn.' *Radical Philosophy*, 150 (July/Aug 2008). www.radicalphilosophy.com/article/the-rush-to-the-intimate (accessed 23 February, 2021).

— 'Eyes in the sky – bodies on the ground'. *Critical Studies on Security*, 6:3 (2018): 347–358.

Halberstam, J. 'Automating gender: Postmodern feminism in the age of the intelligent machine'. *Feminist Studies*, 17:3 (1991): 439–460.

Haley, S. *No Mercy Here: Gender, Punishment and the Making of Jim Crow Modernity*. Chapel Hill: The University of North Carolina Press, 2016.

Haraway, D. 'Situated knowledges: The science question in feminism and the privilege of partial perspective'. *Feminist Studies*, 14:3 (1988): 575–599.

— 'The biopolitics of postmodern bodies'. In *Simians, Cyborgs and Women*. New York: Routledge, 1991.

— 'A cyborg manifesto: Science, technology, and socialist-feminisms in the late twentieth century'. In *Simians, Cyborgs and Women*. New York: Routledge, 1991.

Haritaworn, J., A. Kuntsman, and S. Posocco (eds). *Queer Necropolitics*. Abingdon: Routledge, 2014.

Hayles, N. K. *How We Became Posthuman: Virtual Bodies in Cybernetics, Literature, and Informatics*. Chicago: University of Chicago Press, 1999.

Howell, A. 'Forget "militarization": Race, disability and the "martial politics" of the police and of the university'. *International Feminist Journal of Politics*, 20:2 (2018): 117–136.

Kaplan, C. *Aerial Aftermaths: Wartime from Above*. Durham, NC: Duke University Press, 2018.

Karkazis, K. *Fixing Sex: Intersex, Medical Authority, and Lived Experience*. Durham, NC: Duke University Press, 2008.

Khalili, L. 'Gendered practices of counterinsurgency'. *Review of International Studies*, 37:4 (2011): 1471–1491.

Kindervater, K. H. 'The emergence of lethal surveillance: Watching and killing in the history of drone technology'. *Security Dialogue*, 47:3 (2016): 223–238.

Kinsella, H. 'Securing the civilian: Sex and gender in the laws of war'. In M. Barnett and R. Duvall (eds), *Power and Global Governance*, 249–272. Cambridge: Cambridge University Press, 2005.

— *The Image Before the Weapon: A Critical History of the Distinction between Combatant and Civilian*. Ithaca: Cornell University Press, 2011.

Laastad Dyvik, S. 'Women as "practitioners" and "targets": Gender and counterinsurgency in Afghanistan'. *International Feminist Journal of Politics*, 16:3 (2014): 410–429.

MacKenzie, M. *Beyond the Band of Brothers: The US Military and the Myth That Women Can't Fight*. Cambridge: Cambridge University Press, 2015.

Manchanda, N. 'Queering the Pashtun: Afghan sexuality in the homo-nationalist imaginary'. *Third World Quarterly* 36:1 (2015): 130–146.

Manjikian, M. 'Becoming unmanned: The gendering of lethal autonomous warfare technology'. *International Feminist Journal of Politics*, 16:1 (2014): 48–65.

Masters, C. 'Bodies of technology: Cyborg soldiers and militarized masculinities'. *International Feminist Journal of Politics*, 7:1 (March 2005): 112–132.

Nicholas, L. and C. Agius. 'Drones and the politics of protection'. In L. Nicholas and C. Agius (eds), *The Persistence of Global Masculinism: Discourse, Gender and Neo-Colonial Re-Articulations of Violence*, 115–140. Cham: Springer International Publishing, 2018.

Owens, P. *Economy of Force: Counterinsurgency and the Historical Rise of the Social.* Cambridge, Cambridge University Press, 2015.

Power, M. 'Confessions of a drone warrior'. *GQ*, 13 October, 2013. www.gq.com/news-politics/big-issues/201311/drone-uav-pilot-assassination (accessed 16 February, 2021).

Preciado, P. B. *Testo Junkie: Sex, Drugs, and Biopolitics in the Pharmacopornographic Era*. New York: The Feminist Press at the City University of New York, 2013.

Puar, J. K. *Terrorist Assemblages: Homonationalism in Queer Times*. Durham, NC: Duke University Press, 2007.

— '"I would rather be a cyborg than a goddess"'. *PhiloSOPHIA*, 2:1 (2012): 49–63.

— *The Right to Maim: Debility, Capacity, Disability*. Durham, NC: Duke University Press, 2017.

Reddy, C. *Freedom with Violence: Race, Sexuality, and the US State*. Durham, NC: Duke University Press, 2011.

Repo, J. *The Biopolitics of Gender*. New York: Oxford University Press, 2016.

Richter-Montpetit, M. 'Beyond the erotics of orientalism: Lawfare, torture and the racial-sexual grammars of legitimate suffering'. *Security Dialogue*, 45:1 (2014): 43–62.

Satia, P. 'Drones: A history from the British Middle East'. *Humanity: An International Journal of Human Rights, Humanitarianism, and Development*, 5:1 (2014): 1–31.

Shaw, I. G. R. and M. Akhter. 'The unbearable humanness of drone warfare in FATA, Pakistan'. *Antipode*, 44:4 (2012): 1490–1509.

Somerville, S. *Queering the Color Line: Race and the Invention of Homosexuality in American Culture*. Durham, NC: Duke University Press, 2000.

Spillers, H. J. 'Mama's baby, Papa's maybe: An American grammar book'. *Diacritics*, 17:2 (1987): 65–81.

Suchman, L. 'Situational awareness: Deadly bioconvergence at the boundaries of bodies and machines'. *MediaTropes*, 5:1 (2015): 1–24.

Wiegman, R. *American Anatomies: Theorizing Race and Gender*. Durham, NC: Duke University Press, 1995.

Wiener, N. *Cybernetics, or Control and Communication in the Animal and the Machine*. Cambridge, MA: MIT Press, 1961 [1948].

Wilcox, L. *Bodies of Violence: Theorizing Embodied Subjects in International Relations*. New York: Oxford University Press, 2015.

Wilcox, L. 'Drone warfare and the making of bodies out of place'. *Critical Studies on Security*, 3:1 (2015): 127–131.

— 'Drones, swarms and becoming-insect: Feminist utopias and posthuman politics'. *Feminist Review*, 116:1 (July 2017): 25–45.

— 'Embodying algorithmic war: Gender, race, and the posthuman in drone warfare'. *Security Dialogue*, 48:1 (2017): 11–28.

Wilke, C. 'Seeing and unmaking civilians in Afghanistan: Visual technologies and contested professional visions'. *Science, Technology, & Human Values*, 42:6 (2017): 1031–1060.

Williams, A. J. 'Enabling persistent presence? Performing the embodied geopolitics of the unmanned aerial vehicle assemblage'. *Political Geography*, 30:7 (2011): 381–390.

Williams, L. *Porn Studies*. Durham, NC: Duke University Press, 2004.

7

Borders and migration as seen from above

Rasmus Degnbol and Andreas Immanuel Graae

For those of us who have never experienced war and conflict in the European countries, borders are a somewhat abstract phenomenon. Or at least until 2015, when fences, barbed wire, and armed militant border guards suddenly emerged all around Europe as a response to the so-called 'refugee crisis'. In the early summer of 2015, when the crisis intensified, Danish photographer, Rasmus Degnbol, decided to photograph these new European borders and their impact on the hundreds of thousands of refugees and migrants arriving after perilous journeys. He decided to carry out his task using a technology developed by the military: the drone.

With the drone as medium, Degnbol offers an alternative way of looking at migration, from above. With its ambiguous and distancing gaze on the humanitarian crises unfolding across the borders of Europe, he found the drone uniquely capable of mediating the scale and dehumanisation of European migration politics. Accordingly, Degnbol named his ongoing drone project *Europe's New Borders*,[1] a photo series showing guarded borders, crossing points, camps, shelters, and emptied sites, all from the vertical perspective of the drone. Following the refugees' trail from their initial arrival on Lesbos, Greece, through Eastern and Central European countries, and to infamous refugee camps like 'The Jungle' in Calais, France, Degnbol reports neutrally from the distanced position of the drone. While the photos are beautiful, sometimes almost sublime in their colours, contrasts and compositions, beneath the neatly ordered and sanitised surface, they express a darker and more disturbing reality. With barren landscapes, cleft by border walls and scattered with faceless human beings and their sad belongings, the photos thus uncover a changed Europe and address an inconvenient truth about how we as Europeans protect our Western communities against immigration. Through its clean aesthetics and distanced gaze, the drone captures this tension by mirroring the governmental view from above, which sees no individuals, only faceless numbers.

Andreas Immanuel Graae and Rasmus Degnbol first became acquainted in 2016 when they both spoke at a drone conference at the H. C. Andersen

Airport in Odense, Denmark. Since then they have developed a collaboration, and on several occasions Degnbol has presented his photos at the University of Southern Denmark, most recently as part of the *Drone Imaginaries and Society* conference in 2018. Meanwhile, the international art community began to discover *Europe's New Borders*, which quickly became one of the most critically acclaimed and award-winning photo projects on the migration situation in Europe, with exhibitions at various galleries and museums around the world, among other places at MoMA, the Museum of Modern Art, New York in 2016–2017. Yet, far from MoMA's higher circles, more exactly in Copenhagen's raw but increasingly gentrified north western district, Degnbol and Graae meet at a crowded coffee bar some rainy day in 2019[2] to discuss *Europe's New Borders*, drone photography, and the politics of migration as seen from above.

The journey starts: sensing the distance

Andreas Immanuel Graae (AG): These days we are becoming still more exposed to images of migrants and refugees on television, in global news, on the internet, social media, and so forth. It has often been argued that this massive exposure to images of suffering people has somehow anaesthetised us. We have simply become too used to watching the same images of people in deep misery, which has made us somehow indifferent. Why did you choose to photograph refugees with a drone?

Rasmus Degnbol (RD): Actually, my starting point was exactly rooted in this very experience of overexposure. In normal photo journalism, which is my craft and trade, there is usually just one way of photographing everything from the same perspectives, showing the same motifs. And especially when it comes to refugees and humanitarian crisis, it's typically the same old way of doing it that has dominated. Personally, I was getting tired of this, and as a photographer I did not feel like I was adding anything new to the story. On the beaches on Lesbos we were 40–50 photographers shooting the same images of the same boats in the same way with the same people going through the same tragic emotions. I felt that the photos I was shooting were showing people being either extremely happy – because they believed that they had reached safety in Europe – or in deep sorrow crying from their losses. But the thing was that you could never sell the happy pictures. I was getting frustrated by this mediated reality and the mismatch between what I was able to show and what was really happening.

I therefore stopped shooting these traditional photos in early 2015. Instead, I started asking what type of stories did not hit the mainstream media – and I started mapping them into Google Maps. After a couple of months researching I looked at a map that showed how the stories I found interesting were all happening along the borders: these were 'small stories' – such as refugees being shot on the Bulgarian border and the like – which never became big news. When I looked at the map, I could see that these stories were happening along the borders from Greece and all the way to Denmark and Norway and thought that there must be something extremely interesting to report from these borders. But then I ran into the first problem: how do you photograph borders? In 2015, there were actually no real physical changes going on around the borders yet, and I had no idea of how this crisis would change Europe, although I had an idea that something would definitely change.

But then I looked at my map, and I said to myself: 'You have to photograph this. You have to build your own map of stories.' And if you look on a map, you look from above. So I realised that I needed to shoot this series of photos from above. At this point, I therefore had two choices: I could either hire a helicopter – which would be the normal thing to do – or I could use a drone.

AG: And you did. In fact, you built your own personalised drone and equipped it with a camera. I guess you knew of the drone, but you did not have any actual experience with drone photography in 2015. How did you do it? And did you find any inspiration from other drone photographers – such as Tomas van Houtryve who is also interviewed for this volume?[3]

RD: It is true that I didn't have a clue about drones when I first got the idea. I am not an engineer, and I had never built anything like that before, it was simply learning-by-doing as I tried my best to put the bits and pieces and rotor blades together. Moreover, the technological quality of drones in 2015 was really far from today, where you can easily buy a cheap drone that is superior in all aspects. It was not in any way easy to build something stable enough to photograph with. Anyway, I got it up and it was flying, and although I completely crashed it one of the first times I was out testing it, I still got the feeling that this was very special and that I needed to continue doing it.

At the same time, I already knew Tomas van Houtryve who was the first one to use drones for journalism. I had been following a master class with him in 2014, and also had him as my mentor back then. I had seen his photos and learned that this angle was possible and could be used for reporting. In fact, nobody used drones for this purpose before he started doing it. At that point, the drone was mostly used for wide-angle shots and pretty landscape pictures, which is fine, of course, but would it also be able to work as a tool for photo journalism? Nobody really knew at that point. However, I had an idea of what new capabilities this alternative and ground-breaking perspective could provide.

AG: *Okay, the drone was a novel technology for photography and journalistic reporting in 2015 – but, from a more historical perspective, the view from above was not that new, right? I mean, aerial photos shot from balloons,*[4] *aeroplanes, helicopters and so forth have been there for ages, and in particular since World War I in which Germans first started using the aerial gaze for reconnaissance and strategic planning. How did you experience the drone view as different from a traditional aeroplane or helicopter shot?*

RD: With the drone you could get really close. From a helicopter you are at least 150 metres up in the air, and that makes it more distanced. Even with a good zoom you do not reduce the distance; this is actually not how to make pictures look close. A zoom just makes the picture bigger, but you can still sense the distance. But I wanted closeness. Even for aerial photos, closeness is crucial and it demanded the right altitude, which only the drone could provide. I experimented a lot to find the right height. What was too high, or what is too close?

AG: *This makes me think of the title of Omer Fast's art film* 5,000 Feet is the Best *in which a drone operator explains the ideal altitude of the drone. From that perfect height he 'could tell you what kind of shoes you wore', as he says.*[5] *When you shoot your drone photos, are you going after a similar degree of detailed description and proximity? Do you also have a favourite height?*

RD: Sure I have, although the altitudes are of course very different when flying a smaller drone than the big military ones which the operator in Fast's film is probably talking about. When I fly, I am normally not going above 15–25 metres, perhaps 30 metres as the maximum. In fact, I scrutinised Tomas' [van Houtryve] images in order to find out what height would give the perfect balance between distance and closeness. I even practised with my girlfriend standing beneath the drone in order to create that ideal sense of height. Here, I also discovered that the most optimal camera perspective was my usual reportage optics with 35–50 millimetres focal length by which I normally shoot all my reportages. And it's the same for the drone. If you zoom in more than that, you get this feeling of distance that we are used to from the helicopter. Even from a drone, if you zoom too much it will look like a helicopter shot. This is the visual aesthetics that we have become accustomed to through pre-drone aerial photography such as helicopter footage. We would instinctively think that if it looks this or that way, it must be a helicopter shot. However, I wanted to find out what the drone could actually be used for in journalism. It was a very long experimental phase triggered by my curiosity about what this new tool was capable of in terms of new ways of telling stories.

The journey continues: borderlands, labour camps, and smugglers

AG: You found the drone to be particularly well suited for grasping both the scale of the problem and the concept of borders. You also named the project 'Europe's New Borders'. How did you end up with that title? And what significance does the concept of the border have in your work?

RD: I always thought that borders are fascinating per default. On the one hand, they are imaginary constructions and lines which are invisible and randomly drawn, but at the same time they are very real geopolitical symbols and materialisations of power. In my childhood I had no recollection of showing my passport, whereas today people even have to wait in lines showing their passports when travelling from Denmark to Sweden. And while the internal European borders are still somehow abstract to us European citizens, they are becoming very concrete for refugees, for whom every single border crossing is a life-and-death struggle.

When the number of refugees crossing the borders to Europe intensified in 2015, I sensed that this perspective on borders and on the more long-term changes in Europe's geopolitics was missing. I felt that it was typically very one-sided coverage. Nobody was talking about the politics, which was one of the main reasons for the refugee crisis. Nobody was talking about all the reports in 2011 and 2012 that stated that this was going to happen. I wanted to take a step back and not focus so much on individual tragedies or humanitarian aspects – which had already been well covered – but rather I wanted to enlighten viewers on what was happening on 'both sides of the borders' so to speak. While my photos are of course about refugees, I was actually more interested in the concept of borders, and how they changed – and the refugee crisis was a kind of a driver for this change. My main concern was what this crisis was about to do to the Europe I knew.

AG: How did you experience these geopolitical changes yourself on your own journeys, then?

DG: Well, for one thing I had to show my passport at all border checkpoints. And moreover, I got arrested nine times for flying the drone close to the border, which is prohibited in most countries, where the border is regarded as a military installation. Today it is common knowledge that you are not allowed to fly a drone in military zones, but this was 2015 and there were no rules or legislations regarding drones whatsoever. The border police did not really understand the concept of the drone, and they were basically just detaining me to stop me from doing whatever I was doing. They probably thought that I was spying or planning some kind of illegal activity when I was photographing the fences. However, after spending all this time at the European borders I must admit that I got rather paranoid – something I never thought that I would be. I don't usually get scared easily, but this time I was on high alert constantly. Every time I sent up my drone, I knew that I would most likely get detained. And while most of the border guards were typically nice people who quickly calmed down when I explained what I was really doing, some of them were pretty scary guys, like militia and stuff like this.

AG: What was the most uncomfortable experience you had during detention or when flying your drone in these borderlands?

DG: The scariest experience I had was in Hungary: I wanted a picture of the new fence on the Hungarian border to Serbia, and I did the photo three times in order to get it the way I wanted. The first two days, it was mostly border police or regular police who approached me. But the last day it was clearly some kind of militia – as regular border authorities have to wear visible uniforms or other identification to show that they are officials. But these guys were wearing black masks and no marks. They took me and my drone, put me in a car and drove off with me. Then, they put me in some kind of safehouse and asked me a ton of questions for a couple of hours. It was very uncomfortable – especially because nobody knew where I was. I never found out where I was or who these guys were.

But I also had a lot of trouble with smugglers and people traffickers who were smuggling refugees across the borders. Of course they did not want me to come flying with my drone, taking pictures. But I was going to a lot of remote places to tell the stories that nobody else cared about, of refugees getting killed or turning up dead somewhere – which brought me to these troublesome routes with not-nice people. For instance, I had a couple of close calls with the Kosovo-Albanian mafia. One of them was at this small road from Macedonia to Serbia. When I approached, I expected some kind of border patrol or check point, but there was nothing. I parked my car on the side and started preparing to take my pictures. Then I heard a car coming up really fast, which blocked the road completely. And out of this big black Mercedes five big Kosovo-Albanian mob-looking guys jumped out shouting at me: 'Who are you and what are you doing here?' Then I had to think really fast, concerned as I was with all my extremely expensive drone equipment in my car. In the moment, I just started rabbling something nonsense in my worst Danglish, and they just looked at me, not really trusting me, but one of them said: 'Can we agree that you get into your car, and you never saw us, and we never saw you?' And I said: 'Yes, we absolute can!' Then I hurried into my car, and as I drove off I saw the black Mercedes – which was probably a kind of front patrol car – and following it about forty to fifty cars full of refugees that were being smuggled across the border.

AG: If you could name one thing that you regret not photographing with a drone would that be it?

RD: In fact, I saw a lot of these strange and frightening things because I spent so much time in the borderlands. For example, in the regions between the Bulgarian and Turkish border I saw labour camps where the Syrian refugees were being kept as slaves by people with Kalashnikovs. They captured them in the regions between Turkey and Bulgaria, where they were literally hunting refugees for money. Most often they were just killing them. Typically, one refugee brings about 3,000 or 4,000 Euros with him, so if you can catch a group of 40 it makes a huge salary. And in Bulgaria, where Muslims are extremely looked downed upon, these vigilante groups believe that they protect their country while at the same time earning some money. If they were not killed, they were taken to these labour camps and used as slaves. It was really terrifying to witness. That was probably the one thing I regret the most that I did not photograph. But when people point Kalashnikovs into your car, you don't really show your press card and tell them that you have the right to be here. You just get out of there.

At that moment it was simply not possible to stay and photograph the camp without putting myself in too much danger. One of the reasons was that the 2015 drone technology only allowed me to be about 300 metres away, and it was too big a risk to take. But if I had the drone I have today it would actually have been possible. Then I could have had much more distance – I could probably have been even a couple of kilometres away – which would have allowed me to get the pictures and get out of there.

The politics of the faceless: anonymity, distance, and closeness

AG: Talking about distance, you mentioned previously that you wanted closeness. However, at the same time you use the distance and remoteness of the drone to access all these dangerous places and scenes, but also to create a certain sense of scale when looking at the borders and migrants from above. How do you experience the balance between distance and closeness when photographing from the drone?

RD: One of the key qualities of the drone is that it's somewhat distanced, but still close. It provides a kind of *neutral* look so to speak. In my projects, I find that my photos are strongest when they are as objective as possible; I always strive for this neutrality. That being said, I know, of course, that such a thing as one hundred percent neutrality or objectiveness does not exist. But by keeping the photos as emotionally distanced and neutral as possible, I want them to be open for interpretation, that it is not me telling the viewer what to think, but rather about triggering a process of reflection in the viewer.

AG: But also, on a more practical level, the drone verges between closeness and distance. You can get really close and capture all these details, but at the same time you are 'not there' or at least you are withdrawn from the scene you are shooting. How did that increased distance affect the way you work as a photographer compared to how you used to work without the drone?

RD: That is indeed true, and in the beginning when I started using the drone I was surprised by how technical it made the whole situation and how remote and disconnected it made me feel. When I was standing there looking from the drone to the screen and back to the drone again, I sometimes felt totally detached from the scene. There could be people crying, and I could hear them, but I couldn't feel it the same way that I used to, all because of the drone. I was actually quite surprised how big a deal this was for me. Being trained as a photographer, I'm used to feeling people. Normally when I shoot photos, I'm within a few metres from the people I photograph. It's part of my trade and my training not to have that kind of boundary between me and the object. But with the drone, I started being emotionally disconnected from the people I photographed. I therefore had to make a strategy of switching between the drone and traditional horizontal photographing in order not to become too detached: the one day I did research from the ground with a normal camera, the next day I used the drone, and so forth.

In fact, this strategy also had another purpose. I always wanted to be as close as possible in order to be one hundred percent sure that what I was

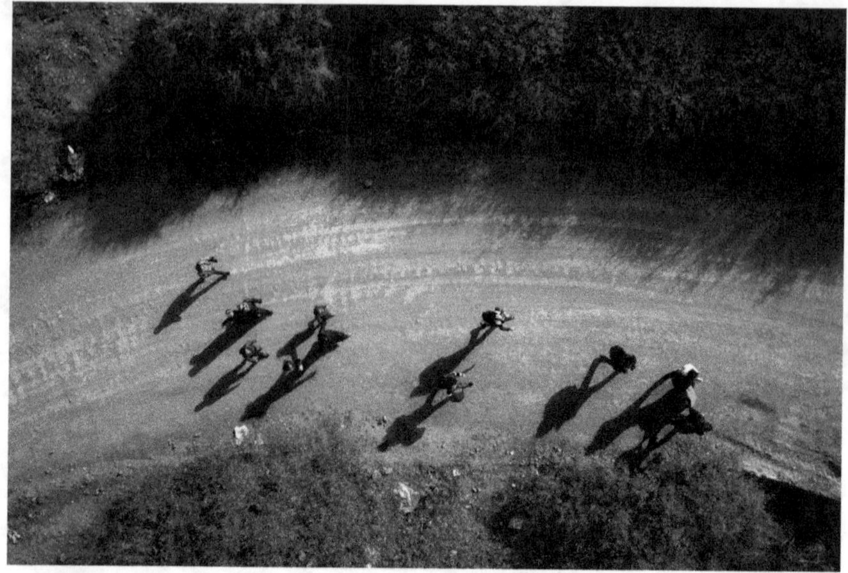

7.1 Rasmus Degnbol, *A Group of Syrian Refugees from Aleppo Walking on a Dirt Track along the Beaches of Lesbos after Arriving with a Boat from Turkey*, 2015.

telling with the photos, including their captions, was true. For instance, if I was standing more than a hundred metres away from what I photographed I didn't have a sense of what was really going on and therefore I couldn't write captions. It was simply impossible. On every picture I am literally just outside the frame. Like on this picture with a group of a Syrian refugees walking on a dirt track along the beaches of Lesbos after arriving with a boat from Turkey. Here, I am actually positioned just a few metres outside of the frame, which was an important way of working with the drone as a journalist. Then I was able to stop people and talk to them afterwards to get to know more about them.

AG: Let's talk a bit more about this photo [figure 7.1]. *What would you say that the drone specifically did in mediating the story of this Syrian family from Aleppo? What qualities, or obstacles, did you encounter using the drone as a medium?*

RD: With this kind of photo of people walking, I would normally have shot it from the ground showing their faces. That's how we usually work in journalism, trying to catch emotional moments by focusing on human gestures and facial expressions. But when shooting from the drone, you almost remove the personality a bit. The drone doesn't show individual faces, it rather displays the bigger picture. In a way the drone perspective mirrors the way politicians and authorities at large look at immigrants and refugees. Clearly, the top-down view makes it all more abstract and anonymous. It anonymises the individual persons on these pictures, which is, in fact, also why I believe that the drone perspective fits my project so well. It shows that this is not about persons, but about numbers.

AG: I totally agree that this is the impression you get when you look at this photo of the walking refugee family, a kind of 'politics of the faceless' if you will. But how do you feel about deploying this anonymising, governmental, and cynical gaze from above – can you even avoid identifying with it to some degree?

DG: I see where you are going, and one of the important aims of the project is indeed to show my viewers that this is how refugees are looked upon politically and bureaucratically, letting them identify with this detached gaze. Then they can perhaps better start understanding why nothing is happening, and why nobody is helping these people – and this is because they are looked upon not as individual human beings, but as crowds, masses, and cool numbers. Whereas in journalism, we would normally tell the story of the walking family as an image of a larger picture, but this is not how politics works. The way the European politicians and law makers respond to the refugee crisis has nothing to do with the family on this photo. It has much more to do with the 'bigger picture' – or what you call 'the politics of the faceless' – that is, the 1.2 million refugees and migrants that entered the European borders in 2015. And from this cynical perspective, the family on the photo has really no meaning.

AG: Okay, but you still have this guy in the hoodie looking straight up at the drone which creates a somewhat personal feeling or a sense of intimacy – almost as if he returns your gaze, as a kind of a counter-stare?

RD: See, that's why the drone is so different from normal aerial photography, because it allows you to get so close and obtain a kind of intimacy. When you photograph people on the ground, you will almost always know if they do not want to be photographed. They can signal it or tell you directly, and then you stop. But when you photograph somebody from the drone, you practically don't give him or her a choice. I had a lot of concerns about these ethical issues of my work. For instance, the Afghan refugees who know the sound of the drone as something that would normally mean military surveillance or bombs. Would I inflect them some kind trauma when flying above them with my drone? Luckily I didn't. In fact, they mostly didn't mind it. I guess that comes with the proliferation of this new technology, that people have already started to get used to it. But even so, I am always very careful to read the situation and ready to land it if people get angry or afraid of it.

For instance, when I first arrived at Lesbos and started photographing the incoming boats with refugees disembarking on the shore. I had a couple of incidents where the refugees hadn't see me and started throwing rocks at the drone because they thought it was a military or police drone surveilling them. But as soon as they saw me and realised that I was the one controlling it, they didn't care.

Arriving at Lesbos: voyeurism and intervention

AG: You arrived at Lesbos in the summer of 2015 when the first huge wave of boats with thousands and thousands of refugees were reaching the beaches from Turkey, many of them half dead or drowned. How did you respond to all this chaos and misery while still keeping your distance from the drone? Did you ever intervene or was it sort of 'against the rules'?

RD: As a journalist and photographer you can sustain quite a bit. You learn to distance yourself and try not to react unless it is absolutely necessary, because the rule is that if you intervene, you cannot photograph it. But if I saw people suffering or in desperate need of help I would of course intervene. This happened several times. For instance, one day when I was on the beach photographing, a boat flipped over and refugees, including children, started drowning. Then I naturally put down my camera and said to the other photographers, 'Guys I'm not watching three kids drowning!' I simply couldn't see why I should photograph this, if I could do anything about it. And I really hope that anybody would do the same in a similar situation. There were certainly moments where I stopped being a photographer and started being a human being.

AG: Let's take a look at one of your most iconic images from the time when refugees disembarked at the beaches of Lesbos. We have seen these horrible pictures of crying people and dead bodies washed ashore dozens of times. Yet in this photo you went for neither human faces nor dead bodies, but instead photographed an enormous pile of discarded life vests – also known as the 'life jacket graveyard' or 'mountain of misery' – from the straight-down perspective of the drone. What do you think of this iconic photo today?

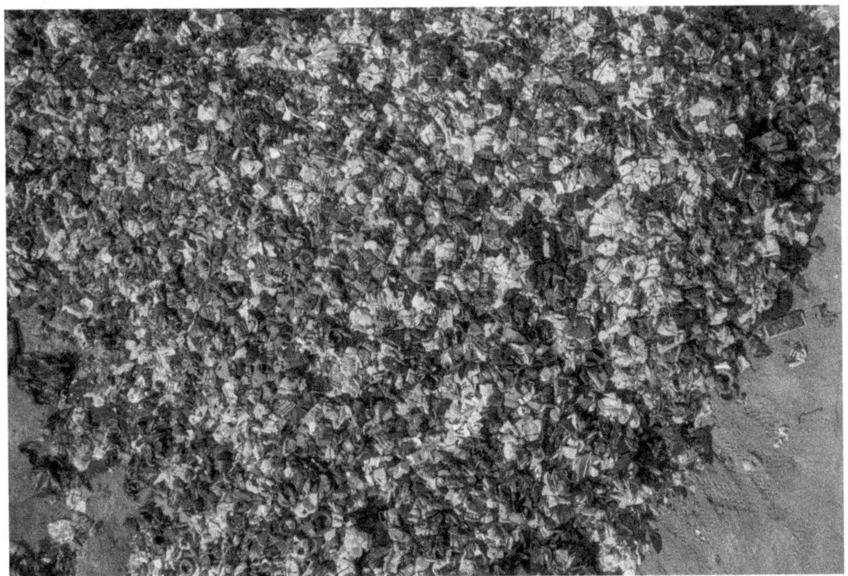

7.2 Rasmus Degnbol, *100,000 Life-Vest Mountain on Lesbos, Greece*, 2015.

RD: Well, first of all I still find it haunting as hell. Personally, I think that this place is one of the toughest places I ever visited; it was the only place where I saw many journalists cry, and I think that somehow this mourning transcends into the picture. At a first glance, however, it can seem rather abstract, and for some people it's hard to figure out what it even represents. But because of the huge sized prints and the high degree of detail you can start identifying all these various discarded items which has been left there by the refugees as a kind of memorial to their desperate and hopeless journey. Besides the 100,000 life vests forming the actual 'mountain', you start noticing all the other kinds of stuff, such as lifebuoys, tyres, bags, clothes, children's shoes, air mattresses, water wings, swim rings, flippers, and much more. Clearly, you would not have been able to spot all these disturbing details from a traditional perspective, and even less so the shocking quantity of discarded objects. Again, this is where the drone view can help the viewer grasp the enormous scale of the humanitarian disaster.

AG: This aspect of scale seems to be recurrent in many of the photos, but it strikes me that there is something more at play in this particular one with the life jackets. Perhaps it has something to do with the composition of the picture and the straight-down perspective – as opposed to the other slightly more tilted images – but perhaps also to the fact that this photo is basically lacking human beings, which might also relate to the abstractness, you mentioned?

RD: Yes, I definitely think that the abstractness has something to do with it, because clearly it is not as easy to decode as many of my other photos. What I personally like most about photography is when the photographer allows me to think, and I believe that this picture is so powerful because it does exactly that. Viewers have now become trained at decoding photos, so if I tell them that 'here is more than one hundred thousand life vests', they can do a story themselves which is way stronger than what I could ever photograph. It is all about triggering the imagination and curiosity, which I believe is best done without too much explanation. And here, the fact that there are no human beings in the picture, that it is much more graphical and abstract, forces the viewer to reflect about what has actually happened, and what will be happening, to the thousands of people who left these objects. I like this more intellectual side of the drone photos; how they demand the viewer to actually reflect in order to understand.

Also, in relation to the abstractness of this photo, I have an anecdote from when I was visiting the exhibition at MoMA. Here, I talked to one of the tour guides who had passed and looked at the photo for months on her tours and kept being puzzled about it. She simply couldn't see what it was and thought that perhaps it was flowers. That shows how abstract it may appear for some viewers.

At the museum: the viewer becoming drone

AG: I sense in your drone photos – and in the way you are talking about them – a sort of openness and resistance to interpretation, or a drive to make them not too easily decoded by viewers. In short, you like them to be abstract and demanding, but then you also mentioned previously how they can be seen as reflecting a certain kind of migration politics. How would you say that the abstract and the political merge in your work?

RD: It is right that I feel, probably mostly in retrospect, that the photos mirror the politics and the neutral or bureaucratic view on the refugees as numbers. But I don't think that this *mirroring*, if we should call it that, is something that is expressed without some kind of ambiguity and openness for interpretation. In fact, I think it's not so much the works themselves as much as the vertical perspective on the human beings that opens up for the political interpretation. For me it is really more important to give the viewer an experience that awakens a process of critical reflection. This is also done more practically through the curation of the project. For instance, at MoMA and other museums, many of the photos are curated on huge light tables where the viewers are not looking horizontally at them, but look down on them from above. That way of displaying the photos almost has the viewers becoming their own drones: they can hover around the images in the same way as a drone, or 'zoom in' on some of the tiny details due to the huge size of the prints, which make even tiny details crystal clear. In this way, the photos stop being regular images and become a full experience, or performative experience, through which the viewer can better connect with the premise of these photos – which is the cynical migration politics behind it all.

AG: It seems to be that the detached, depersonalised view from above – both reflecting the politics of migration, and reflected in exhibition when the viewer looks straight down on the photos like a drone – is key to the particular drone aesthetics in your work. But not all of your photos are shot from the straight-down, ninety-degree angle, in fact many of them are slightly tilted. Is that in order to get more perspective, see more landscape, show more body or […]?

RD: Yes, it's right that at some point I actually stopped photographing directly down since the images simply got too flattened. I experienced scenes where shooting straight down would actually destroy the story: For instance, I have this photo of a huge line of busses, five kilometres long, waiting in line to transport refugees back across the border to Serbia. I tried to get as high up as the drone would allow me, but still I only got eight or nine busses. I started tilting the camera five or ten degrees, just to give the picture slightly more depth and perspective so that I could get the entire line of busses vanishing in the horizon.

Otherwise, when photographing straight down from the drone, it's all about lines and curves, shapes, colours – like in the photo of the life vests, in which the aesthetics becomes much more graphic, almost like an abstract painting. It is due to the colours and contrasts which is, of course, also highly dependent on the sun.

AG: How do you then work with these more formal aspects of drone photographing, such as lines, colours, and contrasts – do you plan for it when researching the area of the scene you are shooting?

RD: Yes, absolutely. For each of my drone photos there are usually three or four days of research, and on top of that there is a lot of research from home. During the project, I normally used Google Maps to pinpoint the

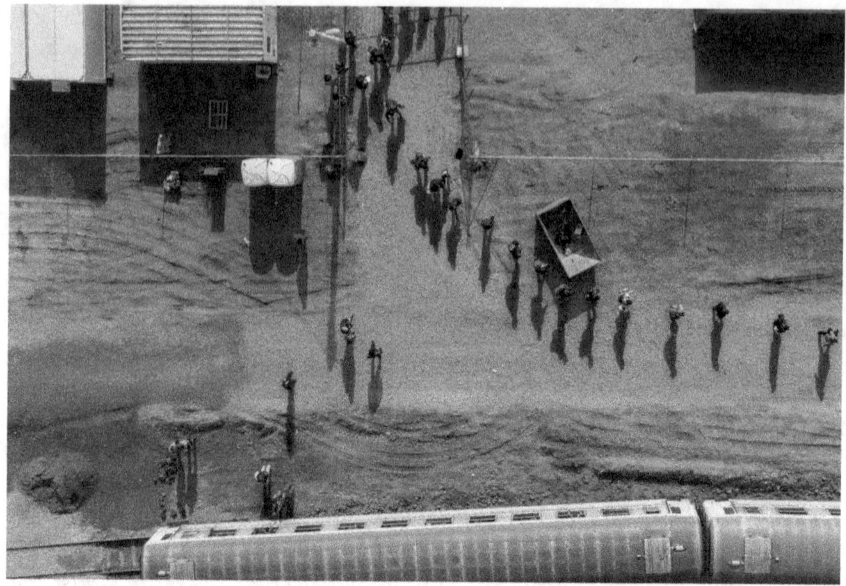

7.3 Rasmus Degnbol, *Refugees Walk to the Train in Slavonski Brod, Croatia*, 2015.

exact GPS location where refugees were crossing the borders in order to see when and where there was a story to be told. Then I travelled there and scouted around the area trying to find out where and how the refugees were passing through. But I also looked carefully at the natural environment such as sun light and shadows when I planned for the perfect time to shoot the photos.

For instance, I used apps on my phone to figure out on what time of the day the light was best and the shadows would be longest – like in one of the photos of refugees on the march to a train in Croatia. Before shooting that photo, I scouted the location for four days in order to not only see what time of the day they were being marched out, but also to find the optimal time in which the shadows were right. In fact, shadows are absolutely key to drone aesthetics. When you see people from above they quickly become flattened and two-dimensional. And when there are no shadows, like in the middle of the day, it becomes even harder to spot individuals. Then you only have a flat image, in which it is almost impossible to see any people, since they basically just become dots with a couple of pixels surrounding them.

AG: It is interesting how the shadows are serving a concrete aesthetic purpose, but – to me at least – there is also something uncanny or almost spectral about them: They are showing humans, but they only show their shadows, it's almost like they have been there, but are not there anymore, as if they have disappeared. Have you ever thought about that in relation to what we talked about earlier about the dehumanising view of the drone?

RD: I never thought about them as ghosts. I guess that in the actual situation I was mostly focused on the practical function of the shadows as providers of contrast and indicators of what was actually going on in the picture. But certainly I can see what you mean about the dehumanising or almost haunting appearance they make as a march of shadows, not human beings. And this also taps well into the overall political theme of the project, which we have already talked a lot about; that when removing their faces, you also remove their individual value. The drone aesthetics is indeed dehumanising, it's depersonalised and sanitised, just like borders and migration politics are dehumanising per se. But once you start reflecting on my photos, I don't think you find them dehumanising, I think they are more a kind of reflection on the dehumanised response to the crisis. The drone is a tool which is very efficient in producing a certain experience in the viewer of how *we* – and I see this very literally as you and me and other European citizens – are looking at people in deep misery through a distanced and cynical view, and will probably keep doing so in the years to come.

Notes

1 For more on the project 'Europe's new borders', see Rasmus Degnbol's website: http://rasmusdegnbol.com/portfolio-item/europes-new-borders/ (accessed 3 March, 2021).
2 Interview conducted on 23 April, 2019, Copenhagen.
3 See Svea Braeunert's interview with Tomas van Houtryve in chapter 4 of this volume.
4 For more on the aerial history of drones, see Kathrin Maurer' historical analysis of nineteenth-century hot air balloon as early drones in this volume's chapter 1.
5 Omer Fast (dir), *5,000 Feet is the Best*, 30 min, originally exhibited at The Imperial War Museum, London, 2011.

Bibliography

Degnbol, R. 'Europe's new borders'. http://rasmusdegnbol.com/portfolio-item/europes-new-borders/ (accessed 3 March, 2021).

Fast, O. (dir). *5,000 Feet is the Best.* Originally exhibited at The Imperial War Museum, London, 2011. 30 min.

Part III

Communities

8

Swarm of steel: insects, drones and swarming in Ernst Jünger's *The Glass Bees*

Andreas Immanuel Graae

> Human subjects thrive on network interaction (kin groups, clans, the social), yet the moments when the network logic takes over – in the mob or the swarm, in contagion or infection – are the moments that are the most disorienting, the most threatening to the integrity of the human ego.[1]

> The fear and enthusiasm we experience at the sight of perfect mechanisms are in contrast to the happiness we feel at the sight of a perfect work of art. We sense an attack on our integrity, on our wholeness. That arms and legs are lost or harmed is not yet the greatest danger.[2]

Since ancient times, insect swarms have triggered uncanny emotions such as anxiety, paranoia and panic within human communities. During the twentieth century, these fears revived, although in an altered form, as they converged with fantasies of automation and emergent behaviour among intelligent machines. For instance, works such as Karel Čapek's *The Insect Play* (1921) and Fritz Lang's film *Metropolis* (1927) captured dystopic fears of an inhuman technological society through the creepy imagery of insectile machines. And during the Cold War, termites, ants and bees became menacing metaphors for the infestation of Western societies by alien agents from totalitarian communities in which the freedom of the individual was sacrificed for the sake of the collective.[3] However, the strange sensorial worlds of insects have also played a less dystopic role in the Western history of thought. Beehives and anthills feature frequently as metaphors and inspirational models for imagining alternative and more efficient ways of organising society and social life,[4] and likewise insects have generated strong interest and inspiration among technical designers and innovators, who recognise the mechanistic principles and alternative sensorial capacities underlying insect anatomy and perception.

The impact of insects in the history of technology is indeed evident in our contemporary drone imaginaries. While insects have been used as weapons in war since antiquity, in the form of catapulted hives, wasp warheads, fighting ants, and bacteria-laden fleas,[5] in modern times, the alternative military use of insects has become increasingly mechanised. In 2006, for instance, the US military research agency DARPA (the Defense Advanced Research Projects Agency) launched a so-called 'Hybrid Insect' programme, with tiny cyborg insects designed for a new 'battle-swarm doctrine'; here, swarming micro-drones are envisioned to play an increasingly important role in military operations, as they can attack from all directions, intermittently but consistently. The military naming of drones – yielding various insectile names such as Black Hornet, Killer-bee, Wasp, Mantis and Gnat – refers metaphorically to their visual and sonic appearance, which is encompassed by the very etymology of the word 'drone', originally denoting both a male honeybee, and the deep, machinic buzzing sound it makes. The latter is indeed one of the reasons why civilian populations living under drone surveillance tend to imagine unmanned vehicles hovering above them as mosquitoes, whose enervating insect-like whirring serves as a constant reminder of the omnipresence of military power patrolling above.[6]

Yet the diverse culturally and historically rooted imaginaries that couple insects and machines often pass unnoticed in current drone studies. While some scholars have explored drone swarming as a sign of a posthuman society to come,[7] others have treated it as a prism exposing the strangeness of the drone (see, for instance, chapter 10 by Claudette Lauzon in this volume), or as way of queering or disrupting the prevailing 'gender-war matrix' (see chapter 6 by Lauren Wilcox).[8] In this chapter, however, I wish to take the drone's entomologic origin literally by focusing on the social and communal dimensions of insect life in order to explore how the peculiar logic of the swarm taps into the larger drone imaginary. Central to this inquiry are questions of emergence and control in relation to how humans, insects and machines interact and are integrated into new forms of co-existence. What emotional responses do swarms trigger in the human? And how has the integration of insects into human-made technologies and networks changed the social order and conduct of war as we know it?

In *The Exploit: A Theory of Networks*, Alexander Galloway and Eugene Thacker address the emergence of networks across various forms, operating at anonymous and often non-human levels that exercise novel forms of control. They approach this 'network logic' – that is, the decentralised, rhizomatic structure of the swarm – through insect metaphors, asserting how we as humans naturally strive to construct social networks, but always in a distributed and dispersed fashion. Yet, in spite of the human habit of building networks, it is the moments when the network logic takes over (such as in the drone swarm) that is supremely threatening to our human integrity. For, as Galloway and Thacker ask, how do we 'control something that is by definition constituted by its own dispersal, by being radically distributed, spread out, and horizontal?'[9] While this question has been discussed over and again in aesthetic, philosophical and technological network studies,[10] my aim here is not to provide a straight answer, but rather to investigate how the human disorientation when encountering the radically material logic of swarming is coloured by a deeper historical imaginary of machines and insects.

For this purpose, the power of aesthetic and literary works to imagine future worlds based on projections of contemporary technologies can prove handy. Rarely has the human encounter with insects and/as machines been more accurately registered than in the writing of German author Ernst Jünger. As an eager entomologist with a keen eye for technology's impact on the human, Jünger puts the baffling human experience of 'entering the swarm' into literary form in his futuristic novel *The Glass Bees* (*Gläserne Bienen*, 1957), which features advanced robotic bees hardly distinguishable from today's micro-drones. In what follows, I will read Jünger's novel as an early literary work on drone swarming and situate it in its proper historical context, which coincides with the dawning era of cybernetics, computers, networks and automation.

Entering the swarm

Although probably best known for his frontline experiences of the First World War, presented in a cool, detached voice in the war diary *Storm of Steel* (*In Stahlgewittern*, 1920), Jünger's entire body of work is in fact preoccupied with understanding technology and its relation to nature, specifically to the realm of insects. The latter is especially pronounced in his literary account from the trenches, in which descriptions of roaring war machinery often merge with records of the natural world and its six-legged inhabitants.[11] In short, Jünger's works literarily swarm with insects and entomological imagery in a mixture of cool, scientific observation and creepy-crawly metaphors. In *Storm of Steel*, the sounds of bombs and shells are thus frequently described as a 'mosquito-like droning', and the bullets 'rushing and buzzing' above as 'swarms of bees.'[12] Not only do these metaphors mark insect-collector Jünger's profound interest in the entomologic world; they also, as we will see, propose a distinct focus on insects as a way of understanding the increasingly non-human logic of networks, swarms and automation.[13]

Winding forward in time to 1957, the peculiar coupling of insects and machines is particularly explicit in Jünger's futuristic novel *The Glass Bees*. The novel is set in a not too distant future where advanced micro-robots are rapidly taking over human jobs. The narrator, Captain Richards, an unemployed former cavalry officer, feels lost in this new world of autonomous machines. Nonetheless he accepts a job interview with the mysterious Zapparoni, an industry magnate specialising in designing miniature automatons to do the most risky and undesirable tasks, such as 'handling explosives, dangerous viruses, and even radio-active materials.'[14] Moreover, it is implied that the robots could be used for military purposes as they are described as 'ingenious weapons'. The robots' coercive potential is further implied by Zapparoni when he, in a key scene during the job interview, leaves our narrator alone for a while in a picturesque garden with a 'beware of the bees'. The comment points to the insidious nature of the insects swarming at the far end of the garden, the so-called glass bees, whose true robotic nature Richards soon discovers as he starts observing them through a pair of binoculars that seems to have been left there just for him:

> I distinguished diverse models – almost colonies – of automatons [*Automatenvölker*] which combed the surrounding fields and shrubs. Creatures of especially strong structure bore a whole set of proboscises which they dipped into umbels and flower clusters. Others were equipped with tentacles that closed around the tufts of the blossoms like delicate pincers, squeezing out the nectar. Still others remained a puzzle [*rätselhaft*] to me.[15]

The passage reveals the narrator's epistemic uncertainty as he struggles to identify what the swarming insect-machines really are. Are they mechanical 'models', or more like organic 'colonies'?[16] Are they 'automatons' or 'creatures' [*Tiere*])? Do they use mechanical 'pincers', or are these organic 'proboscises' and 'tentacles'? These questions do not only puzzle the narrator; they also mark a crucial problem in the drone imaginary; namely, that of determining the hybrid status and prosthetic relation between man and machine – or, in the case of Jünger's robotic insects, between nature and technology.

Jünger thereby touches upon a century-long tendency among entomologists and technical designers of seeing insects not merely as metaphors, but rather as *models* for imagining and creating new and innovative technologies. For instance, in 1869, artist and scientist Etienne-Jules Marey created an artificial insect as a case study for measuring the flight patterns and the locomotion of insect wings. Marey's mechanical reconstruction of insect movement received massive attention in newspapers and was furthermore noticed by the US military, who saw great potential in the machine as a model for aerial warfare. Marey himself expressed deep interest in the sensory potentialities of his mechanical insect, noting how it represented a new and much more precise mode of perception: 'When the eye ceases seeing, the ear hearing and the sense of touch feeling, or when our senses give us deceptive appearances, these machines are like new senses of astounding precision.'[17] In other words, Marey's insect opened up a whole new dimension for technical imagination of alternative ways of sensing – insights which are also recognised today by engineers and technical designers who use insects as sensorial models for developing new generations of robotic pollinators.

In fact, the organic design of natural bees has recently been mimicked by Japanese engineers in their fabrication of micro-aerial vehicles that employ hairy structures which stick to pollen by virtue of an ionic liquid gel.[18] Understanding 'how animals can quickly detect and then home in on pollinating structures within a flower could inspire the development of sensors for robotic pollinators', the engineers state in their effort to 'relieve the natural honeybees of the burdens that have steadily driven them towards collapse.'[19]

A similar fascination with insect's sensorial capacities is certainly at play in *The Glass Bees*, where the mechanical principles underlying insect anatomy are pointedly emphasised through comparison of the insect's sensory apparatuses to 'pincers' squeezing out the blossom's nectar. In short, Jünger shared nineteenth-century entomologists' view of insects as windows into a new dimension, described it in one of his insect diaries as a 'remote, hopeful, and mystical world'.[20] However, in this world, the isolated sensorial capabilities of any single insect are not the most astonishing discovery; more striking is how the insects work together as one collective sensory organism, as a *swarm*. Observing the bees with great curiosity, the narrator thus notices that 'Given the flying speed, the fact that no collision occurred during these flights back and forth was a masterly feat.'[21] He therefore concludes that a 'high degree of methodical planning' must be behind the invention, and while it has taken 'centuries to discover the secret of the bees'[22] he sees that it has now been technically copied and perfected by Zapparoni.

Accordingly, the artificial bees look and behave much like real insects, embodying the basic rules of biological self-organisation in the form of *swarming*; that is, the way in which 'a set of simple, local interactions culminates in complex, collective organisation, problem solving, and task fulfilment.'[23] Confronted with this complexity and networked logic, the narrator's immediate response is to look for a central agent or command, and, as he sees no humans around, he starts focusing on a particularly large insect, which he names the 'Smoky Gray', from which he senses a 'controlling force or a cell transmitting orders.'[24] While Richards keeps a sharp eye on this apparent leader of the swarm, trying to discover 'whether changes in the crowd of swarming automatons corresponded to its movements or followed upon them',[25] he reformulates topical ideas of the time; theories of feedback, control and communication in mechanical and natural systems, also known as *cybernetics*.

Cybernetic models and organic constructions

As the novel was published in 1957, a few years after the famous Macy conferences on cybernetics (1946–1953), it is natural to read Jünger's narrative of the glass bees as a reflection of a new set of techno-scientific imaginaries that flourished in this Cold War period. The Macy conferences were a series of post-war meetings that synthesised research into animal worlds and technological systems in order to rethink human–machine interaction, communication and control. Insects and animals were a major focus at these conferences, generating a veritable 'cybernetic zoo',[26] including William Grey Walter's robot tortoise[27] and Norbert Wiener's moth automaton. It is worth mentioning here that Wiener, one of the founding fathers of cybernetics, originally formulated his theory of feedback systems as a model for describing the challenges faced by ground-based anti-aircraft cannoneers trying to hit rapidly moving aircrafts during the German bomb raids over London in the Second World War. Given Jünger's profound interest in military technologies – and his own personal experience of watching aeroplanes being shot down during the First World War – it is not surprising that there are quite some similarities between the fictive robots in *The Glass Bees* and Wiener's cybernetic models.[28] When the narrator above describes how changes in the behaviour of the swarming drone bees correspond to the movements of the large 'Smoky Gray' insect, he is therefore basically describing a cybernetic feedback mechanism. In other words, the closed signal loop between the artificial insects generates a change in the environment, triggering a system change.

Returning to Wiener's moth automaton, Wiener's idea was to test feedback loops in early phototropic and computing machines. The goal was to create simple autonomous machines that – based on imitations of moths' reaction to light – were able to learn with the help of light sensors and feedback data. In the same way, Jünger's drone bees imitate the circular feedback processes of natural bees, for instance through 'the way they radiated from the hives in clusters, threw themselves like a glittering veil over the display of bright flowers, then darted back, stopped short, hovered in a compact swarm.'[29] Indeed, this depiction of the organisational principles and networked logic guiding the glass bees is not unlike contemporary theories that frame drone swarms as something radically 'dispersed, distributed, and yet in constant communication.'[30]

The keyword here is *communication*. For Wiener, the most essential discovery of cybernetics was that both social organisations and individual nervous systems are 'bound together by a system of communication […] in which circular processes of a feedback nature play an important part.'[31]

Following a similar logic, the narrator in *The Glass Bees* notes how the robotic bees communicate with each other 'by inaudible calls and invisible signs', and that 'the gatherers, one by one, were swiftly summoned to deliver the harvest.'[32] Significantly in this context, The Macy conferences also fostered a strong interest in ant and bee communication as social and military tools required for the new post-industrial turn to informatics and networked societies. In particular, Karl von Frisch's studies of bee language in the 1953 book *The Dancing Bees* (*Aus dem Leben der Bienen*) emphasised the capacity of bees to communicate complex navigational directions and share information about nearby food sources through dancing.[33] It is beyond doubt that Jünger – as an acclaimed entomologist – was acquainted with von Frisch's ground-breaking discoveries. This is evident, for instance, when Jünger's narrator notes how he is essentially mesmerised by 'the dancelike force of the spectacle'.[34] Clearly, the way the glass bees communicate through an 'inaudible' and 'invisible' language corresponds well to von Frisch's observations of how natural bees communicate information to each other through dancing and swarming, like a holistic artificial organism, or as an *organic construction*.

The latter term is particularly significant in the larger context of Jünger's writings. In part, this is due to the narrator's initial puzzlement at the bees' hybrid status; he specifically refers to them as 'distinct units working as mechanisms, that is, not at all in a purely chemical or organic fashion.'[35] But the description of them as *organic mechanisms* also echoes a darker phase of Jünger's authorship – namely, his controversial writings during the interwar period, among which the 1932 essay *The Worker* (*Der Arbeiter*) stands out as the most important, and at the same time most disturbing, precursor to *The Glass Bees*. Throughout this essay, Jünger envisions the so-called worker-gestalt as a new class of warriors rising from the ashes of the First World War in the manifest form of a new caste of hardened, steely warrior-machines incapable of feeling pain or pleasure. Jünger consistently defined these new 'workers' as 'organic constructions',[36] that is, as a fusion of the organic and mechanical in a prosthetic coupling of man and machine, or sometimes of *insect* and machine. The transformation of human beings into insects (Jünger's favourite metaphor) communicates the message of his essay well. In Jünger's fascist writings, the worker-gestalt inaugurates an age of objectification of human life in which the individual is nothing but an insignificant part of the mass, 'the sum of a saleable quantity of individuals',[37] which presents itself in 'rows, in networks, in chains and bands of faces, scurrying past at lightning speed, or in *ant-like* columns whose forward movement is no longer from choice, but subjected to an automatic discipline'.[38]

It is worth noting here how Jünger's vision of the worker-gestalt as a hybrid between man, machine and insect – a 'unity of organic and mechanical' in which 'the technique becomes an organ'[39] – again coincides with Wiener's idea of cybernetics as the prosthetic coupling of machines with living organisms (when he, for instance, explains the cybernetic system of an aeroplane as being prosthetically coupled to the pilot, and the gunner to his anti-aircraft cannon). However, while Jünger's totalitarian essay embraced technology's transformative power to change society into an ant-like colony of machine-workers, Wiener's thoughts on insect communication were more critical at the sociological level. For instance, Wiener warned against fascist aspirations for a human state based on the model of ants as resulting from 'a profound misapprehension both of the nature of the ant and of the nature of the man.'[40] Rather, Wiener regarded the variety and possibility of the human organism and community as superior to those of ants – since, if 'condemned and restricted to perform the same functions over and over again [the human being] will not even be a good ant, not to mention a good human being'.[41] According to Wiener, the cybernetic systems of communication and control among both ants and bees should therefore be used mainly as cybernetic models for engineering intelligent machines and computer networks, not as social models for imagining or redesigning human communities.

While the subjection of human life to a society of insect-like masses and machines mainly belongs to Jünger's early interwar writings, with their fascist-warrior dreams of a 'total mobilisation' of the worker-gestalt, it could seem that Jünger later redefined his view on insects and social change to be more in line with Wiener's. And indeed, at least on the surface, *The Glass Bees* appears to be a techno-critical story about the loss of human integrity in the encounter with intelligent machines and swarming networks. Yet, when taking a closer look, the violent fantasy of technical perfection and insect-like communities lingers on in *The Glass Bees*, though in camouflaged form. As Andreas Huyssen has pointed out, Jünger's withdrawal into the entomologic world of nature in the late 1930s remains embedded in the discourse of violence and danger 'which was discursively explicit in Jünger's writing in 1929, [but] had become implicit and ever more hidden in ekphrastic descriptions of strangely beautiful flowers, dangerous plants, and destructive insects by 1938.'[42]

In other words, the insects that featured so prominently in Jünger's early war writings became implicit carriers of the violent imagery of the heavily armoured machine-worker in his later works.[43] In this context, *The Glass Bees* can be read as a postscript to Jünger's interwar writings, with the drone bees concretising the earlier more figurative use of insects as a metaphor for the radical transformation of human communities into violent and totalitarian ant-states. In this light, the robotic insects in *The Glass Bees* are merely a natural continuation, or perhaps even the ultimate consummation, of Jünger's drive towards armouring himself by way of machinic and insect-like automation.

The technical perfection of the swarm

While the drone bees in Zapparoni's garden could be taken as signs of Jünger's continuous fascination with violent technologies and cybernetic models, there might also, however, be another possibility: namely, that the swarming insects are at the same time symptoms of a traumatising and alienating machine culture which strives towards the perfection of nature, including an eradication of all unnecessary elements – such as humans. This line of thought is certainly palpable in *The Glass Bees*, where the narrator reflects on the incompatibility of human and technical perfection: 'If we strive for one, we must sacrifice the other [...] Technical perfection strives toward the calculable, human perfection toward the incalculable.'[44] Here, the robotic bees clearly represent a grey zone between the two forms of perfection: the mechanical and the natural, the calculable and the incalculable, but it is a grey zone in which nature has already become 'inadequate, both in its beauty and logic, and should be surpassed.'[45]

This superiority of technology over nature becomes even more manifest when the narrator discovers how Zapparoni had 'simplified nature' by eliminating all redundant elements from his beekeeping, so that the 'whole establishment radiated a flawless but entirely unerotic perfection'.[46] This basically implies a sterilisation of nature in which there 'were no eggs or cradles for the pupae, and neither drones nor a queen [since] Zapparoni approved only of sexless workers.'[47] Moreover, the narrator notes how the biological process of 'slaughtering of the drones' – that is, how in nature the drone bees are immediately killed after they have fertilised the queen bee – had been cut out of Zapparoni's masterplan, which included 'neither males nor females, neither mothers nor nurses.'[48] Noticeable here is also Jünger's pronounced misogyny, as *The Glass Bees* features no women at all (except for an implicit reference to the narrator's wife), and even the queen bees have been eradicated. This is, however, in contrast to the rather queer imagination of the 'sexless' swarming community of robotic bees.[49] A remarkable parallel to this peculiar imagination – in particular to the 'slaughtering of the drones' – is Jünger's contemporary science fiction writer colleague, Kurt Vonnegut, whose short story 'The Drone King', from the early 1950s, features an experiment in which drones (here, natural male bees) are spared from otherwise inevitable death by a rich madman, who proposes them as an ingenious new means of communication. In contrast to Jünger's glass bees, however, Vonnegut's 'drone kings' turn out to be a huge failure, since they are not carrying out their communication tasks at all, and eventually end up being killed.[50]

The two different outcomes of the stories are significant for Jünger's techno-fetishism: while Vonnegut makes use of a significant amount of black humour in his story, Jünger simply takes the prospect of insect communication and automation way too seriously to joke about it. Yet Zapparoni's optimisation is not only made in order to rationalise, but also to eradicate, the feudal hierarchy in nature's own formation of the hive into workers, drones and female queens, which is yet another echo of *The Worker*. With the nullification of the biological order, resembling a Victorian model of society in which the social insects embody a tidy hierarchical structure,[51] Jünger thus continues his revolt against bourgeois society. Although, rather than the fascist model of the ant-state he imagined in *The Worker*, Zapparoni's sterilised worker bees are the perfect image of a new social order shaped by the emerging dynamics of liberal capitalism, with its economic optimisation of labour and control of markets and data.

Lacking all the differentiated traits and feudal structures known from natural bee organisation, this type of social formation, in the form of machinic communities of sexless worker-bees, essentially anticipates the fluid nature of capitalism. To paraphrase Jussi Parikka, the speculative market structure and monetary flows of capitalism follow a kind of 'swarm logic', working as part of its own 'algorithmic perfection machine.'[52] In other words, Jünger's robotic glass bees are characterised by being dispersed and decentralised, distributed, spread out and horizontal. As such, they come uncannily close to how current military researchers of artificial intelligence and automation predict how future warfare will look; that is, a future battlefield without human soldiers or individualised robots, but with swarms of decentralised operational units, a so-called 'swarm force', that can 'help turn the military into a "sensory organization."'[53] Again we see how inspiration from insects – particularly ants and bees – has coloured the specific branch of drone imaginaries related to future conflict and swarm intelligence. In the oft-quoted report *Swarming and the Future of Conflict* (2000), military strategists John Arquilla and David Ronfeldt use bees and ants as exemplary metaphors for their vision of a 'Battleswarm Doctrine', in which swarming formations and strategies such as 'swarm raiding' and guerrilla tactics are 'based on the dispersed deployment and robust internetting of myriad, mostly small units of maneuver, some dedicated to close-in combat and others to distant fire.'[54]

A similar deployment of swarming robots features in *The Glass Bees*, as the narrator notices a variety of models among the insects that 'clearly hadn't the slightest connection with bees and beekeeping.'[55] Rather, they confirm his suspicion that the bees are a kind of dual-use technology with the potential of serving a military purpose as 'genius weapons' that could contribute 'not only to the improvement but also to the shortening of life.'[56] He further senses that the glass bees could have the 'disgusting habit of mutual spying – the cowardly triumph of calculating brains over courage to live' – which strengthens his feeling of being constantly monitored by Zapparoni, whose presence he senses as an 'invisible master'.[57] Richards' feeling of being put under ubiquitous surveillance by the bees is probably the reason why several scholars have read the novel as an explicit critique of technology. For instance, Roger Berkowitz warns that the 'danger posed by Zapparoni's bees is the one we face today: that we allow our fascination with technology to dull our humanity.'[58] In my reading, however, loss of humanity is not what concerns Jünger the most in *The Glass Bees*. Although the perfection of the autonomous machines undoubtedly arouses mixed feelings in the narrator, he is still fascinated by the 'perfect mechanisms' from which an 'uncanny but fascinating halo of brilliance' emanates, evoking 'both fear and Titanic pride.'[59]

Rather, it is Jünger's personal techno-neuroses and traumatic past which are at play here, as there are evident parallels between Jünger and the narrator, Captain Richards. As one of the most highly decorated German soldiers of the First World War,[60] Jünger idolised the old virtues of warfare – the bravery, danger, risk, and, of course, violence, which finds an echo in Captain Richards' nostalgic memories of his military time in the cavalry, contrasted by the era of automation in which he has now been left helpless. As the narrator's melancholically notes, 'These were not the great days of the cavalry.'[61] This lament for the old martial code – unfolded through numerous flashbacks to his past as a cavalry man – is thus in stark contrast to the high-tech mechanisms that surround him in Zapparoni's garden. The transition from an old to a new conduct of war – symbolised by the substitution of cavalry with insects (marking the prosthetic coupling of man and machine/animal) – thus becomes emblematic of the technological reconfiguration of the battlefield through the new networked logic of automation and swarm intelligence.

Crushing the drone

This technological reorganisation and disintegration of the human body in favour of machines becomes particularly clear in one of the final scenes in Zapparoni's garden. Here, Richards – still where we left him, studying the bees through the binoculars – discovers something even more bizarre. In a pond at the far end of the garden, he spots some strange objects which, to his horror, appear to be severed human ears. Shocked by the 'brutal exhibition', Richards instantly feels nauseous, yet, somehow, he also finds the scene familiar:

> But it was inevitable as motif. Wasn't it necessarily the result of a perfection of technique to whose initial intoxication it had put an end? Had there been at any period in the history of the world as many mutilated bodies, as many severed limbs as in ours?[62]

Here we perhaps find one of the strongest echoes of Jünger's own military past. The narrator's uncanny encounter with severed ears and mechanised glass bees – both markers of a new technological order that breaks with the anthropocentric norms of the industrial age – thus comes to mirror Jünger's traumatic war memories.[63] But it also suggests something else. In fact, in psychoanalytical theory, severed body parts represent the epitome of trauma, that is, the disturbing confrontation with a body in bits and pieces as a retrospective projection of the child's becoming-self. To Richards, the vision leads 'to a lower level of reality' and strengthens his impression that 'everything might have been a mirage.'[64]

Indeed, the entire novel, with its multiple anecdotes and flashbacks to memories from Richards' cavalry past, can be regarded as a reflection of a 'before' when battlefields had not yet been technologically reorganised into armies of swarming robots and networks. Yet Richards' memories of the glorious past have a hollow ring, distorted as they are by the mirage caused by optical distortion and the trauma of dismembered body parts. Again, the fragility and 'organic vulnerability' of the human body is the root of trauma for Jünger, and as always the solution is not therapy, but violence. Consequently, Richards ends up smashing the large 'Smoky Gray' hornet with the flat end of an iron golf club, causing a coil of wires to spring from out of its belly. A 'rust-brown cloud' then rises from the golf club, and a splash hits Richards, burning a hole in his sleeve. The traumatic loss and dismembering of the human body is thus projected onto the desperate crushing of the machine. What is more, the violence inherent in the crushing of the insect – whether manifest or symbolic – is by and large similar to the violence that characterises Jünger's writings, armouring him against his haunting war memories of mechanised battlefields.[65]

Whether we understand Richards' crushing of the threatening hornet-drone as an urge to find satisfaction and remedy through violence, or simply as a desperate act of self-defence, his situation would in any case have been much different, and definitely less secure, had there been not just one drone attacking him, but an entire swarm of drones attacking from all directions like a 'systematic pulsing of force and/or fire by dispersed, internetted units'.[66] The narrator's meticulous and clearly fascinated descriptions of the glass bees' technical design, their navigation capacities, organisation in hives, swarming intelligence, subtle communication forms, surveillance capabilities and so on all seem to indicate the Janus head of this technological wonder, should it unexpectedly decide to harm you. As we have seen, it is essentially this uncertainty and loss of control when faced with the networked logic of swarming intelligence that evokes the narrator's feelings of both fascination and anxiety. This is particularly clear in his depiction of the 'uncanny but fascinating halo of brilliance'[67] that surrounds the robotic insects, enclosing the ambivalent configuration of automation in the novel as well as into the larger drone imaginary. These emotional responses – such as fear, fascination and uncanniness – are key to the affective infrastructure that constitutes the drone imaginary. And, in the case of the robotic glass bees, these feelings are even more profound, as they locate drone swarming at the delicate balance between technical ingenuity and human catastrophe.

In this context, Richards' words can be seen to prefigure Lauren Berlant's idea of 'cruel optimism', whose desire for and promise of a better life 'makes it impossible to attain that expansive transformation for which [it] is striving.'[68] The narrator's disturbing experience of being surveilled, or even attacked, by the superiorly designed machines in Zapparoni's garden very much embodies the cruelty of this 'technical optimism',[69] for which Jünger (cf. his early technophilic writings) can be considered a proponent. According to Berlant, the promise provided by this form of technical optimism nurtures in the human being an aspiration to 'a life without risk, in proximity to plenitude without enjoyment.'[70] Following this logic, Captain Richards does not have much to be happy about. Rather, the increased automation of labour has not only removed the elements of risk and danger from the battlefield, but has also drained society of jobs, leaving him and his fellow cavalrymen unemployed. Because, as we recall, it was indeed unemployment that initially brought Richards to Zapparoni's garden, with prospects of a job in the robotics industry. As we now know, these prospects did not materialise, as Richards' destruction of the hornet-drone did certainly not recommend him for employment.

However, the changed prospects of labour are not merely the most disturbing thing in the novel's dystopic imagination of insect automation. It also conveys a creeping sensation that humans' very existence is threatened by the proliferation of autonomous machines, especially those that 'hadn't the slightest connection with bees and beekeeping.'[71] From here, it is only a short step to the imagined prospect of armies of swarming, lethal robots which, as Richards notes, could easily be even more disturbing than glass bees, as they are constantly replaced with more advanced models: 'The struggle for power had reached a new stage; it was fought with scientific formulas. The weapons vanished in the abyss like fleeting images, like pictures one throws into the fire. New ones were produced in protean succession.'[72]

As this chapter has argued, the technological reconfiguration of warfare towards ever smaller, more advanced autonomous systems – which is also evidently the case in today's drone wars – was thus already accurately registered by Jünger in 1957. As a highly sensitive cultural seismograph, Jünger was keen to translate this decentralisation of human control entailed by high-tech warfare into a literary form. Yet his prolonged fascination with the world of insects and machines also made him embrace technological progress as not only a natural process but also an almost mythic force. Here, the techno-entomologic thread running through Jünger's writing, forming a peculiar link between insects and machines, can be read as the embodiment of this force – or, more generally, of the reconfigured technological order of warfare in the age of swarming and intelligent machines.

Notes

1 A. R. Galloway and E. Thacker, *The Exploit: A Theory of Networks* (Minneapolis: University of Minnesota Press, 2007), 5.

2 E. Jünger, *The Glass Bees*, trans. L. Bogan and E. Mayer (New York: The Noonday Press, 1991), 113.

3 For more on insects as metaphors and models in the social imaginary, see: J. A. Lockwood, *The Infested Mind: Why Humans Fear, Loathe, and Love Insects* (Oxford; New York: Oxford University Press, 2013). See also: C. Hollingsworth, *Poetics of the Hive: The Insect Metaphor in Literature* (Iowa City: University of Iowa Press, 2001).

4 Philosophers from Aristotle to Thomas Hobbes have reflected on the biological self-organisation of insect life when formulating their models for body politics and sovereignty. See A. R. Galloway and E. Thacker, *The Exploit: A Theory of Networks* (Minneapolis: University of Minnesota Press, 2007), 67.

5 For a thorough history of entomological warfare, see J. A. Lockwood, *Six-Legged Soldiers: Using Insects as Weapons of War* (New York: Oxford University Press, 2009).

6 See, for instance, A. A. Saif, *The Drone Eats with Me: A Gaza Diary* (Manchester: Comma Press, 2015).

7 See, for instance, R. Berkowitz, 'Drones and the question of the human', *Ethics & International Affairs*, 28:2 (2014): 159–169; J. Packer and J. Reeves, 'Taking people out: Drones, media/weapons, and the coming humanectomy', in L. Parks and C. Kaplan (eds), *Life in the Age of Drone Warfare* (Durham, NC: Duke University Press, 2017), 261–281.

8 For more on the gender-war matrix, see also: C. Daggett, 'Drone disorientations: How "unmanned" weapons queer the experience of killing in war', *International Feminist Journal of Politics*, 17:3 (2015): 361–379.

9 Galloway and Thacker, *The Exploit*, 68.

10 Galloway and Thacker, *The Exploit*, 67.

11 As Andreas Huyssen notes, 'When storm trooper Jünger was not leading an attack on English troops, he kept himself busy at the front as a botanist and bug collector.' A. Huyssen, *Miniature Metropolis, Literature in an Age of Photography and Film* (Cambridge, MA: Harvard University Press, 2015), 239.

12 E. Jünger, *Sämtliche Werke*, bd. 1 (Stuttgart: Klett-Cotta, 1978), 193, 253, 95.

13 According to Jussi Parikka, in the nineteenth century 'entomology spread much beyond its confines and interfaced its agenda with those of technology and philosophy.' J. Parikka, *Insect Media: An Archaeology of Animals and Technology* (Minneapolis: University of Minnesota Press, 2011), 2.

14 Ernst Jünger. *Gläserne Bienen. Sämtliche Werke*, bd. 9, *Erzählende Schriften I* (Stuttgart: Ernst Klett Verlag, 1978), 459. This and the following English translations are from the 1960 translation of the book by Louise Bogan and Elizabeth Mayer: E. Jünger, *The Glass Bees*, trans. L. Bogan and E. Mayer (New York: The Noonday Press, 1991), 93. The following paging refers to this translation, while all other references from Jünger's texts refer to the above edition of *Sämtliche Werke*.

15 Jünger, *The Glass Bees*, 7.

16 The German word *Völker*, i.e. 'people', has even more anthropomorphic connotations to human-like communities than the translators' choice 'colonies' implies.

17 Étienne-Jules Marey, *La Méthode Graphique* (Paris: G. Masson, 1878), 108. Quoted in Parikka, *Insect Media*, 17.

18 G. J. Amador and D. L. Hu, 'Sticky solution provides grip for the first robotic pollinator', *Chem*, 2:2 (2017): 162.

19 The collapse alludes to the co-called 'Colony Collapse Disorder' that currently threatens the natural bees with extinction. The engineers have further declared that their suggested robotic solution would be 'one small step for pollen, one giant leap for robotic pollination.' Amandor and Hu, 'Sticky solution provides grip', 164.

20 Jünger, *Sämtliche Werke*, bd. 2, 199.

21 Jünger, *The Glass Bees*, 94.

22 Jünger, *The Glass Bees*, 94.

23 Galloway and Thacker, *The Exploit*, 67.

24 Jünger, *The Glass Bees*, 140.

25 Jünger, *The Glass Bees*, 107.

26 Parikka, *Insect Media*, 123.

27 For instance, Niels Werber has noticed how Jünger sends his subtle regards to Walter's tortoise as Richards notes how Zapparoni's robots 'had started with tiny turtles'. N. Werber, 'Ants and aliens: An episode in the history of entomological and sociological construction of knowledge', *Berichte zur Wissenschaftsgeschichte*, 34:3 (2011): 254.

28 For more on Jünger's inspiration from the Macy Meetings and Norbert Wiener's theory of cybernetics, see Werber, 'Ants and aliens' and W. Kittler, 'From

Gestalt to Ge-stell: Martin Heidegger reads Ernst Jünger', *Cultural Critique*, 69:1 (2008).

29 Jünger, *The Glass Bees*, 96.
30 Galloway and Thacker, *The Exploit*, 66.
31 N. Wiener, *Cybernetics or Control and Communication in the Animal and the Machine*, 2nd edn (Cambridge, MA: MIT Press, 1976), 24.
32 Jünger, *The Glass Bees*, 97.
33 Parikka, *Insect Media*, 126–127.
34 Jünger, *The Glass Bees*, 97.
35 Jünger, *The Glass Bees*, 6.
36 Jünger, *Sämtliche Werke*, bd. 6; *Der Arbeiter*, 127.
37 Jünger, *Der Arbeiter*, 254.
38 Jünger, *Der Arbeiter*, 254.
39 Jünger, *Der Arbeiter*, 92.
40 N. Wiener, *The Human Use of Human Beings: Cybernetics and Society* (London: Eyre and Spottiswoode, 1950), 51.
41 Wiener, *The Human Use of Human Beings*, 52.
42 Huyssen places the source of all this technological and natural destruction in Jünger's past as traumatic response to the unprocessed memories of the horrors of the First World War. Huyssen, *Miniature Metropolis*, 239.
43 As Huyssen notes in an early text on Jünger: 'Jünger's entomological texts about birds and insects, snakes and flowers have the same function as the increasingly aestheticized descriptions of his war experience and the fantasies of the armored, machine-like body with its petrified camera-like gaze.' A. Huyssen, 'Fortifying the heart – totally: Ernst Jünger's armored texts', *New German Critique*, 59 (1993): 16.
44 Jünger, *The Glass Bees*, 113.
45 Jünger, *The Glass Bees*, 29.
46 Jünger, *The Glass Bees*, 94.
47 Jünger, *The Glass Bees*, 94.
48 Jünger, *The Glass Bees*, 95.
49 For more on the disruption and queering of the gender-war-matrix, see chapter 6 in this volume by Lauren Wilcox.
50 Vonnegut's short story was unknown until recently when it was found among his papers in the Lilly Library at Indiana University and subsequently published in *The Atlantic*, 2017. K. Vonnegut, 'The drone king', *The Atlantic* (October 2017), www.theatlantic.com/magazine/archive/2017/10/kurt-vonnegut-the-drone-king/537870/ (accessed 3 March, 2021).
51 As Parikka notes, 'in Victorian society, bees (and spiders) were considered to be superior insects'. Parikka, *Insect Media*, 40.
52 Parikka, *Insect Media*, 31
53 J. Arquilla and D. F. Ronfeldt, *Swarming and the Future of Conflict* (Santa Monica: RAND National Defense Research Institute, 2000), 46.
54 Arquilla and Ronfeldt, *Swarming*, 85.
55 Jünger, *The Glass Bees*, 105.

56 Jünger, *The Glass Bees*, 66.
57 Jünger, *The Glass Bees*, 114.
58 Berkowitz, 'Drones and the question of the human', 159–169.
59 Jünger, *The Glass Bees*, 113.
60 Jünger was wounded seven times during the war, and among other medals of honour he received the highest military decoration of the German empire, Pour le Mérite.
61 Jünger, *The Glass Bees*, 43.
62 Jünger, *The Glass Bees*, 112
63 As Devin Fore has remarked, this 'depot of dismembered human parts on display before him is a fitting complement to posthuman, de-organized technologies such as glass bees.' D. Fore, 'The entomic age', *Grey Room*, 33 (2008): 35.
64 Jünger, *The Glass Bees*, 110.
65 As Huyssen has put it, 'this identification with the destructive forces of modernity that overwhelmed Jünger on the battlefield is a traumatic reaction formation, which resulted in a compulsive repudiation of his own body as organic and vulnerable.' Huyssen, 'Fortifying the heart', 13. For more on the same, see Devin Fore's essay on *The Glass* Bees in which he extrapolates Huyssen's point: 'If the pathologically armored bodies of Jünger's Weimar writings revealed their author's anxiety about the fragility of the human body in the face of modern warfare, in postwar works such as *The Glass Bees* it is technoscientific progress and invention rather than weaponry that threaten to violate the organic soundness of the human frame'. Fore, 'The entomic age', 35.
66 Arquilla and Ronfeldt, *Swarming*, 8.
67 Jünger, *The Glass Bees*, 113.
68 L. Berlant, *Cruel Optimism* (Durham, NC: Duke University Press, 2011), 2.
69 Berlant, *Cruel Optimism*, 41.
70 Berlant, *Cruel Optimism*, 41.
71 Jünger, *The Glass Bees*, 105.
72 Jünger, *The Glass Bees*, 54.

Bibliography

Amador, G. J. and D. L. Hu. 'Sticky solution provides grip for the first robotic pollinator'. *Chem*, 2:2 (2017): 162–164.

Arquilla, J. and D. F. Ronfeldt. *Swarming and the Future of Conflict*. Santa Monica: RAND: National Defense Research Institute, 2000.

Berkowitz, R. 'Drones and the question of the human'. *Carnegie Journal of Ethics & International Affairs*, 28:2 (2014): 159–169.

Berlant, L. *Cruel Optimism*. Durham, NC: Duke University Press, 2011.

Daggett, C. 'Drone disorientations: How "unmanned" weapons queer the experience of killing in war'. *International Feminist Journal of Politics*, 17:3 (2015): 361–379.

Fore, D. 'The entomic age'. *Grey Room*, 33 (2008): 26–55.
Galloway, A. R. and E. Thacker. *The Exploit: A Theory of Networks*. Minneapolis: University of Minnesota Press, 2007.
Hollingsworth, C. *Poetics of the Hive: The Insect Metaphor in Literature*. Iowa City: University of Iowa Press, 2001.
Huyssen, A. 'Fortifying the heart – totally: Ernst Jünger's armored texts'. *New German Critique*, 59 (1993): 3–23.
— *Miniature Metropolis, Literature in an Age of Photography and Film*. Cambridge, MA: Harvard University Press, 2015.
Jünger, E. *Sämtliche Werke*. Stuttgart: Klett-Cotta, 1978.
— *The Glass Bees*, trans. L. Bogan and E. Mayer. New York: The Noonday Press, 1991.
Kittler, W. 'From gestalt to ge-stell: Martin Heidegger reads Ernst Jünger'. *Cultural Critique*, 69:1 (2008): 79–97.
Lockwood, J. A. *Six-Legged Soldiers: Using Insects as Weapons of War*. New York: Oxford University Press, 2009.
— *The Infested Mind: Why Humans Fear, Loathe, and Love Insects*. Oxford; New York: Oxford University Press, 2013.
Marey, E. *La Méthode Graphique*. Paris: G. Masson, 1878.
Packer J. and J. Reeves. 'Taking people out: Drones, media/weapons, and the coming humanectomy'. In L. Parks and C. Kaplan (eds), *Life in the Age of Drone Warfare*, 261–281. Durham, NC: Duke University Press, 2017.
Parikka, J. *Insect Media: An Archaeology of Animals and Technology*. University of Minnesota Press, 2011.
Saif, A. A. *The Drone Eats with Me: A Gaza Diary*. Manchester: Comma Press, 2015.
Vonnegut, K. 'The drone king'. *The Atlantic*, October 2017. www.theatlantic.com/magazine/archive/2017/10/kurt-vonnegut-the-drone-king/537870/ (accessed 3 March, 2021).
Werber, N. 'Ants and aliens: An episode in the history of entomological and sociological construction of knowledge'. *Berichte zur Wissenschaftsgeschichte*, 34:3 (2011): 242–262.
Wiener, N. *The Human Use of Human Beings: Cybernetics and Society*. London: Eyre and Spottiswoode, 1950.
— *Cybernetics or Control and Communication in the Animal and the Machine*. Cambridge, MA: MIT Press, 2nd edn, 1976.

9

Artificial intelligence and the socio-technical imaginary: on Skynet, self-healing swarms and *Slaughterbots*

Jutta Weber

> If even senior defense officials with responsibility for autonomous weapons programs fail to understand the core issues, then we cannot expect the general public and their elected representatives to make appropriate decisions.[1]

Slaughterbots, a video that went viral on YouTube shortly after its release in November 2017, may be one of the most influential drone imaginaries to date.[2] Within a few days it had received more than two million views, even though it was not a Hollywood science fiction trailer but a science communication by arms control advocates. In *Black Mirror* style,[3] the video pictures the dangerous potential of the deployment of autonomous swarms of self-flying mini-drones equipped with artificial intelligence (AI) capabilities, cameras, sensors, face recognition and explosives. The video was released by the Future of Life Institute[4] together with AI expert Stuart Russell, a professor of computer science at the University of California, Berkeley. Russell explains at the end of the video that the capabilities of autonomous weapons shown in the film are a very near-future possibility, the 'results of integrating and militarizing technologies that we already have'[5] – and that this development needs to be stopped: 'Allowing machines to choose to kill humans will be devastating to our security and freedom. We have an opportunity to prevent the future you just saw, but the window to act is closing fast.'[6]

Technoscientific imaginaries

After a decade of academic debate and years of slow-moving negotiations at the United Nations Convention on Certain Conventional Weapons, Stuart Russell and the Future of Life Institute decided to choose a more popular and hopefully effective method of science communication to stimulate critical debate and achieve a ban on lethal autonomous weapons in the long run, because 'serious discourse and academic argument are not enough to get the message through.'[7] Negotiations over a ban on lethal autonomous weapons have been ongoing at the Convention on Certain Conventional Weapons in Geneva since 2014,[8] with few results. At the same time, many non-governmental organisations and investigative journalist organisations such as the Campaign to Stop Killer Robots,[9] Code Pink,[10] the Bureau of Investigative Journalism[11] and the academic International Committee for Robot Arms Control[12] have been trying to draw attention to massive violations of human rights by drones, with little effect so far. According to Russell's understanding, one of the great obstacles to a realistic debate about the potentials of contemporary AI-based technologies seems to be the traditional socio-technical imaginaries of AI, shaped by films such as the *Terminator* series, *I, Robot* and *Ex Machina*. Thanks to the influence of Hollywood science fiction blockbusters, autonomous AI is often seen as a *conscious* and evil super-intelligence working towards the erasure of the human race. This socio-technical imaginary emphasises the power of technology but is implausible in its overstatement of the capabilities of AI. One of the effects of this imaginary has been repetitive discussions of whether AI can gain consciousness or not, while the concrete effects of applied AI, such as the loss of meaningful human control, have often been neglected.

Against this cliché, arms control advocates point out that we do not need to fear that emergent drone swarms will turn into conscious superhuman entities that do us evil. The real problem is that they can easily be turned into weapons of mass destruction (WMDs) – not only by the military or terrorists, but by *any* perpetrator:

> We have witnessed high-level defense officials dismissing the risk on the grounds that their 'experts' do not believe that the 'Skynet thing' is likely to happen. Skynet, of course, is the fictional command and control system in the *Terminator* movies that turns against humanity. The risk of the 'Skynet thing' occurring is *completely unconnected* to the risk of humans using autonomous weapons as WMDs or to any of the other risks [...]. If even senior defense officials with responsibility for autonomous weapons programs fail to understand the core issues, then we cannot expect the general public and their elected representatives to make appropriate decisions.[13]

Obviously, neither politicians, the general public nor defence experts have fully understood the logic, functioning and dangerous potential of contemporary AI-based autonomous weapons systems. Therefore, arms control advocates believe that a new, more realistic imaginary of AI weapon assemblages-in-the-making is greatly needed. They want 'to give people a clear sense of the kinds of technologies and the notion of autonomy involved: This is not "science fiction"; [...] and the capabilities are not "decades away" as claimed by some countries at the UN talks in Geneva'.[14]

Given that today many military and university research laboratories are intensively investigating so-called swarm intelligence – in the form of swarming algorithms and micro-robots respectively – researchers fear that the technology projected in *Slaughterbots* will soon be in place. When this happens, the weapons will proliferate very fast and globally, so that the window for a ban on autonomous weapons will be closed – or at least, the ban will become much harder to obtain.

Contemporary research in many high-tech nations is directed towards the development of complex and adaptive swarms of autonomous drones.[15] In October 2017, the US Department of Defence announced 'one of the most significant tests of autonomous systems'[16] when it released a swarm of 103 Perdix drones from three F/A-18 Super Hornet fighter aircraft over China Lake in California: 'The micro-drones demonstrated advanced swarm behaviors such as collective decision-making, adaptive formation flying, and self-healing.'[17] In 2017, Chinese researchers made successful tests with even more (119) micro-drones.[18] China Electronics Technology Group Corporation, a partner in the project, claimed that swarm intelligence was at 'the core of artificial intelligence of unmanned systems and the future of intelligent unmanned systems'.[19]

Images and narratives about drone technology, according to Kathrin Maurer and Andreas Immanuel Graae, are a prism of cultural knowledge from which the complex interplay between drone technology and human communities can be investigated (as noted in the Introduction above). The concept of the imaginary has been very well developed in science and technology studies,[20] perhaps most prominently by Sheila Jasanoff and Sang-Hyun Kim. They claim that socio-technical imaginaries are always also imaginaries about our way of life, about collectively shared visions of our social order and desirable futures, which are often seen as something that can be achieved with the help of technological progress. Nevertheless, they are co-produced in the discourses and practices of science, technology and society.[21]

Donna Haraway has pointed out that 'figures and stories [...] run riot throughout the domains of technoscience. Not only is no language, including mathematics free of troping; not only is facticity always saturated with metaphoricity; but also, any sustained account of the world is dense with storytelling.'[22] Technoscientific narratives and imaginaries are central to the understanding of our world and its reconfiguration, because stories, imaginations, epistemologies and materialities are intimately linked. We need 'better' imaginaries, metaphors and narratives to change dominant and problematic discourses, to invent 'better worlds'. But what are the imaginaries of AI – in the military, in everyday discourse and pop culture, in the

Slaughterbots video that went viral? What do they look like? In the following I will give a brief overview of the drone imaginary sketched by the *Slaughterbots* video, the military imaginary of intelligent drone swarms, and the popular culture/Hollywood imaginary of AI, and I will discuss whether the old, Hollywoodesque imaginary is being replaced by a new one.

Slaughterbots: the video

The *Slaughterbots* video pictures the application of drone swarms not in the military but in the civilian realm. It starts with a typical CEO presentation in which the protagonist demonstrates the capabilities of the new technology. The CEO promises that emergent drone swarms, released in hundreds or thousands from an aeroplane, allow an 'airstrike of surgical precision [...] A 25 million dollar order now buys this [...] Enough to kill half a city, the bad half', because it 'allows you to separate the good guys from the bad'.[23] The drones are equipped with face recognition software to follow and kill selected targets – according to their social media profiles, for example. With this new weapons system, the CEO claims, 'nuclear is obsolete'.[24] The rest of the video develops two main scenarios in which sitting members of parliament and hundreds of politically engaged students are lethally attacked by drone swarms that have been released by unknown actors.

At the end of the video clip, Russell warns of the problems and effects of autonomous weapons: 'What we were trying to show was the property of autonomous weapons to turn into WMDs automatically, because you can launch as many as you want.'[25] The video impressively sketches the potential for mass destruction which becomes possible with autonomous drone

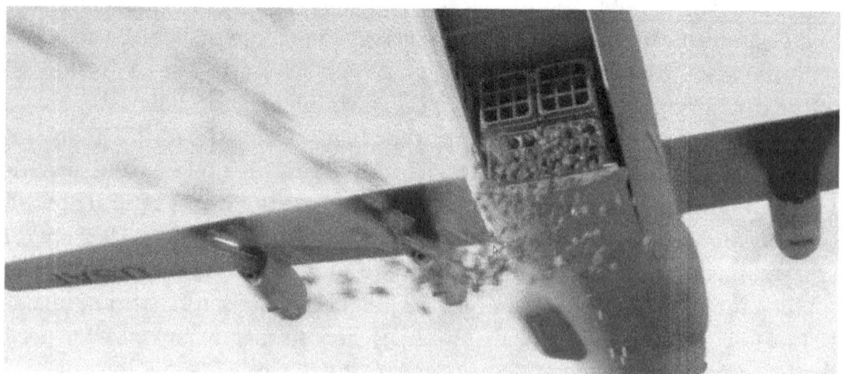

9.1 Screenshot from *Slaughterbots*, 2017, directed by Stewart Sugg. Written by Matt Wood. *YouTube*.

swarms. What is not very clear is what kind of 'autonomy' these drones have, how they select their targets and how they get access to relevant data.

The confusion is partly grounded in the fact that autonomy has different meanings in the humanities and in computer science/engineering. From the Enlightenment onwards, autonomy has been related to the free and self-aware subject which chooses its own maxims self-determinedly and consciously – as famously formulated by Immanuel Kant. Even though this concept has been challenged by theorists such as Karl Marx, Sigmund Freud, Michel Foucault and Judith Butler, it still predominates in many realms – for example, ethics, law, economics and also everyday life. At the same time, the concept of autonomy is also central to AI and robotics, but its basic assumptions are very different from traditional humanistic approaches to free will. It goes back to the cybernetic idea of purposeful behaviour in the sense of a pragmatic physiological automated mechanism: think for example of a torpedo with a target-seeking mechanism. Today's control mechanisms in AI systems – for example, in drone swarms – are much more sophisticated than traditional servomechanisms. Nevertheless, these systems still do not follow their own maxims. They are fenced in by norms, values and categories programmed into their software – and although the complexity of software layers might lead to unpredictable effects, these are not intentional.[26]

The *Slaughterbots* drones are autonomous in finding and following their targets, but the profiles of the people to be killed are preprogrammed. It is exactly this sophisticated mixture of autonomous and preprogrammed behaviour that makes it so difficult to understand the challenges posed by this technology.

The military imaginary: self-healing swarm intelligence

In military discourse, swarm intelligence – the next version of AI – is a big topic.[27] It is regarded as a highly productive feature of self-organising systems which enables them to solve complex tasks on the basis of simple, synchronised behaviour beyond central control. As the systems' entities communicate with each other, they can adapt their behaviour to new situations swiftly. The biomimetic concept is inspired by the behaviour patterns of bird, ant, insect or fish swarms. The military and the defence sector hope for autonomous swarms (of drones, tanks etc.) with emergent, more flexible and adaptive behaviour, which will be capable of solving more complex tasks beyond central control.

William Roper, director of the Strategic Capabilities Office, which is involved in the development of the Perdix micro-drones for the US Department of Defense, writes:

> Due to the complex nature of combat, Perdix are not pre-programmed synchronized individuals, they are a collective organism, sharing one distributed brain for decision-making and adapting to each other like swarms in nature [...]. Because every Perdix communicates and collaborates with every other Perdix, the swarm has no leader and can gracefully adapt to drones entering or exiting the team.[28]

To date, it is not possible to preprogram and operate a swarm of drones: the Perdix drone experiment and other, similar military endeavours are attempts to achieve this, but so far they have been only short-lived attempts with little success. Researchers hope, however, that with the help of decentralised self-control and emergent properties of the autonomous systems, they will be able to adapt faster (know where to move), make faster decisions (know whom to kill) and evolve higher cognitive capabilities (have awareness in the battlespace). With this new quality of autonomy, researchers anticipate that it will become more difficult to identify (and thereby target/eliminate) the drones. Military defence strategists dream of deploying enormous swarms of drones with different tasks simultaneously, to overpower the enemy by sheer brute force.[29]

> Uninhabited and autonomous systems will enable the next evolution, as forces shift from fighting as a network to fighting as a swarm, with large numbers of highly autonomous uninhabited systems coordinating their actions on the battlefield. This will enable greater mass, coordination, intelligence and speed than would be possible with networks of human-inhabited or even remotely controlled uninhabited systems.[30]

The promises of biomimetic approaches – which try to learn from natural behaviour or use it as inspiration for new design strategies – reach back to the early days of cybernetics, and became dominant in artificial life research and behaviour-based robotics from the 1980s onwards. Even back then, researchers hoped that complex behaviour might spring from the cooperation of simple entities, with simple rules emerging into a more coherent, intelligent whole. With the help of the biomimetic approach, decisive progress could be made, for example, with regard to robots' movement abilities (climbing stairs, dancing, moving smoothly etc.), but the new quality of (cognitive) autonomy was never achieved.[31]

The Hollywood/blockbuster AI imaginary

Many Hollywood or blockbuster science fiction films portray AI as an unpredictable or evil force that develops a superhuman intelligence (HAL in *2001: A Space Odyssey*; Skynet in the *Terminator* series; VIKI in *I,*

Robot). AI is often shaped like a human (see *Terminator* or *Ex Machina*); it can develop intentions and strategies like a human, but it has no morality or ethical guidelines. Often it runs amok or tries to take over the world, producing an apocalypse or even wiping the human race from the planet. In these dystopian films, AI is conscious, highly intelligent, dangerous and non-transparent. One might say that these imaginaries are the flipside of imaginaries of the ethical robot (such as in the film *Bicentennial Man*) based on Isaac Asimov's three laws of robotics,[32] ethical AI design principles which prohibit harm to any human being, but which do not play a central role in contemporary popular culture.

Stuart Russell and the scientists at the Future of Life Institute strive towards an imaginary of AI beyond that which dominates discourses of the military or popular culture. They do not share the biomimetic military imaginary of autonomous self-healing drone swarms. The military narrative may be different from the Skynet narrative of the evil, conscious, human-like super-intelligence, since it does not run amok, even though it develops its own strategies; nevertheless, it is based on a naturalised, mythological, socio-technical imaginary of AI as an evolving, learning, beehive-like organism that has become intelligent and is capable not only of adapting but also of making strategic decisions – and killing. This dream is pursued in the hope of ultimately making so-called autonomous systems intelligent, and thereby making it possible to 'sustain American military technological dominance'.[33]

What we see in the *Slaughterbots* video is quite different from this US military dream of self-healing, intelligent drone swarms. The swarms of small, fast and cheap drones are deployed by unknown (and hard-to-identify) protagonists to kill political enemies via AI, face recognition/machinic vision and shaped charges. But the target selection is based on preprogrammed criteria applied to the social media profiles of parliamentarians and students. The targeting of individuals on the basis of data analytics is not far from US military insurgency/kill list strategies that are already in place: kill lists (such as the 'disposition matrix') are produced via data-mining, by sifting through enormous amounts of data – from drone feeds and military and security service databases to social media profiles.[34] Governments hope thereby to find hidden threats/terrorists, and the collected data is used to select and rank targets for assassination via drone attacks or raids.[35] While non-governmental protagonists may not have access to or be able to hack into military and secret service databases, it is nevertheless possible to build one's own (kill) list of political enemies on the basis of public social media profiles.

The autonomous drone swarms in the *Slaughterbots* video are not staged as self-conscious, intelligent organisms following their own self-determined

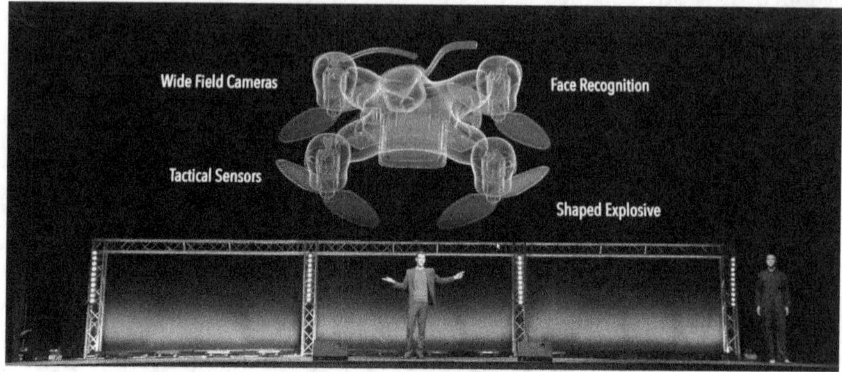

9.2 Screenshot from *Slaughterbots*, 2017, directed by Stewart Sugg. Written by Matt Wood. *YouTube*.

goals. The slaughterbots are obviously programmed to select their targets via social media data analytics according to pregiven criteria (for example, leftist students engaged in an anti-corruption non-governmental organisations), and they seek their targets using facial recognition, to kill them with explosives. In following these preprogrammed goals, the slaughterbots may show coordinated, flexible and dynamic behaviour to fulfil their tasks (avoiding obstacles, following humans etc.). But these swarms are neither conscious nor capable of setting their own agendas.

The open question is whether the eminent difference between the imaginary of the self-conscious, intelligent, autonomous AI[36] and the *Slaughterbots* imaginary of tomorrow's AI as a collection of smart software programs is observable. The imaginary of *Slaughterbots* (hopefully) shows that today's or tomorrow's AI makes possible the automation of sophisticated tasks that we would normally expect to be performed by humans. This does not mean that the software programs are intelligent in themselves. Nevertheless, the adaptive, coordinated drone swarms can easily be turned into WMDs.

Matt McFarland of CNN wrote of *Slaughterbots*: 'Perhaps the most nightmarish, dystopian film of 2017 didn't come from Hollywood.'[37] Maybe the arms control advocates' *Slaughterbots* video was an important step towards the development of a new AI imaginary that is not occupied with the old trope of the evil, almighty wrongdoer, but which helps us to debate the 'core issues' of AI, to take responsibility for its development, and to understand the close entwinement of science, technology and society. Another interesting step in this direction – also not from Hollywood – is the *Black Mirror* TV series episode 'Hated in the Nation'.[38] In this episode, a viral Twitter game called the Game of Consequences invites users to choose the hashtag #DeathTo, picking a person to be killed by hacked killer bees. The person who is subject to the most #DeathTo tweets dies the same day. Users are supposedly chosen because of their bad behaviour – from peeing on war monuments to writing clickbait. The killer bees – originally planned as substitutes for natural bees, and now used for government surveillance – kill the victim by penetrating the brain after entering through the nose or eyes. At the end of the episode, all those who have participated in the ranking of victims are killed by drone swarms. The episode is a bitter satire on the enthusiasm for public shaming and the ugly consequences of hate speech and abusive social media usage. Nevertheless, it shows the possibility of turning autonomous drones with profiling technologies and facial recognition into deadly weapons, including in the civil realm.

We certainly need more detailed studies of the multidimensional socio-technical imaginaries of AI and autonomous weapon systems. For now, it seems that this is a rather contested field that certainly needs alternative world-making discourses and practices. The imaginary of AI as a decision-making entity is not only part of the Hollywood science fiction narrative, but is also partly implemented in contemporary military discourses that build on biomimetic concepts of emergent and adaptive behaviour, which is the precondition of the idea of swarms as distributed brains that can solve complex problems. At the same time, defence officials deflect urgent questions of arms control, referring to *Slaughterbots* as the product of a Skynet/*Terminator*-style fantasy, while arms control advocates try out new ways of making their point about the growing danger of drones as WMDs. I think we need more interventions to enable new and productive imaginaries which will help us to understand the consequences of lethal autonomous weapon systems.

Notes

1 S. Russell, A. Aguirre, A. Conn and M. Tegmark, 'Why you should fear "slaughterbots": A response', *IEEE Spectrum*, 2018. https://spectrum.ieee.org/automaton/robotics/artificial-intelligence/why-you-should-fear-slaughterbots-a-response (accessed 28 December, 2019).
2 *Slaughterbots*, directed by S. Sugg, written by M. Wood, *YouTube*, 2017, www.youtube.com/watch?v=9CO6M2HsoIA (accessed 28 December, 2019).
3 *Black Mirror* is a contemporary dystopian science fiction TV series focusing on possible but unpredicted effects of new technologies.
4 Future of Life Institute, https://futureoflife.org (accessed 24 January, 2020).
5 *Slaughterbots*.
6 *Slaughterbots*.

7 Russell et al., 'Why you should fear "slaughterbots"'.
8 United Nations Geneva, www.unog.ch (accessed 24 January, 2020).
9 *Campaign to Stop Killer Robots*, www.stopkillerrobots.org (accessed 24 January, 2020).
10 *Code Pink*, www.codepink.org (accessed 24 January, 2020).
11 Bureau of Investigative Journalism, www.thebureauinvestigates.com (accessed 24 January, 2020).
12 International Committee for Robot Arms Control, www.icrac.net (accessed 24 January, 2020).
13 Russell et al., 'Why you should fear "slaughterbots"'.
14 Russell et al., 'Why you should fear "slaughterbots"', emphasis in original.
15 M. Rubenstein, A. Cornejo and R. Nagpal, 'Programmable self-assembly in a thousand-robot-swarm', *Science*, 345:6198 (2014): 795–799.
16 US Department of Defense, 'Department of Defense announces successful micro-drone demonstration', 2017, www.defense.gov/Newsroom/Releases/Release/Article/1044811/department-of-defense-announces-successful-micro-drone-demonstration/ (accessed 28 December, 2019).
17 US Department of Defense, 'Department of Defense announces successful micro-drone demonstration'.
18 Xinhua, 'China launches record-breaking drone swarm', *Xinhuanet*, 2017, www.xinhuanet.com//english/2017-06/11/c_136356850.htm (accessed 28 December, 2019).
19 Xinhua, 'China launches record-breaking drone swarm'.
20 M. McNeil, M. Arribas-Ayllon, J. Haran, A. Mackenzie and R. Tutton, 'Conceptualizing imaginaries of science, technology, and society', in U. Felt, R. Fouché, C. A. Miller and L. Smith-Doerr (eds), *The Handbook of Science and Technology Studies* (Cambridge, MA: MIT Press, 4th edn, 2017), 435–463.
21 S. Jasanoff and S.-H. Kim, 'Containing the atom: Sociotechnical imaginaries and nuclear power in the United States and South Korea', *Minerva*, 47:2 (2009): 119–146, 120; S. Jasanoff, 'Future imperfect: Science, technology, and the imaginations of modernity', in S. Jasanoff and S.-H. Kim (eds), *Dreamscapes of Modernity: Sociotechnical Imaginaries and the Fabrication of Power* (Chicago: University of Chicago Press, 2015), 1–33; McNeill et al., 'Conceptualizing imaginaries of science, technology, and society'.
22 D. Haraway, *Modest_witness@second_millennium: FemaleMan_meets_oncomouse* (New York: Routledge, 1997), 64.
23 *Slaughterbots.*
24 *Slaughterbots.*
25 *Slaughterbots.*
26 L. Suchman and J. Weber, 'Human-machine autonomies', in N. Bhuta, S. Beck, R. Geiss, H.-Y. Liu and C. Kress (eds), *Autonomous Weapon Systems: Law, Ethics, Policy* (Cambridge: Cambridge University Press, 2016), 75–102.
27 J. Arquilla and D. F. Ronfeldt, *Swarming and the Future of Conflict* (Santa Monica: RAND National Defense Research Institute, 2000); J. Kosek, 'Ecologies

of the empire: On the new uses of the honeybee', *Cultural Anthropology*, 25:4 (2010): 650–678; R. O. Work and S. Brimley, '20YY: Preparing for war in the robotic age', *Center for a New American Security*, 2014, www.cnas.org/publications/reports/20yy-preparing-for-war-in-the-robotic-age (accessed 28 December, 2019); P. Scharre, 'Robotics on the battlefield part II: The coming swarm', *Center for a New American Security*, 2014, www.cnas.org/publications/reports/robotics-on-the-battlefield-part-ii-the-coming-swarm (accessed 29 December, 2019).

28 US Department of Defense, 'Department of Defense announces successful micro-drone demonstration'.

29 Scharre, 'Robotics on the battlefield'; Work and Brimley, '20YY: Preparing for war in the robotic age'. For a critique, see J. Altmann, 'Autonomous weapon systems: Dangers and need for an international prohibition', in C. Benzmüller and H. Stuckenschmidt (eds), *KI 2019: Advances in Artificial Intelligence: 42nd German Conference on AI, Kassel, Germany, 23–26 September, 2019: Proceedings* (Cham: Springer 2019), 1–17.

30 Scharre, 'Robotics on the battlefield', 14.

31 Suchman and Weber, 'Human-machine autonomies'.

32 I. Asimov, 'Run around', *Astounding Science Fiction*, 29:1 (1941): 94–103.

33 Scharre, 'Robotics on the battlefield', 7.

34 J. Weber, 'Keep adding: Kill lists, drone warfare and the politics of databases', in M. de Goede, A. Leander and G. Sullivan (eds), 'The politics of the list: Law, security, technology', special issue, *Environment and Planning D: Society and Space*, 34:1 (2016): 107–125.

35 Weber, 'Keep adding: Kill lists, drone warfare and the politics of databases'.

36 Whether it be the evil Skynet as a caricature of the 'rational', conscious human, or the quasi-natural, self-healing drone swarm that emerges towards 'real' intelligence.

37 M. McFarland, '"Slaughterbots" film shows potential horrors of killer drones', *CNN Business*, 2017, https://money.cnn.com/2017/11/14/technology/autonomous-weapons-ban-ai/index.html (accessed 24 January, 2020).

38 *Black Mirror*, 'Hated in the Nation' (series episode), directed by J. Hawes, written by C. Brooker, Netflix, 2016.

Bibliography

Altmann, J. 'Autonomous weapon systems: Dangers and need for an international prohibition'. In C. Benzmüller and H. Stuckenschmidt (eds), *KI 2019: Advances in Artificial Intelligence: 42nd German Conference on AI, Kassel, Germany, 23–26 September, 2019: Proceedings*, 1–17. Cham: Springer 2019.

Arquilla, J. and D. F. Ronfeldt. *Swarming and the Future of Conflict*. Santa Monica: RAND National Defense Research Institute, 2000.

Asimov, I. 'Run around'. *Astounding Science Fiction*, 29:1 (1941): 94–103.

Black Mirror. 'Hated in the Nation' (series episode). Directed by J. Hawes. Written by C. Brooker. Netflix, 2016.

The Bureau of Investigative Journalism (2020). www.thebureauofinvestigatives.com (accessed 24 January, 2020).

Campaign to Stop Killer Robots (2020). www.stopkillerrobots.org (accessed 24 January, 2020).

Code Pink (2020). www.codepink.org (accessed 24 January, 2020).

Future of Life Institute (2020). https://futureoflife.org (accessed 24 January, 2020).

Graae, A. I. and K. Maurer (eds). *Drone imaginaries: The power of remote vision*. Manchester: Manchester University Press, 2021.

International Committee for Robot Arms Control (ICRAC) (2020). www.icrac.net (accessed 24 January, 2020).

Jasanoff, S. 'Future imperfect: Science, technology, and the imaginations of modernity'. In S. Jasanoff and S.-H. Kim (eds), *Dreamscapes of Modernity: Sociotechnical Imaginaries and the Fabrication of Power*, 1–33. Chicago: University of Chicago Press, 2015.

Jasanoff, S. and S.-H. Kim. 'Containing the atom: Sociotechnical imaginaries and nuclear power in the United States and South Korea'. *Minerva*, 47:2 (2009): 119–146.

Kosek, J. 'Ecologies of the empire: On the new uses of the honeybee'. *Cultural Anthropology*, 25:4 (2010): 650–678.

McFarland, M. '"Slaughterbots" film shows potential horrors of killer drones'. *CNN Business*, 2017. https://money.cnn.com/2017/11/14/technology/autonomous-weapons-ban-ai/index.html (accessed 24 January, 2020).

McNeil, M., M. Arribas-Ayllon, J. Haran, A. Mackenzie and R. Tutton. 'Conceptualizing imaginaries of science, technology, and society'. In U. Felt, R. Fouché, C. A. Miller and L. Smith-Doerr (eds), *The Handbook of Science and Technology Studies*, 435–463. Cambridge, MA: MIT Press, 4th edn, 2017.

Rubenstein, M., A. Cornejo and R. Nagpal. 'Programmable self-assembly in a thousand-robot-swarm'. *Science*, 345:6198 (2014): 795–799.

Russell, S., A. Aguirre, A. Conn and M. Tegmark, 'Why you should fear "slaughterbots": A response', *IEEE Spectrum*, 2018. https://spectrum.ieee.org/automaton/robotics/artificial-intelligence/why-you-should-fear-slaughterbots-a-response (accessed 28 December, 2019).

Scharre, P., 'Robotics on the battlefield part II: The coming swarm'. *Center for a New American Security*, 2014. www.cnas.org/publications/reports/robotics-on-the-battlefield-part-ii-the-coming-swarm (accessed 29 December, 2019).

Slaughterbots. Directed by S. Sugg. Written by M. Wood. *YouTube*, 2017. www.youtube.com/watch?v=9CO6M2HsoIA (accessed 28 December, 2019).

Suchman, L. and J. Weber. 'Human-machine autonomies'. In N. Bhuta, S. Beck, R. Geiss, H.-Y. Liu and C. Kress (eds), *Autonomous Weapon Systems: Law, Ethics, Policy*, 75–102. Cambridge: Cambridge University Press, 2016.

United Nations Geneva (2020). www.unog.ch (accessed 24 January, 2020).

US Department of Defense. 'Department of Defense announces successful micro-drone demonstration'. 2017. www.defense.gov/Newsroom/Releases/Release/Article/1044811/department-of-defense-announces-successful-micro-drone-demonstration/ (accessed 28 December, 2019).

Weber, J. 'Keep adding: Kill lists, drone warfare and the politics of databases'. In M. de Goede, A. Leander and G. Sullivan (eds), 'The politics of the list: Law, security, technology', special issue, *Environment and Planning D: Society and Space*, 34:1 (2016): 107–125.

Wikipedia, 'Slaughterbots'. 2019. https://en.wikipedia.org/wiki/Slaughterbots (accessed 28 December, 2019).

Work, R. O. and S. Brimley. '20YY: Preparing for war in the robotic age'. *Center for a New American Security*. 2014. www.cnas.org/publications/reports/20yy-preparing-for-war-in-the-robotic-age (accessed 28 December, 2019).

Xinhua. 'China launches record-breaking drone swarm'. *Xinhuanet*, 2017. www.xinhuanet.com//english/2017-06/11/c_136356850.htm (accessed 28 December, 2019).

10

Stranger things: a techno-bestiary of drones in art and war

Claudette Lauzon

> Our machines are disturbingly lively, and we ourselves frighteningly inert.[1]

> The promise of monsters is a regenerative politics, an invitation to explore new ways of being in touch, new forms of becoming, new possibilities for kinship, alliance, and change.[2]

When Donna Haraway penned 'A cyborg manifesto' in the last quarter of the twentieth century, little could she have anticipated the rapid acceleration of technological innovation in the first quarter of the twenty-first, as our machines become ever more lively and we ourselves ever more frighteningly inert. But with the prescient acknowledgement that increasingly 'leaky distinctions' between human, animal and machine threatened to open the floodgates to a host of worryingly techno-deterministic outcomes, Haraway proposed that the ascending figure of the cyborg might instead augur a utopian world to come. Cyborgs, she wrote, 'are monstrous and illegitimate; in our present political circumstances, we could hardly hope for more potent myths for resistance and recoupling.'[3]

It would be exceedingly difficult – and perhaps ill-advised – to suggest at this juncture in world history that the figure of the drone likewise represents opportunities for resistance, let alone a utopian worldview. Since 2004, the US-led drone wars have killed thousands in Yemen, Somalia, Afghanistan and Pakistan, including up to 1,700 civilians.[4] During the period 2016–2018 alone, the US government under President Donald Trump further escalated drone strikes in those countries, while eliminating many of the Obama-era restrictions intended to reduce civilian deaths. In 2018, according to the United Nations, twice as many civilians were killed and injured by US military operations in Afghanistan as in the previous year.[5] However, and in conversation with recent explorations of the drone imaginary as a space for imagining other (better) worlds, in this chapter I want to think closely about the drone, itself an assemblage of human/nonhuman agents and affects, as a speculative site to investigate Karen Barad's call for 'kinship, alliance, and change.'[6] Inspired by a rich feminist history of grappling with monsters and the monsterisation of others,[7] I bring a series of recent artworks to bear on the figure of the drone through three rhetorical lenses: the swarm, the blob, and the living dead.

My question is twofold: to what extent have the monsters that populate the Western social imaginary come to shape what the editors of the present collection identify as a contemporary drone imaginary? And how might critical visual cultural practices work to reshape our consequent fears and desires? Taking seriously what both Haraway and Barad identify as the 'promise of monsters' to double back on their makers, I suggest that the monstrous bodies of drone warfare might paradoxically cultivate a praxis of uneasy kinship, or what Jean-Luc Nancy would call an 'inoperative community'[8] among the human and nonhuman actors that together constitute the stranger things of drone warfare.

The swarm

Picture a space, about the size of a small classroom, nondescript and unadorned but for a window and a radiator along one of the drably painted white walls. On the floor sit dozens of miniature toy helicopters, still and silent in neat military formation. Almost immediately the silence is pierced by the mechanical whirring of tiny engines coming to life as the helicopters raise themselves off the floor, seeming to evince a sudden collective will to power. But just as quickly, the collective devolves into noisy chaos. Now more like a swarm of angry and disoriented insects, the helicopters begin to careen around the room, bouncing off the walls, the ceiling and each other until one after another they fall lifeless to the floor. A few of the toys fail even to achieve takeoff, and are soon knocked off their feet by others on their flailing descent. Within minutes, the squadron of tiny aircraft once again goes silent, and the neat military grid is now a scene of quiet disarray – the miniature battlefield strewn with mangled bodies of twisted metal.

At first sight, Swiss artist Roman Signer's three-minute video *56 Small Helicopters* is an artwork that has little purchase with the contemporary drone imaginary – and even less so with any serious experiments with swarm intelligence. Certainly *56 Small Helicopters* calls to mind not artificial intelligence so much as what Hito Steyerl terms 'artificial stupidity' – the idea, simply put, that the machines we task ever increasingly with decision-making functions are alarmingly prone to communication breakdown and malfunction.[9] Like Steyerl's insights into the many ways in which artificial intelligence actually *produces* artificial stupidity (examples include bots creating fake news, recognition software misidentifying

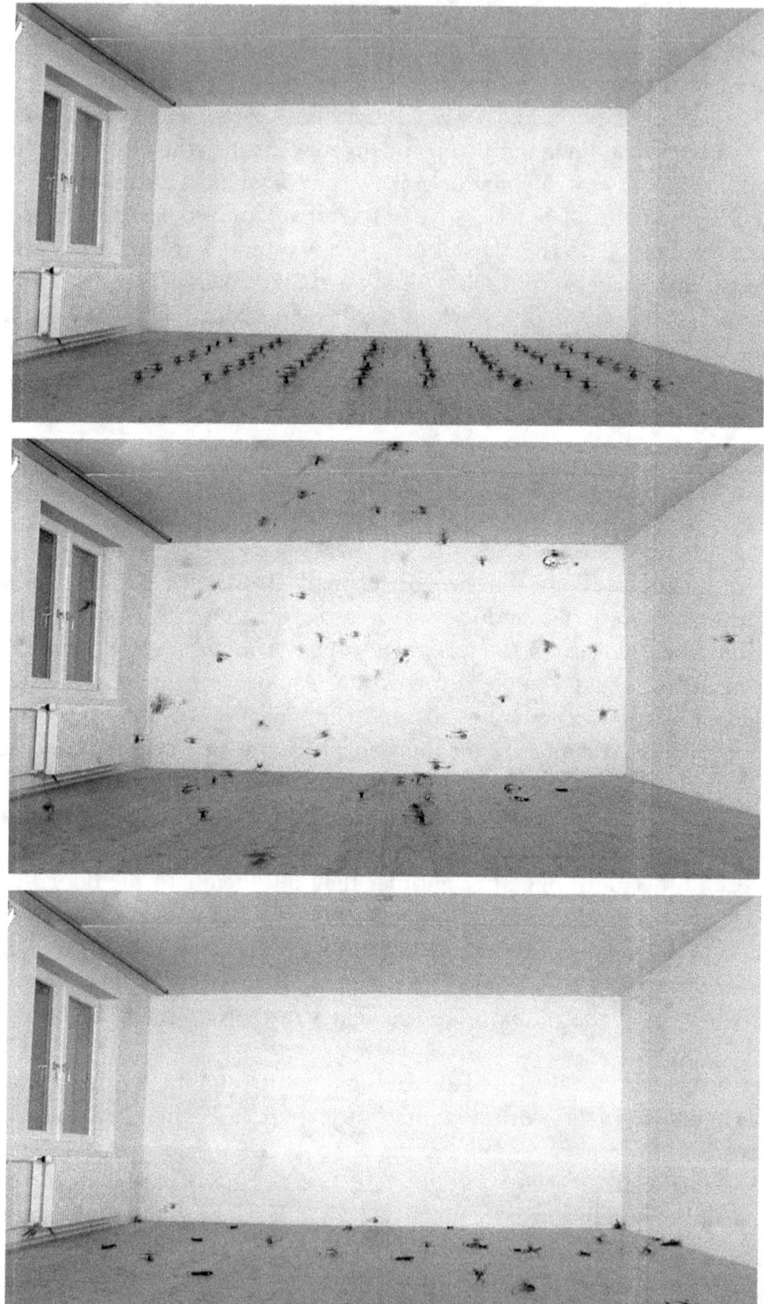

10.1a–c Roman Signer, *56 Kleine Helikopter* ('56 Small Helicopters'), 2008, Atelier St. Gallen. Single-channel video, 3 min., 10 sec. Video: Aleksandra Signer.

subjects, and algorithms producing un-processable amounts of metadata), Signer's errant helicopters give us pause to reconsider our increasingly awe-struck relationship with new technologies and the non-human entities (whether spam bots or autonomous vehicles) that they produce. And today, that awe is directed nowhere more enthusiastically than toward swarming drones, whether in the one-minute 2013 Lexus car advert (fittingly called 'Swarm') in which a group of quadrotors manoeuvre themselves in and out of various buildings in Vancouver, Canada,[10] or on the June 2018 cover of *Time Magazine*, which saw its iconic masthead spelled out by almost one thousand drones lit up against the night sky above a headline heralding 'The Drone Age'.[11] If the figure of the lone drone will trigger a range of emotions and responses depending on whether it is surveilling or delivering pizza to a remote village, it would seem that a squadron of drones appearing to dance gracefully in unison arouses only joy and amazement.

It is perhaps this collective sense of technophilic wonder, and the criticality that it seems to defer, that provoked the art group Random International in 2017 to produce *Zoological*, an installation of enormous helium-filled white foil balloons equipped with motors, rotors, cameras, and onboard computers. Programmed with a custom swarm algorithm that uses LIDAR technology to afford them relative autonomy in the space, the spheres interact with each other and their human visitors according to a series of pre-programmed environmental triggers that cause them to hover over certain individuals and avoid others.[12] *Zoological* was developed, according to Random International, as a deliberation on lived experience 'in a world increasingly run by algorithms, [in which] we are having to adapt rapidly to a continually developing cohabitation with autonomous machines whose presence is often intangible or discrete.'[13] At once deeply wondrous and deeply troubling, the installation looks back in time to the paranoia-fuelled dystopian science fiction of the 1950s and 1960s (recalling especially the ambiguously sentient white orb known as Rover in the British television series *The Prisoner*), but also forward to an uncertain (but near) future in which fleets of autonomous drones conduct ubiquitous surveillance at home and endless wars abroad. It is a future to which the Western military-industrial complex is also, without doubt, attuned.

Most modern dystopian narratives of terrifyingly sentient mechanical entities are actually predated by the military history of drone technology, which arguably begins with the development of remotely controlled aircraft prior to the First World War.[14] But it was only in the early twenty-first century that advanced sensor capacities enabled remotely piloted aircraft to take centre stage in the so-called Global War on Terror waged by the US and its allies. And no sooner did the dream of a war 'fought by airplanes with no men in them at all'[15] come to near fruition than a new dream – of wholly autonomous swarms of weaponised drones – began to take shape. As Jeremy Packer and Joshua Reeves observe in regards to what they cheekily refer to as an inevitable 'humanectomy' (literally the expulsion of human subjects) in military intelligence and operations, the swarm has emerged as a powerful figure as automation becomes an overriding operational principle. For while conventional military networks 'had to safeguard their principal nodes of intelligence against enemy attack, [...] the swarm cloud possesses a continuously refined, emergent collective intelligence that is far beyond the grasp of humans' physiological capacity.'[16]

To that apparent end, in January 2017 the US Department of Defense (DoD) released a video showing a fleet of 103 micro-drones performing a coordinated test mission at a weapons station in California's Mojave Desert. As explained in a fact sheet distributed by the Office of the Secretary of Defense, Perdix drones measure 16.5 cm in length with a wing span of 30 cm.[17] In development since 2013, they are presently distinguished by a 'distributed brain' and the capacity for adaptation and self-healing, 'much like swarms in nature.' The next generation, the fact sheet states, will 'likely include more advanced autonomy.'[18] Interestingly, like the implicit reference to buzzing insects in Signer's *56 Small Helicopters* and to non-human animals in Random International's *Zoological* installation, the DoD clearly invokes the natural world in its description of the Perdix drone. And indeed, the initiative is emblematic of a long and ongoing (if only varyingly successful) set of programs to conscript flighted animals into both the practice and the imaginary of military technology. From Julius Neubronner's carrier pigeons equipped with still cameras in the early twentieth century, to DARPA's Hybrid Insect-Micro Electro-Mechanical System programme (which from the 1940s to the present has been tasked with creating cyberinsects),[19] to the taxonomy of militarised drones today, with monikers like Eagle, Hawk, Mantis, Dragon, Heron, Raven, Hummingbird and Wasp, military powers have long sought to harness the unique powers of non-human animals to wage aerial war.[20]

Indeed, recent developments in contemporary military technology have produced what Rosi Braidotti calls a 'techno-bestiary' of robotic dogs, fleas and cockroaches.[21] But while this contemporary techno-bestiary of mediated violence – and especially its swarm-based representatives – is certainly at the heart of the drone imaginary, it is also useful to consider the deeply ambivalent, even abject figuration of non-human animals and the swarm, in particular, in the *human* imaginary. Lauren Wilcox carefully unpacks this ambiguity in her analysis of subversive feminist appropriations of swarm imagery. From speculative fiction such as Charlotte Perkins Gilman's *Herland Trilogy* of 1915 (in which feminist collectives are presented as insect-like swarms), through to the insect metaphors that dominate representations of Beyoncé (or Queen B) and her legions of fans (the Beyhive), Wilcox underscores that the swarm has been 'reimagined in ways that transcend [its] contemporary militaristic politics.'[22]

This brings us back to Roman Signer's *56 Small Helicopters*. First, and like much of Roman Signer's art practice, this work fails to fulfil any technophilic desire for posthuman militaristic mastery and precision that drone swarm technologies seem to promise.[23] This is signalled in the very installation of the artwork: At the Laboral Centro de Arte y Creación Industrial in Gijón, Spain, where it was shown in 2014–2015 as part of the group exhibition *A Screaming Comes Across the Sky*, the HD video was screened on a small, low-resolution cathode ray tube television that sat on the floor of the gallery. Likewise, the fifty-six helicopters themselves betray an indifference to technological innovations of the early twenty-first century. These are hardly the beautifully self-choreographed drones of the Lexus advert or the Perdix programme. It is this spectacularly unruly scene of drones going feral – acting out an almost comical artificial stupidity – that sparks a rethinking of our common conceptions of precision, even metaphysical transcendence, or what Kroker and Kroker call 'the sublime seduction of drone technology.'[24] Signer's is a swarm that refuses to swarm.

But if we return to my description of the film's end as reminiscent of a battlefield strewn with fallen bodies, I would like to suggest that this artwork makes another significant intervention into the drone imaginary. As Wilcox notes, the swarm signals not only the future of remote warfare but also its discontents. In fact, in Western military parlance the 'terrorist threat' is regularly presented as 'the threat of the multitude, of the swarm, of the concerted action of that which does not necessarily have a single head.'[25] With this vision of the dehumanised enemy other in mind, let us alter the perspective of this last screen shot (and does art not *always* ask us to alter our entrenched perspectival positions?) and flip it upward towards us, so that the floor of the room becomes the screen. Like so, we might then be induced to squint and imagine these tiny helicopters as bug splats on a windshield or, more saliently, on the screen of the drone pilot's monitor. Now keeping in mind that 'bug splat' – which was once the name of a programme used by the Pentagon to predict the likelihood of civilian casualties in an air strike – has now become a term used colloquially in the military to refer to collateral casualties of drone violence,[26] Signer's helicopters come to stand in both for posthuman killing machines on a spectacularly failed mission *and* the victims of remote warfare, both agents of necropower and the objects of its relentless gaze. Or rather, they are situated messily somewhere in-between. It is to this messy in-between place that we now turn as we explore first the blob, and then the living dead, both exemplars of the monster as 'a form suspended between forms that threatens to smash distinctions.'[27]

The blob

Picture a large pink balloon with two tiny translucent wings that flutter gently as it floats around a dark room. About the size of the white orbs of *Zoological*, it is more organic in appearance, mostly due to a richly painted surface of sinewy streaks and splotches resembling the topography of an alien planet, an internal body organ, or perhaps a human eyeball. Buoyed by helium and guided by a small commercial drone to which it is tethered with rope, the balloon has a languid gait and appears somewhat indifferent to its surroundings and visitors, but unafraid of transgressing the boundaries of personal space.

The sinewy pink balloon is the centrepiece of the multimedia installation *Drones with Desires*, created in 2015 by London-based artist and designer Agi Haines to speculate on the future of machine learning based on the human brain's neural procedures. To make the piece, the artist worked with a team of neuroscientists at Erasmus University Medical Centre in Rotterdam, who scanned her brain with a diffusion tensor MRI. The scan was then used as a blueprint to algorithmically encode an artificial neural network into the drone's operating system. As it moves through a space, learning about its environment through visual sensors, the drone makes

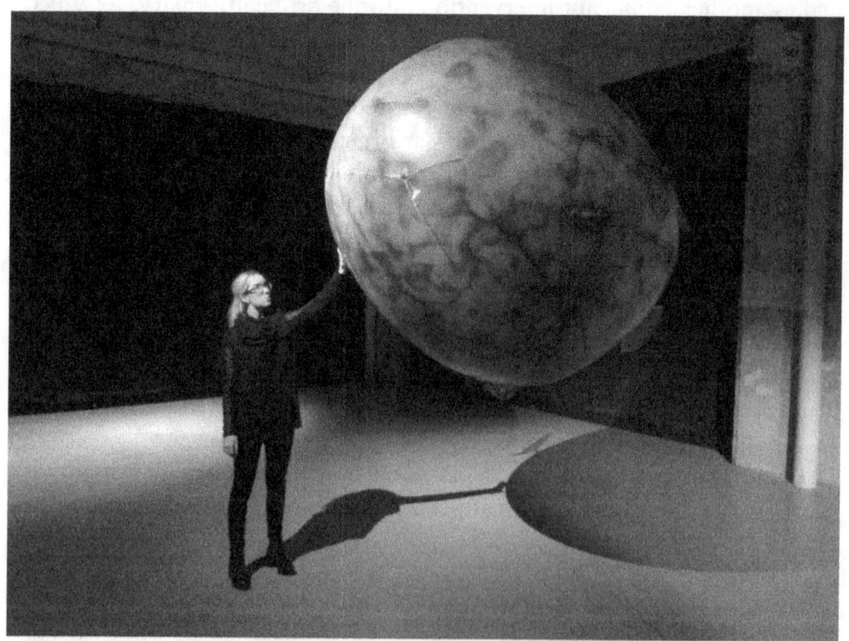

10.2 Agi Haines, *Drones with Desires*, 2015.

navigational decisions based on the replication of the brain's patterns and pathways, which then feed back into its learning behaviours. As Haines describes it, 'we tried to imagine at what point a robot might be considered representative of "me" through the decisions it makes.'[28] She refers playfully to the object as the blob.

For a reader familiar with American horror cinema of the mid-twentieth century, the word 'blob' will conjure the eponymously titled 1958 teen film in which a human-devouring amoeba-like alien organism, which has fallen to earth in a meteorite, terrorises a small town and threatens to eventually engulf the entire planet but for the valiant efforts of two quick-thinking teenagers.[29] Eventually flash frozen and transported to the north pole, the blob is left there to hibernate for 'as long as the arctic stays cold' – a chillingly prescient cliff-hanger if ever there was one. But putting aside the unwitting allusion to the present true-life horror of climate change, the fact that the blob's only weakness is the cold helped to position the now-classic B-movie as one of many horror and science fiction films in the Cold War period to traffic in collective paranoia regarding the so-called red menace and the even more menacing threat of nuclear annihilation.[30] Zombies, body snatchers, Martian invaders, and gelatinous commie-red blobs: there seemed to be no end to the monsters upon whom fear of the geopolitical other could be projected. Fast forwarding thirty years, the oblique Cold War symbolism would be literalised in the 1988 Chuck Russell remake, in which the blob turns out to be a biological weapon that was manufactured by a mysterious US government agency during the Cold War, launched into orbit because of its uncontrollable destructive power, and has now fallen back to earth – a plot twist that turns the alien invader into a self-inflicted wound of the twentieth century's ever more apocalyptic military-industrial complex.[31]

Let us fast forward again to the early twenty-first century, when 'blob' takes on an entirely new meaning in the cultural lexicon. No longer just an amorphous, free-floating, territorialising monster that engulfs and consumes human bodies indiscriminately, blob now refers – in the realm of computer vision and image processing – to the targeted body itself. Blob detection is a simple but effective method for differentiating objects (or collections of pixels) against their surroundings based on pixel density and texture intensity. Used in applications as diverse as tumour identification on MRIs and the tracking of pedestrians by unmanned aerial vehicle (UAV) cameras, blob detection would seem to endorse Steyerl's observation, in the video *How Not to Be Seen: A Fucking Didactic Educational .MOV File* (2013), that 'resolution determines visibility.'[32] Of course, blob detection makes up only a small part of the extraordinarily high-tech realm of drone surveillance and warfare, which today sees weaponised UAVs like the US Air

Force's MQ-9 Reaper equipped with 368 still and video cameras, along with high-definition multi-spectral targeting systems designed for maximum depth and breadth of vision. As a testament to the presumed clarity that these systems afford, drone operators often assert that the video feeds during surveillance and strike operations are so sharp as to create a sense of intimacy with the tracked target.[33] A pivotal scene in Omer Fast's 2011 documentary/fiction hybrid *5,000 Feet is the Best* is exemplary here, as an anonymised ex-drone operator, his face obscured, intones dispassionately:

> I can tell you what type of shoes you're wearing from a mile away. I can tell you what type of clothes a person's wearing, and their hair colour and everything else. So there are very clear cameras on board. We have the IR, infrared, which we can switch to automatically, and that'll pick up any heat signatures or cold signatures. I mean if someone sits down let's say on a cold surface for a while and gets up, you'll still see the heat from that person for a long time. It kind of looks like a white blossom, just shining up into heaven. It's quite beautiful.[34]

The description in this scene is not uncharacteristic. In a 2013 interview on NBC News, former sensor operator Brandon Bryant describes watching one of his victims 'bleed out' on the screen before him: 'When the smoke clears, there's a crater there, and I watch this guy bleed out. I can almost see the agony on this guy's face. It's really more intimate for us, because we see everything.'[35] Assertions such as these are often accompanied by claims, like Bryant's, that remote pilots are actually *closer* to the front lines than conventional soldiers, and therefore comparably (or even more) likely to experience post-traumatic stress. While these claims have yet to be backed up by any objective measure,[36] they are regularly rehearsed in mainstream media – seemingly to establish drone operators as sympathetic characters in a war in which the designation of victimhood is a complicated business.[37]

On the other hand, interviews with pilots and sensor operators, in addition to transcripts of drone strikes, point to contradictory evidence that the bodies in a drone camera's field of vision appear on the screens of drone operators as tiny nondescript figures, oftentimes referred to as 'just black blobs on the screen.'[38] In one chilling example, the father of a US serviceperson accidentally killed in a US drone strike in April 2011 was shown footage of the strike recorded by the Predator drone, and in an interview with the *Los Angeles Times* he describes seeing 'three blobs in really dark shadows' on the screen. 'You couldn't even tell they were human beings – just blobs', he is reported as saying.[39] It is a curious contradiction, perhaps due to the exaggeration of claims of precision in debates over drone vision, and perhaps also partly indicative of what Thomas Stubblefield describes as 'a self-defence mechanism against this closeness, an attempt to compensate for the loss of distance by freeing operators from the messy obligations of intersubjectivity.'[40] Stubblefield is referring here to the use of the term 'bug splat' to refer to casualties of drone strikes. His mistrust of what he calls a 'tempting' narrative displacement, wherein soldiers must dehumanise their victims only to retain their own humanity, is one that I share. What distinguishes the blob from the bug splat, I want to suggest, is a subtle but significant difference between the bug splat as non-human animal and the blob as inanimate data source. 'Bug splat' is only the most recent in a long history of what Stubblefield calls the 'beastialization' of the enemy – 'a shifting set of rhetorical and technical operations by which subjects are deprived of human status in order to justify their status as targets'[41] (he reminds us that during the Second World War, Jews were referred to by the Nazis as rats, while US soldiers called their Japanese counterparts mad dogs). The blob, on the contrary, is the monstrous figure of the pixel come alive, but only by virtue of an infrared camera that translates heat signatures into signs of life and cold signatures into proof of death. Whether targeted insurgent, roadside wedding guest, a grandmother sowing seeds in a field or even a US soldier caught accidentally in the crosshairs of a Predator drone, it is impossible to escape the a priori dehumanising gaze of the drone stare.

This is not to infer that all bodies are treated equally under the many eyes of the drone, nor that greater visual accuracy would somehow reduce the harm that is triggered by its violent stare. Enthusiastic narratives of a precise surgical gaze, as Anjali Nath observes, falsely and dangerously conflate 'precision, categorization, and knowability with a more humane, less damaging form of killing.'[42] For when, as she continues, 'the enemy body is produced through his or her appearance as an indistinct shape that, because of its unrecognizability, is killable', the inevitable killing of civilians that follows 'is not simply a technological error but rather a *technocultural* practice, animated by the criminalization of Orientalized bodies.'[43] What the figure of the blob *can* help elucidate is the troubling disavowal of the human from the contemporary battlefield. As Katherine Chandler rightly points out, debates regarding the so-called 'coming humanectomy' tend to operate according to a 'dissociative logic' that wilfully ignores the complex human–machine assemblages that both produce and are produced by the drone wars.[44] Even the terms most widely used to describe the technology, 'drone' and 'unmanned vehicle', contribute to this occlusion. But drones themselves are '*unbearably human*', to quote Caroline Holmqvist, 'in the sense that they are deeply embedded within the imperial and military apparatus behind them, though those human relations are *masked and mystified*.'[45]

In what she calls a drone manifesto, Chandler returns to Haraway's figure of the cyborg to posit the drone as an exemplar of its twenty-first-century resonance, challenging us to replace the discursive (and material) negation embedded in the term 'unmanned' with a double negation – 'I am not *not* a drone' – in order to begin to come to terms with 'the responsibility for the human and machine synthesis that would be taken up through such a statement.'[46] And perhaps it is unsurprising that today, as in the 1950s, it is science fiction B-movies that are best equipped to perform the grammatical gymnastics required to take this call seriously. A case in point is *The Drone*, a 2019 low-budget horror film about a commercial UAV whose owner, a serial killer known as The Violator, implants his consciousness into the drone's operating system moments before he is killed in a police raid. The rest of the movie follows the drone on a murderous spree of its own, as it tracks and then attacks the killer's ex-wife and her new husband.[47] Entering the pantheon of B-movie monsters – from the Blob and the Thing to King Kong and Godzilla – the Drone, however, departs from now-familiar narratives that rely, as Eugene Thacker notes, on a 'fairly conventional relationship of inside and outside' that is then horrifically compromised by the invasion of 'them' into the space of 'us'.[48] What renders the villainous drone deadly is not its autonomic agency but rather the disastrous coupling of man and machine. And this is truly curious, given how the drone has been positioned as specifically *post*human in the cultural imaginary – a positioning that, as many theorists have noted, sets up a 'singular feedback loop […] between "drone" and "target"'[49] that disavows the participation of humans, both perpetrators and victims. In *The Drone*, the repressed human–machine assemblage returns with a vengeance.

If it is the case, as it surely must be, that the monsters we create reflect our cultural fears and desires, is it possible that in the twenty-first century, what we in the Western world fear most is not the monster outside the door, nor even the monster we have created, but, rather, the possibility that *we* are in fact the monster, *we* the invasive alien with unfettered and uncontrollable reach and power? Certainly, this is again not the context in which to raise the topic of climate change to which this question undeniably points, nor is it necessary to rehearse the extent to which the Western world – the US and its NATO allies specifically – have, for much of the world, become the menace that we once attributed to the Soviet Union. Of course, the Global War on Terror has only exaggerated an already 'blobular' modern history of expansion and encroachment, displacement and occupation that has seen the US intervene in extranational politics with disastrous consequences. What *is* new is the extent to which drone technologies have enabled an unprecedented blurring of the borders of late modern war, to the extent that Derek Gregory speaks of an 'everywhere war' and asks: 'If the United States is fighting a global war, if it arrogates to itself the right to kill or detain its enemies wherever it finds them, where does it end?'[50] In twenty-first-century geopolitics, the creeping, menacing threat is an increasingly powerful global conglomeration whose capitalisation of the military-industrial complex seems to know no bounds.

Returning to the assemblage that is Agi Haines's *Drones with Desires*, I want to suggest that the work undermines both the territorialising logic of the blob *and* the posthuman logic of the drone, as if fulfilling what Lucy Suchman (invoking Haraway) identifies as the promise of monsters to turn on their creators, 'questioning the normative orders that are the conditions of possibility for their monstrosity.'[51] First, like the serial killer-cum-drone, Haines's drone has been implanted with a replication of a human brain, but Haines's brain patterns are only simulated, as the artist readily admits.[52] While the drone's learning behaviour might offer speculative insights into neuroplasticity, its movements and decision-making processes are linked only superficially – algorithmically – to a specific human brain. Here, the blob's putative function as a collection of human data is invoked but just as quickly withdrawn.

At the same time, however, inverting Chandler's provocative turn of phrase, Agi Haines's drone is not *not* human. With its pink skin, vein-like markings and strange propensity to follow its visitors, Haines's is furthermore, as its title suggests, a drone 'with desires'. Those desires are whimsical, unpredictable, and impossible to make sense of, but in a sense this makes the blob even more unbearably human, more unbearably *us*. Neither alien creature, nor Soviet menace, nor a gathering of military-aged males on a road in Yemen, but rather a messy human-animal-machine assemblage that fulfils yet another promise of monsters, to 'refuse easy categorization' and instead occupy a space 'between forms, that threatens to smash distinctions.'[53] But if our understanding of humanness has always been circumscribed by our relationship to our machines, Haines's blob reveals to us that this set of relations is now beginning to show also its *in*humanness.

The living dead

Picture, finally, a large darkened warehouse space in which the ghostly outline of a human body is suspended from a ceiling with dozens of barely visible wires. Four metres in length and about a metre off the floor, the body itself is also composed of copper wire – eight kilometres of it. The figure is furthermore a screen of sorts, through which passes a collection of public and leaked video footage of US military drone strikes. The floor underneath the suspended body is a dynamic, shimmering satellite image of Beirut overlaid with the shadow of the body and the restless, relentless drone vision projected from the ceiling. As you circumnavigate the figure, a

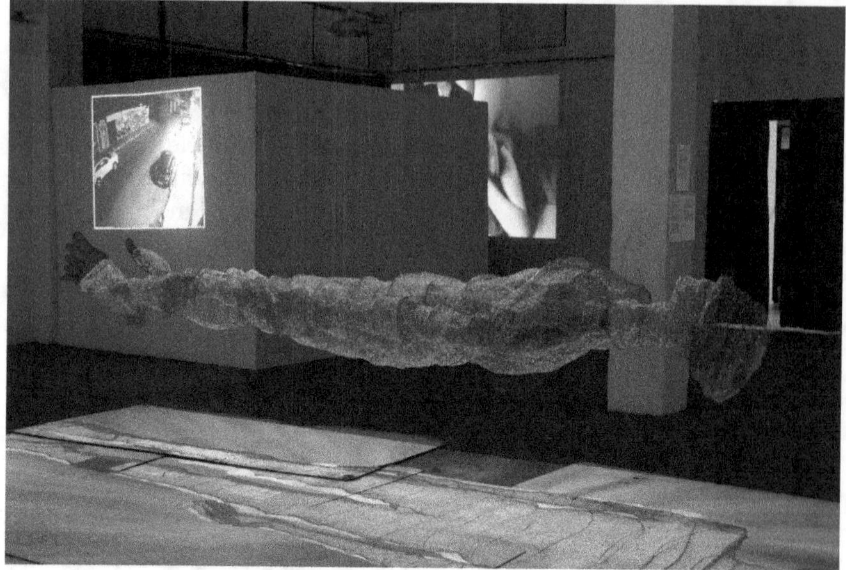

10.3 Miha Vipotnik, Lisa Parks, Elie Mouhanna, Marc Abou Farhat and Tadej Fius, *Spectral Configuration*, Station Beirut, 2015. Photo: Elie Mouhanna.

motion detection camera tracks your movements, mapping and then translating your coordinates onto the map.

Spectral Configuration, an installation conceived by Slovenian artist Miha Vipotnik and US scholar Lisa Parks in collaboration with Elie Mouhanna, Marc Abou Farhat and Tadej Fius,[54] is striking for its resemblance to one of the most thought-provoking artworks of the twentieth century, a collage by German dada artist Max Ernst known as *Murdering Airplane* (1920). Here, what can only be described as an early cyborg with the nose, tail and wings of a fighter plane, but the torso and limbs of a human body, hovers over a barren landscape and three soldiers, at least one of whom is wounded and possibly wearing a prosthetic leg. Produced during the aftermath of the First World War, which saw the invention of mass mechanised warfare, the tiny artwork troubles easy distinctions not only between man and machine, but between body and prosthetic. It also uncannily predicts the particular human–machine assemblage that constitutes today's murdering airplanes, except for the fact that Ernst's hybrid creature is sightless – with no eyes or cameras to guide its destructive mission. Mechanised war, Ernst seems to signal, is blinder than justice. Like Ernst's murdering airplane, the centrepiece of *Spectral Configuration* struggles to cohere when we learn that the artists who collaborated on the piece refer to it officially as the 'lone drone' but colloquially as 'the corpse.'[55] Floating above the spectral city of Beirut to the constant din of active drone missions but prone on its back, without eyes, without ordinance, without engine, this murdering airplane is also much messier – more *unbearably human*, even in its lifelessness. And it is this unsettling of categories of animacy and agency that positions the work as fundamentally concerned with the logic of dehumanisation that underwrites drone warfare.

'How long does it take to make a body? How long does it take to destroy one?'[56] These questions, posed by Lisa Parks, point first to the conditions of the work's production. Artist Elie Mouhanna spent two months working twelve-hour days to hand crochet the eight kilometres of copper wire into a human form, and himself refers to the labour-intensive process as an experiment in thinking of the artist as a proto-computer: 'The eyes and hands are used to scan the body, transforming it into a set of data (measurements). The data is then analysed in order to generate the instructions necessary to create a representation of the body. The new body is formed as the hands follow the generated instructions. The entire body is an endless set of instructions.'[57] But Parks's provocative questions point even more compellingly to the human–machine coupling that activates what Achille Mbembe would call the necropolitical imperative of drone power. For Mbembe, Foucault's concept of biopolitics cannot fully account for contexts of conflict and war wherein 'murder of the enemy [is the] primary and absolute objective.'[58] He introduces necropolitics and necropower to account for the 'ways in which, in our contemporary world, weapons are deployed in the [...] creation of death-worlds, new and unique forms of social existence in which vast populations are subjected to conditions of life conferring upon them the status of living dead.'[59]

With this in mind, I want to consider *Spectral Configuration* in relation not to Ernst's prophetic figure of the murdering airplane, but instead to another figure whose presence calls out and interrogates the necropolitical properties of drone warfare. In 2014, the now-iconic photograph of a young girl was installed as an oversized portrait in a field in North Waziristan, Pakistan. Intended to complicate the perceptive field of drone pilots circling overhead, *#NotABugSplat* also sought to meet the broader imperial gaze with those unforgettable piercing eyes looking up into the sky.[60] The result is a recalibration – if only symbolic – of those operations that so deftly transform perpetrators into victims, victims into bug splats, and human beings into blobs. As Thomas Stubblefield notes incisively, the girl portrayed in *#NotABugSplat* was not killed by a drone but is rather a survivor (her family was killed in a drone strike in Dande Darpa Khel, Waziristan, in 2009).[61] And yet, the girl's presence in this artwork establishes her as both a stand-in for the dehumanised victim of the drone wars and a representative of the necropolitical subject whose 'conditions of life confer […] upon them the status of living dead.'[62] She is, to borrow from Lisa Parks, a 'spectral subject.'[63] Turning to Parks's own work, *Spectral Configuration*, here the child on the ground is supplanted with the body of an adult hovering overhead, and so the perspective of the objectified other shifts from ground to figure, from victim/putative bug splat to military-aged-male/putative target. But further complicating this reading is the fact that here, the victim – that is, the corpse – is also the perpetrator – that is, the drone. This oversized but fragile outline of a figure incorporates both of these nebulous subject positions, and this, I suggest, marks the provocation of this particular installation, which underscores the drone's irreducibility to the binary logic of non/human. Indeed the drone and/or corpse is here imagined as *doubly* non-human: both posthuman, an anthropomorphised but nevertheless mechanical object of war, and inhuman, insofar as the military-aged male occupies the position of what Mbembe calls 'a form of death-in-life.'[64] Captured in the crosshairs of necropower, his very existence calls to mind Judith Butler's insistence that in order to respond to 'the question of who will be treated humanely', we must first attend to 'the question of who does and does not count as a human.'[65] But in this compromised position, the shimmering metallic human figure hovering in a warehouse space, through whom are projected the visual and audio evidence of a war that now operates (to borrow from Stubblefield) both 'everywhere' and 'everywhen',[66] the logics of the drone imaginary are symbolically upended by the illogic of the living dead.

Conclusion

Peter Adey writes about the curious, if purely speculative, symmetries and synergies between drone technologies on one hand and human levitation in Surrealist art and literature on the other. Acknowledging that the contemporary drone imaginary – what he refers to as the aesthetic orders of the drone – works to both naturalise and invisibilise specific geo-political relations, Adey suggests that if we want to challenge these aesthetic orders and the political systems they sustain, we might begin by 'tak[ing] the drone from a side-long view, a kind of squint.'[67] For me, Adey's point is not to prove, nor even to stay loyal to, any particular *counter*-order that might be activated by comparison with human levitators (or for that matter with non-human monsters). Instead, he urges us to bring 'different aesthetic regimes to a juncture with the drone' so as to 'begin to reveal those orders and invisibilities, and start to challenge them more consistently.'[68] In bringing a bevy of monsters into dialogue with drones, my aim in this chapter has been to take seriously, if also irreverently, Adey's invitation to make the drone strange, in order to better understand drones as humanity's disavowed but ineluctable 'companion monsters'.[69] In a world in which the putative extraction of the human from drone warfare continues to structure conversations around remote warfare, then it is surely the work of artists to bring to life the blobs, swarms and corpses that populate the drone imaginary, and to pursue the promise of these monsters to imagine 'new possibilities for kinship, alliance, and change.'[70] For if, as Suchman suggests, the monsters we create are uniquely capable of challenging 'the conditions of possibility for their monstrosity',[71] then perhaps they are also capable of enabling us to challenge our own.

Notes

I wish to thank Kathrin Maurer, Andreas Immanuel Graae and T'ai Smith for their insightful comments on drafts of this chapter, and the Social Sciences and Humanities Research Council of Canada (SSHRC) Insight programme for funding support. Special thanks to Agi Haines, Roman Signer, Lisa Parks and Miha Vipotnik for generously sharing their thoughts and work with me.

1 D. Haraway, 'A cyborg manifesto: Science, technology, and socialist-feminisms in the late twentieth century', in *Simians, Cyborgs and Women* (New York: Routledge, 1991), 152.
2 K. Barad, 'Transmaterialities: Trans/matter/realities and queer political imaginings', *GLQ: A Journal of Lesbian and Gay Studies*, 21:2–3 (2015): 387–422, 410.
3 Haraway, 'A cyborg manifesto', 154.
4 This is according to a June 2019 update by the London-based Bureau of Investigative Journalism, which meticulously and comprehensively tracks US drone strikes and other military actions in Pakistan, Afghanistan, Yemen and Somalia. See www.thebureauinvestigates.com/projects/drone-war (accessed 24 January, 2020).
5 Human Rights Service of the United Nations Assistance Mission in Afghanistan and the Office of the United Nations High Commissioner for Human Rights, *2018 Annual Report on the Protection of Civilians in Armed Conflict in Afghanistan* (Kabul, Afghanistan, February 2019), https://unama.unmissions.org/sites/default/files/unama_annual_protection_of_civilians_report_2018_-_23_feb_2019_-_english.pdf (accessed 2 March, 2021).
6 Barad, 'Transmaterialities, 387–422.
7 In addition to Haraway's germinal 'Cyborg manifesto', see her 'Promises of monsters: A regenerative politics for inappropriate/d Others', in L. Grossberg, C. Nelson and P. A. Treichler (eds), *Cultural Studies* (New York: Routledge, 1992), 295–337; B. Creed, *The Monstrous-Feminine: Film, Feminism, Psychoanalysis* (London and New York: Routledge, 1993); and M. Shildrick,

Embodying the Monster: Encounters with the Vulnerable Self (London: Sage Publications, 2002).

8 J.-L. Nancy, *The Inoperative Community*, ed. P. Connor, trans. P. Connor et al. (Minneapolis: University of Minnesota Press, 1991).

9 H. Steyerl and K. Crawford, 'Data streams', *The New Inquiry* (23 January, 2017), https://thenewinquiry.com/data-streams/ (accessed 2 March, 2021).

10 The&Partnership, 'Lexus launches "swarm" for "amazing in motion"', *Little Black Book* (blog), 4 November, 2013, https://lbbonline.com/news/lexus-launches-swarm-for-amazing-in-motion/ (accessed 2 March, 2021).

11 The photo caption points to one of the speck-like drones and reads: 'One of 958 illuminated drones above Folsom, Calif., at 8:31 pm on May 3.' *Time Magazine*, 6 June, 2018.

12 K. Marchese, 'These flying spheres monitor human activity and emotional data to flock nearby preferred people', *designboom* (blog) (30 June, 2018), https://designboom.com/art/zoological-autonomous-flying-spheres-lidar-drones-06-29-2018/ (accessed 2 March, 2021).

13 See www.random-international.com/zoological (accessed 11 March, 2021).

14 See T. Hippler, *Governing from the Skies: A Global History of Aerial Bombing* (London: Verso, 2017) and M. Sherry, *The Rise of American Air Power: The Creation of Armageddon* (New Haven: Yale University Press, 1987).

15 Second World War General Henry Arnold, quoted in Sherry, *The Rise of American Air Power*, 87.

16 J. Packer and J. Reeves, 'Taking people out: Drones, media/weapons, and the coming humanectomy', in L. Parks and C. Kaplan (eds), *Life in the Age of Drone Warfare* (Durham, NC: Duke University Press, 2017), 274.

17 US Office of the Secretary of Defense Strategic Capabilities Office, 'Perdix fact sheet' (1 September, 2017) https://dod.defense.gov/Portals/1/Documents/pubs/Perdix%20Fact%20Sheet.pdf?ver=2017-01-09-101520-643 (accessed 2 March, 2021). See also S. Gallagher, 'DOD successfully tests terrifying swarm of 104 micro-drones', *Ars Technica* (blog), January 12, 2017, https://arstechnica.com/information-technology/2017/01/dod-successfully-tests-terrifying-swarm-of-104-micro-drones/ (accessed 11 March, 2021).

18 'Perdix fact sheet'.

19 Packer and Reeves, 'Taking people out', 275.

20 See A. J. Nocella, I. C. Salter and J. K. C. Bentley (eds), *Animals and War: Confronting the Military-Animal Industrial Complex* (Lanham: Lexington Books, 2014), for a comprehensive collection of essays on the use of nonhuman animals for war; and T. Stubblefield, 'The animal remainder: Excavating non-human life from contemporary drones', in *Drone Art: The Everywhere War as Medium* (Berkeley: University of California Press, 2020), for a thoughtful examination of the contemporary military-industrial complex's zoological impulse.

21 R. Braidotti, *The Posthuman* (Cambridge: Polity Press, 2013), 124–125.

22 L. Wilcox, 'Drones, swarms and becoming-insect: Feminist utopias and posthuman politics', *Feminist Review* 116:1 (July 2017): 29–38.

23 Signer is known especially for staged collisions, such as *Unfall als skupltur* (Accident into Sculpture) of 2008, in which a driverless 3-wheeled Piaggio van loaded with four casks of water sped down a ramp and flipped over, spilling its contents like a waterfall. See S. Dünser, *Roman Signer: 'Installation', Unfall als Skulptur* (Nürnberg: Verlag für moderne Kunst Nürnberg, 2008).
24 A. Kroker and M. Kroker, 'Exits to the posthuman future: Dreaming with drones', in D. Banerji and M. R. Paranjape (eds), *Critical Posthumanism and Planetary Futures* (New Delhi: Springer India, 2017), 75.
25 Wilcox, 'Drones, swarms, and becoming-insect', 34.
26 See B. Cronin, *Bugsplat: The Politics of Collateral Damage in Western Armed Conflicts* (Oxford: Oxford University Press, 2018).
27 J. J. Cohen, *Monster Theory: Reading Culture* (Minneapolis: University of Minnesota Press, 1996), 6.
28 'Agi Haines: Re-designing the human race', *The Front* (blog), https://thefront.tv/read/agi-haines-interview (accessed 1 May, 2019).
29 *The Blob*, directed by I. Yeaworth (Los Angeles: Jack H. Harris Enterprises, 1958), 86 min.
30 See M. K. Booker, *Monsters, Mushroom Clouds, and the Cold War: American Science Fiction and the Roots of Postmodernism, 1946–1964* (Santa Barbara: Praeger, 2001); T. Shaw, *Hollywood's Cold War* (Edinburgh: Edinburgh University Press, 2007); J. Sharlet, *The Family: The Secret Fundamentalism at the Heart of American Power* (New York: Harper, 2008); and S. Sontag, 'The imagination of disaster', in *Against Interpretation and Other Essays* (New York: Farrar, Strauss and Giroux, 1966).
31 *The Blob*, directed by C. Russell (Los Angeles: TriStar Pictures, 1988), 95 min. *The Blob* was also revisited in the sequel *Beware! The Blob*, directed by Larry Hagman (Los Angeles: Jack H. Harris Enterprises, 1972), 91 min.
32 *How Not to be Seen: A Fucking Didactic Educational .MOV File*, directed by H. Steyerl (2013), 14 min.
33 See D. Gregory, '"The rush to the intimate": Counterinsurgency and the cultural turn', *Radical Philosophy*, 150 (July/August 2008), www.radicalphilosophy.com/article/the-rush-to-the-intimate (accessed 23 February, 2021); and N. Gertz, 'Drone operators, cyber warriors, and prosthetic gods', in *The Philosophy of War and Exile* (London: Palgrave Macmillan, 2014), 92–117.
34 *5,000 Feet is the Best*, directed by O. Fast (Copenhagen: Commonwealth Projects, 2011), 30 min.
35 'Ex-drone operator: We see everything', The Today Show, Richard Engel, NBC News, 6 June, 2013. See also B. Bryant, 'Letter from a sensor operator', in Parks and Kaplan (eds), *Life in the Age of Drone Warfare*, 315–323.
36 As Grégoire Chamayou puts it in *A Theory of the Drone* (New York: The New Press, 2015), 'the media picture of empathetic drone operators suffering psychic trauma … has no empirical basis' (108–109), as numerous studies have found that the incidence of PTSD among drone operators is equal to, or even lower than, that found in the general population. For Chamayou, the upshot is that

'this supposed empathy with the victims is, paradoxically, what now makes a public rehabilitation of homicide by drones possible', 108.

37 Chamayou describes the 'victimization' of drone operators as 'that of the crocodile shedding tears, the better to devour its prey', Chamayou, *A Theory of the Drone*, 108.

38 Former sensor operator M. Haas, in E. Pilkington, 'Life as a drone operator: "Ever step on ants and never give it another thought?"' *The Guardian* (19 November, 2015), www.theguardian.com/world/2015/nov/18/life-as-a-drone-pilot-creech-air-force-base-nevada (accessed 2 March, 2021).

39 D. Zucchino and D. S. Cloud, 'US deaths in drone strike due to miscommunication, report says', *Los Angeles Times* (14 October, 2011), www.latimes.com/nation/la-xpm-2011-oct-14-la-fg-pentagon-drone-20111014-story.html (accessed 2 March, 2021).

40 Stubblefield, *Drone Art*, 118.

41 Stubblefield, *Drone Art*, 118.

42 A. Nath, 'Stoners, stones, and drones: Transnational South Asian visuality from above and below', in Parks and Kaplan (eds), *Life in the Age of Drone Warfare*, 248. See also Chamayou, *Theory of the Drone*, 140–149; and D. Gregory, 'From a view to a kill: Drones and late modern war', *Theory, Culture & Society*, 28:7–8 (2011): 188–215.

43 Nath, 'Stoners, stones, and drones', 248.

44 K. F. Chandler, 'A drone manifesto: Re-forming the partial politics of targeted killing', *Catalyst: Feminism, Theory, Technoscience*, 2:1 (2016): 1.

45 C. Holmqvist, 'Undoing war: War ontologies and the materiality of drone warfare', *Millennium*, 41: 3 (2013): 11, emphasis added. See also I. Graham, R. Shaw and M. Akhter, 'The unbearable humanness of drone warfare in FATA, Pakistan', *Antipode*, 44:4 (2012): 1490–1509.

46 Chandler, 'A drone manifesto', 19, emphasis in original.

47 *The Drone*, directed by J. Rubin (2019), 82 min., premiered at the Slamdance Film Festival in January.

48 E. Thacker, *In the Dust of This Planet* (London: Zero Books, 2011).

49 Chandler, 'Drone manifesto', 13.

50 D. Gregory, 'The everywhere war', *The Geographical Journal*, 177:3 (September 2011): 242.

51 L. Suchman, 'Frankenstein's problem', in U. Schultze, M. Aanestad, M. Mahring, C. Osterlung and K. Riemer (eds), *Living with Monsters? Social Implications of Algorithmic Phenomena, Hybrid Agency, and the Performativity of Technology* (Proceedings of the WG 8.2 Working Conference on the Interaction of Information Systems and the Organization, IS&O 2018, San Francisco, CA, 11–12 December, 2018, Cham, Switzerland: Springer, 2018), 17.

52 'Drones with desires: A machine with inbuilt human memories', *We Make Money Not Art* (blog) (23 November, 2015), http://we-make-money-not-art.com/drones-with-desires-a-machine-with-inbuilt-human-memories/ (accessed 2 March, 2021).

53 Cohen, *Monster Theory*, 6.

54 *Spectral Configuration* was exhibited as part of the Vertical Collisions exhibition at Station Gallery in Beirut in 2015. See www.inmediasres-lb.com/vertical-collisions/miha-vipotnik.html (accessed 11 March, 2021).
55 L. Parks in conversation with the author (15 December, 2017). See also www.inmediasres-lb.com/vertical-collisions/lisa-parks.html (accessed 11 March, 2021).
56 L. Parks, *Spectral Configurations* contributor statement, www.inmediasres-lb.com/vertical-collisions/lisa-parks.html (accessed 11 March, 2021).
57 E. Mouhanna, *Spectral Configurations* contributor statement, www.inmediasres-lb.com/vertical-collisions/elie-mouhanna.html (accessed 11 March, 2021).
58 A. Mbembe, 'Necropolitics', *Public Culture*, 15: 1 (2003): 12.
59 Mbembe, 'Necropolitics', 40.
60 See https://notabugsplat.com/about (accessed 8 December, 2019).
61 Stubblefield, *Drone Art*, n. p.
62 Mbembe, 'Necropolitics', 40.
63 L. Parks, 'Vertical mediation and the US drone war in the Horn of Africa', in Parks and Kaplan (eds), *Life in the Age of Drone Warfare*, 145.
64 Mbembe, 'Necropolitics', 21.
65 J. Butler, *Precarious Life: The Powers of Mourning and Violence* (London: Verso, 2004), 91.
66 Stubblefield, *Drone Art*, 33.
67 P. Adey, 'Making the drone strange: The politics, aesthetics and surrealism of levitation', *Geographica Helvetica* 71 (2016): 320.
68 Adey, 'Making the drone strange', 321.
69 Haraway, 'Promises of monsters', 300.
70 Barad, 'Transmaterialities', 410.
71 Suchman, 'Frankenstein's problem', 17.

Bibliography

Adey, P. 'Making the drone strange: The politics, aesthetics and surrealism of Levitation'. *Geographica Helvetica*, 71 (2016): 319–329.

Allinson, J. 'The necropolitics of drones'. *International Political Sociology*, 9 (2015): 113–127.

Barad, K. 'Transmaterialities: Trans/matter/realities and queer political imaginings'. *GLQ: A Journal of Lesbian and Gay Studies*, 21:2–3 (2015): 387–422.

Booker, M. K. *Monsters, Mushroom Clouds, and the Cold War: American Science Fiction and the Roots of Postmodernism, 1946–1964*. Santa Barbara: Praeger, 2001.

Braidotti, R. *The Posthuman*. Cambridge: Polity Press, 2013.

Bryant, B. 'Letter from a sensor operator'. In L. Parks and C. Kaplan (eds), *Life in the Age of Drone Warfare*, 315–323. Durham, NC: Duke University Press, 2017.

Butler, J. *Precarious Life: The Powers of Mourning and Violence*. London: Verso, 2004.

Chamayou, G. *A Theory of the Drone*. New York: The New Press, 2015.
Chandler, K. F. 'A drone manifesto: Re-forming the partial politics of targeted killing'. *Catalyst: Feminism, Theory, Technoscience*, 2:1 (2016): 1–23.
Cohen, J. J. *Monster Theory: Reading Culture*. Minneapolis: University of Minnesota Press, 1996.
Creed, B. *The Monstrous-Feminine: Film, Feminism, Psychoanalysis*. London and New York: Routledge, 1993.
Cronin, B. *Bugsplat: The Politics of Collateral Damage in Western Armed Conflict*. Oxford: Oxford University Press, 2018.
'Drones with desires: A machine with inbuilt human memories'. *We Make Money Not Art* (blog) (23 November, 2015), http://we-make-money-not-art.com/drones-with-desires-a-machine-with-inbuilt-human-memories/ (accessed 2 March, 2021).
Dünser, S. *Roman Signer: 'Installation', Unfall als Skulptur*. Nürnberg: Verlag für moderne Kunst Nürnberg, 2008.
'Ex-drone operator: We see everything', The Today Show, Richard Engel, NBC News, 6 June, 2013.
Fast, O. (dir). *5,000 Feet is the Best*, Copenhagen: Commonwealth Projects, 2011. 30 min.
Fitzpatrick, A. 'Here's how Lady Gaga's Super Bowl drones worked'. *Time Magazine*, 6 February, 2017. http://time.com/4661063/lady-gaga-super-bowl-drones/ (accessed 2 March, 2021).
Gallagher, S. 'DOD successfully tests terrifying swarm of 104 micro-drones'. *Ars Technica* (blob), 12 January, 2017. https://arstechnica.com/information-technology/2017/01/dod-successfully-tests-terrifying-swarm-of-104-micro-drones/ (accessed 11 March, 2021).
Gertz, N. 'Drone operators, cyber warriors, and prosthetic gods'. In *The Philosophy of War and Exile*, 92–117. London: Palgrave Macmillan, 2014.
Gregory, D. '"The rush to the intimate": Counterinsurgency and the cultural turn'. *Radical Philosophy*, 150 (July/August 2008), www.radicalphilosophy.com/article/the-rush-to-the-intimate (accessed 23 February, 2021).
— 'The everywhere war'. *The Geographical Journal*, 177:3 (September 2011): 238–250.
— 'From a view to a kill: Drones and late modern war'. *Theory, Culture & Society*, 28:7–8 (2011): 188–215.
Haines, A. 'Agi Haines: Re-designing the human race'. *The Front* (blog). https://thefront.tv/read/agi-haines-interview (accessed 1 May, 2019).
Haraway, D. 'A cyborg manifesto: Science, technology, and socialist-feminism in the late twentieth century' [1985]. In *Simians, Cyborgs and Women: The Reinvention of Nature*, 149–181. New York: Routledge, 1991.
— 'Promises of monsters: A regenerative politics for inappropriate/d others'. In L. Grossberg, C. Nelson and P. A. Treichler (eds), *Cultural Studies*, 295–337. New York: Routledge, 1992.
Hippler, T. *Governing from the Skies: A Global History of Aerial Bombing* (London: Verso, 2017).
Holmqvist, C. 'Undoing war: War ontologies and the materiality of drone warfare'. *Millennium*, 41:3 (2013): 535–552.
Human Rights Service of the United Nations Assistance Mission in Afghanistan and the Office of the United Nations High Commissioner for Human Rights.

2018 Annual Report on the Protection of Civilians in Armed Conflict in Afghanistan (Kabul, Afghanistan, February 2019). https://unama.unmissions.org/sites/default/files/unama_annual_protection_of_civilians_report_2018_-_23_feb_2019_-_english.pdf (accessed 2 March, 2021).

Ingold, T. *The Life of Lines* (London: Routledge, 2015).

Kroker, A. and M. Kroker. 'Exits to the posthuman future: Dreaming with drones'. In D. Banerji and M. R. Paranjape (eds), *Critical Posthumanism and Planetary Futures*, 75–90. New Delhi: Springer India, 2017.

Lynn, G. *Folds, Bodies, and Blobs: Collected Essays*. Brussels: La lettre volée, 2004.

Marchese, K. 'These flying spheres monitor human activity and emotional data to flock nearby preferred people'. *designboom* (blog), 30 June, 2018. www.designboom.com/art/zoological-autonomous-flying-spheres-lidar-drones-06-29-2018 (accessed 2 March, 2021).

Mbembe, A. 'Necropolitics'. *Public Culture*, 15:1 (2003): 11–40.

Munster, A. *An Aesthesia of Networks: Conjunctive Experience in Art and Technology*. Cambridge, MA: MIT Press, 2013.

Nancy, J. *The Inoperative Community*, edited by P. Connor. Transl. P. Connor, L. Garbus, M. Holland and S. Sawhney. Minneapolis: University of Minnesota Press, 1991.

Nath, A. 'Stoners, stones, and drones: Transnational South Asian visuality from above and below'. In L. Parks and C. Kaplan (eds), *Life in the Age of Drone Warfare*, 241–258. Durham, NC: Duke University Press, 2017.

Nocella, A. J., I. C. Salter and J. K.C. Bentley (eds). *Animals and War: Confronting the Military-Animal Industrial Complex*. Lanham: Lexington Books, 2014.

Packer, J. and J. Reeves. 'Taking people out: Drones, media/weapons, and the coming humanectomy'. In L. Parks and C. Kaplan (eds), *Life in the Age of Drone Warfare*, 261–281. Durham, NC: Duke University Press, 2017.

Parks, L. 'Drones, vertical mediation, and the targeted class'. *Feminist Studies*, 42:1 (2016): 227–235.

— 'Vertical mediation and the US drone war in the Horn of Africa'. In L. Parks and C. Kaplan (eds), *Life in the Age of Drone Warfare*, 134–157. Durham, NC: Duke University Press, 2017.

Pilkington, E. 'Life as a drone operator: "Ever step on ants and never give it another thought?"' *The Guardian*, 19 November, 2015. www.theguardian.com/world/2015/nov/18/life-as-a-drone-pilot-creech-air-force-base-nevada (accessed 2 March, 2021).

Rubin, J. (dir). *The Drone*. 2019. Premiered at the Slamdance Film Festival in January. 82 min.

Sharlet, J. *The Family: The Secret Fundamentalism at the Heart of American Power*. New York: Harper, 2008.

Shaw, T. *Hollywood's Cold War*. Edinburgh: Edinburgh University Press, 2007.

Sherry, M. *The Rise of American Air Power: The Creation of Armageddon*. New Haven: Yale University Press, 1987.

Shildrick, M. *Embodying the Monster: Encounters with the Vulnerable Self*. London: Sage Publications, 2002.

Sontag, S. 'The imagination of disaster'. In *Against Interpretation and Other Essays*. New York: Farrar, Strauss and Giroux, 1966.

Steyerl, Hi. (dir). *How Not to be Seen: A Fucking Didactic Educational .MOV File*, 2013. HD video, 14 min.

Steyerl, H. and K. Crawford. 'Data streams'. *The New Inquiry* (23 January, 2017). https://thenewinquiry.com/data-streams/ (accessed 2 March, 2021).

Suchman, L. 'Frankenstein's problem'. In U. Schultze, M. Aanestad, M. Mahring, C. Osterlung and K. Riemer (eds), *Living with Monsters? Social Implications of Algorithmic Phenomena, Hybrid Agency, and the Performativity of Technology*, 13–18. Proceedings of the WG 8.2 Working Conference on the Interaction of Information Systems and the Organization, IS&O 2018, San Francisco, CA, 11–12 December. Cham, Switzerland: Springer, 2018.

Thacker, E. 'Nekros: Or, the poetics of biopolitics'. In S. J. Lauro (ed.), *Zombie Theory*, 361–380. Minneapolis: University of Minnesota Press, 2017.

The&Partnership. 'Lexus launches "swarm" for "amazing in motion"'. *Little Black Book* (blog), 4 November, 2013. https://lbbonline.com/news/lexus-launches-swarm-for-amazing-in-motion/ (accessed 2 March, 2021).

US Office of the Secretary of Defense Strategic Capabilities Office. 'Perdix fact sheet', 1 September, 2017. https://dod.defense.gov/Portals/1/Documents/pubs/Perdix%20Fact%20Sheet.pdf?ver=2017-01-09-101520-643 (accessed 2 March, 2021).

Wall, T. and T. Monahan. 'Surveillance and violence from afar: The politics of drones and liminal security-scapes'. *Theoretical Criminology*, 15:3 (2011): 239–254.

Wilcox, L. 'Drone warfare and the making of bodies out of place'. *Critical Studies on Security*, 3:1 (2015): 127–131.

— 'Drones, swarms and becoming-insect: Feminist utopias and posthuman politics'. *Feminist Review*, 116:1 (July 2017): 25–45.

— 'Embodying algorithmic war: Gender, race, and the posthuman in drone warfare'. *Security Dialogue*, 48:1 (2017): 11–28.

Zucchino, D. and D. S. Cloud. 'US deaths in drone strike due to miscommunication, report says'. *Los Angeles Times*, 14 October, 2011. www.latimes.com/nation/la-xpm-2011-oct-14-la-fg-pentagon-drone-20111014-story.html (accessed 2 March, 2021).

11

Eyes in the skies: *Repellent Fence* and trans-Indigenous time-space at the US–Mexico border

Caren Kaplan

> Here, things matter not because of how they are represented but because they have qualities, rhythms, forces, relations, and movements.[1]

There were 'eyes in the skies' along a portion of the US–Mexico border in October 2015. While the term 'eyes in the skies' often refers colloquially to drones or remote sensing satellites, in this case the 'eyes' were iconographic, printed on the surface of 26 ten-foot diameter balloons that were anchored to the ground at evenly spaced intervals for two miles between the towns of Douglas, Arizona in the US and Agua Prieta, Sonora in Mexico. *Repellent Fence/Valla Repelente*, the result of a multi-year project directed by the artist collective, Postcommodity, crossed an international border that had become the subject of bellicose political discourse and, accordingly, increasingly militarised. Although the border that runs between the two communities was not marked by any kind of a fence until the late 1920s, by 2012 an 18-foot high fence had been erected. This border wall not only separates and isolates the two towns of Douglas and Agua Prieta, it also threatens to divide the 62 miles of Tohono O'odham reservation land that stretches nearby along the international border (not to mention the 2.8 million acres of ancestral lands that reach considerably further in each direction or the scattered but significant Yaqui native population as well as *mestizaje* in the region).[2] While most art projects that address the violent effects of the militarised border focus on migrant flows from the south, the launch of *Repellent Fence*, which coincided with the celebration of the first Indigenous People's Day, aimed to create a 'visual and conceptual link' that 'remembered' and 're-conceived' the space as 'temporarily disrupted Indigenous space'.[3]

Launching balloons into the ether while tying them firmly to the hardscape of the Sonoran desert epitomises the tensions at work in the time and space of the border zone. Whose eyes in whose skies? Images of singular and tandem eyes are found throughout the ancient and Indigenous world and across epistemological or religious frameworks through the ages.[4] In European modernity, the 'eye in the sky' is most often associated with

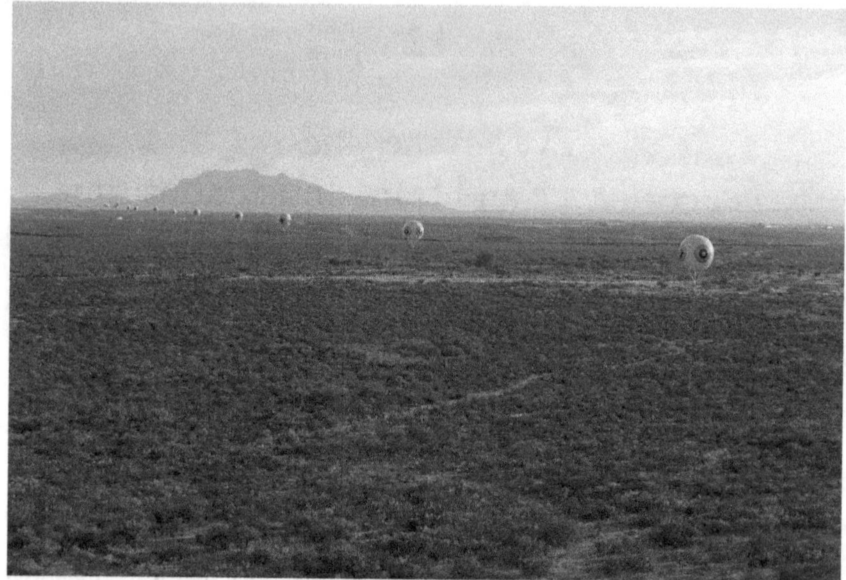

11.1 *Repellent Fence/Valla Repelente*, 2015, land art installation and community engagement, US–Mexico Border, Douglas, Arizona/Agua Prieta, Sonora.

Greek classicism and Christian philosophy and the emergence of a foundational paradox – a universal presence which became expressed as an individualised viewpoint.[5] In the eighteenth century the 'eye in the sky' or 'eye of Providence' became adopted by the new Western European secular republics as a symbol of rational Enlightenment objectivity and democracy.[6] Since the advent of industrialisation at the very least, this 'view' has become mechanised and instrumental to national and commercial security on many scales. Today, as an influential marker of universal knowledge, the global reach of 'eye in the sky' discourse reinforces the foundational aspect of its classical Western origins even as the sweeping powers of 'seeing all' disturb the boundaries of domestic privacy and national security. In a moment when news headlines blare that 'large military-grade drones could soon be flying over your backyard', the launching of 'eyes in the skies' for any purpose can elicit fear, awe, or uncertainty.[7]

Postcommodity's use of large brightly coloured balloons adorned with 'scare-eyes' – menacing eyes surrounded by bold concentric circles – engaged the cultural ambivalence that surrounds aerial views and atmospheric politics[8] in the age of drone warfare, persistent surveillance systems, and No-Fly Zones. Simultaneously regarding and transgressing a militarised international border, *Repellent Fence*'s 26, helium-filled balloons mimicked, even mocked, the instruments of aerial surveillance employed by US Customs and Border Patrol (CBP) which include drones, helicopters, light aircraft, and all manner of remote sensing. Positioned like silent sentinels, the tethered balloons not only occupied airspace, they bridged the relationship between earth and sky as well as time and space. Composed of bright synthetic objects, filled with helium, installed only through extended bureaucratic wrangling between the border authorities of two nation-states, along with considerable community organising – *Repellent Fence* could be understood to be a product of contemporary time. Yet, in conception, design, and location, the installation 'rescaled' and 'repatriated' time and space as 'time-space',[9] as Postcommodity member Cristobal Martinez put it. The balloon launch and installation revived and recalled Indigenous modes of thought and ways of being, bringing Indigenous 'survivance'[10] into view as a generator of atmospheric politics.

Kristen Simmons has argued that the militarised terrain and airspace of the US Southwest borderzone creates a mystified effect: the construction of an open and barren expanse that makes invisible to the point of destruction the 'life and lives' that have always flourished in deserts.[11] As Angelique EagleWoman has pointed out, the US–Mexico border region was 'historically a shared territory of Tribal Nations, including the Apache, Aztec, Hohokam, Hopi, Mayan, Navajo, Pima, Pueblo, Tohono O'odham, and Zuni, among others'.[12] Reflecting the violent displacement of this universe of Indigenous life, the fabricated emptiness of settler colonialism extends into the sky, weaponising the atmosphere and producing dispositions of risk, anxiety, and disappearance. *Repellent Fence* mobilised the well-known trope of the 'eye in the sky' to revive Indigenous presence across relations of space and time, an aerial stewardship as well as a grounded sovereignty. Simmons asks: 'What would it take for individuals to reconceptualise the embeddedness in which we all already are *with* and the potential to be *for* – to stage the grounds for a collective reimagining, a conspiration, an atmospheric otherwise?'[13] The installation of *Repellent Fence* offers a response to that vital question.

The sovereignty of context: trans-Indigenous time-space

> How does one compose meaning, animate space, trouble the cultural policies of placemaking, trouble white sovereignty as manifest in the laws of property, trouble reason with eyes from the sky, the ground, the past present, and future manifest in the Sonoran Desert via some Postcommodity play, noise and 'we' making, *como* un balloon in the sky?[14]

In creating immersive, multi-sensorial, transnational, trans-Indigenous[15] art work that makes us aware of the limits and possibilities of movement through times and spaces, *Repellent Fence* reimagined sovereignty not only as the tension between two nation states – the US and Mexico – but as the enduring force of Indigenous presence. This presence, which includes what Mark Rifkin describes as 'belonging to that shared, unified "now"' as well as to a 'shared "then"' refuses the relegation of native people solely to 'tradition', the 'past', or 'culture'.[16] The romantic myth of 'vanishing natives' and lost ways of life doubly erases native peoples of the Americas from their ancestral land and even, in many ways, from life itself.[17] But as Maria Josefina Saldana-Portillo argues, Indigenous space is 'never simply absorbed' by settler colonialism but 'heterotemporally remains'.[18] Heterotemporality, which Dipesh Chakrabarty defines as 'the plurality that inheres in the "now"', is one way of conceptualising the non-synchronous elements of everyday life.[19] Particularly in the aftermath of violence, the present is hauntingly disturbed by a past that makes its presence known in various forms, fragmenting as well as knitting together disparate perceptions of time and space.[20] The relational plurality of trans-Indigenous time-space co-exists with attempts to eradicate and remove native peoples from historical time and the settler colonial space of the modern nation state. Yet, as Marisol de la Cadena has argued, the 'destruction of these worlds' is inextricably linked to the 'impossibility of such destruction'.[21] Across modernity's differences of race, region, nation, religion, and location, trans-Indigenous time-space revives relations from other times and places – past and future – and brings them into the realm of possible presents.

Many of Postcommodity's works explore this resilient heterotemporality, making and disturbing trans-Indigenous time-spaces. For example, in *Do You Remember When?* (2009), they broke through the floor of the Arizona State University Art Museum to reveal the earth beneath, creating what they called a 'spiritual, cultural and physical portal – a point of transformation between worlds' to activate an 'Indigenous worldview'.[22] Since the university occupies what was once tribal land, the revelation of the earth below the concrete made possible a simultaneous and also discontinuous sense of time and place.[23] Always already present, accessible in uneven, sometimes discontinuous ways, tribal lands exist heterotemporally in material and creative forms in Postcommodity's work. While land plays a major role in arguments for Indigenous sovereignty and reparations, Mishuana Goeman reminds us that land should not be reified on settler colonial terms. Rather, Goeman argues, land can best retain its political vitality for Indigenous social movements by '(re)opening' its meaning beyond confined boundaries or property per se to metaphorical or aesthetic practices.[24] Thus, she writes, 'Indigenous peoples make place by relating both personal and communal experiences and histories to certain locations and landscapes – maintaining these spatial relationships is one of the most important components of identity.'[25] *Repellent Fence* materialises this commitment to reopened and reimagined spaces and places in and through heterotemporality as revitalised protest. As Roberto Bedoya put it in his comments at the launch of *Repellent Fence*:

> On the border and in the indigenous worldview in Southern Arizona, land is not just property to be owned but space that demands stewardship as a 'we' activity, that acknowledges what is sacred in the land via vistas, ceremony, song and care. This worldview is an obligation embedded in the sovereignty of context, a form of governance that the land asserts, that shapes the 'we', that disorders the Great Divide, promoting an aesthetic ordering that lies in the sublime and/or troubling beauty [...] of being with image, song, gesture, pronouns, color, lyric [...] the inhabitants of an aesthetic belonging.[26]

The 'sovereignty of context' is not simply another way of adjudicating claims on bounded territory (although it is capacious enough to include such actions for political justice), just as *Repellent Fence* is not just another example of land art, border art, or site-specific art (although it is also legible to the art world through those terms).[27] Rather, Bedoya and Postcommodity are asking us to take the elements seriously – air and water as well as earth – through the creation of 'aesthetic portals' as a ceremonial practice of trans-Indigeneity. These 'doorways' that 'puncture' moments can transport participants between 'physical and spiritual planes', enabling awareness of 'precolonial history and traditions'.[28] Just as Indigenous peoples live both inside and outside the nation-state, works like *Do You Remember When?* and *Repellent Fence* require us to acknowledge that there are more than European Enlightenment notions of space and time, much more beyond the 'imperial logics of the cartographic and topographic'.[29] The sovereignty of context as Indigenous presence in works like *Repellent Fence* exists alongside and against the governmentality of settler colonialism, opening to what Joanne Barker describes as 'the polity of the Indigenous: the unique governance, territory, and culture of an Indigenous people in a system of (non) human relationships and responsibilities to one another'.[30]

While dedicated to producing and engaging Indigenous spaces, places, and times, Postcommodity has resisted representing a singular tribal identity or authentic perspective.[31] Emphasising connections through a trans-Indigenous deconstruction of the transnational, the collective can be situated within what Shanna Ketchum has termed 'Native American cosmopolitan modernisms'; that is, practices that 'blast open the continuum of history' in settler colonial times and spaces.[32] The diverse and shifting membership of the collective has reflected these complex, trans-Indigenous relational communities and politics.[33] While *Repellent Fence* was created with long-time collaborator Raven Chacon (Navajo), at present the collective is composed of two members: Kade Twist (Cherokee) and Cristobal Martinez (who identifies himself as mestizo, Alcadeno, or Chicano).[34] Resolutely interdisciplinary, the group works with experimental sound as well as visual materials with an emphasis on immersive performance. The group has become known for works that display an 'edgy humor' as well as 'striking imagery' and 'layers of critique', eschewing narrow identity politics for what they term 'complexity'.[35] Speaking of *Repellent Fence*, Martinez has explained that they were not interested in creating 'simple models' but rather in 'mediating the complexity', adding 'we entrench ourselves with the entanglements and in many ways create even more entanglements.'[36]

The entanglements of *Repellent Fence* include the politics and cultures of the US–Mexico border, specifically the tension between purely land- or heritage-based arguments for self-determination and strategies that destabilise identity politics.[37] In an interview in 2015, Postcommodity members pointed out that they 'try to test and bend expectations' in order to 'move beyond stereotypes'.[38] Exploring the transformational relationship between ceremony and the aesthetic, they 'invite people to have a performative and experiential relationship with metaphorical environments'.[39] The emphasis on ceremony in Postcommodity's art practice is made complex not only by the convergence of the members' diverse tribal affiliations but also, as they put it, by the 'intersecting' of 'all sorts of media' which are 'at the heart of the very systems we critique, such as the global economy'.[40] This form of 'reimagined ceremony' shifts 'de-colonial practice' to an 'enquiry-based and discursive process underpinned by Indigenous knowledge systems'.[41]

Although *Repellent Fence* was one of the first projects conceived by the group in their early days, it took almost a decade to bring it into being. The distinctive bright yellow balloons were inspired by a commercial product called the 'Scare Eye Balloon Bird Repellent' or 'Bird Scare Predator Eye' that is sold to frighten birds away from agricultural produce in fields and residential gardens. An inexpensive product, each plastic balloon is about ten inches high and imprinted with concentric circles that comprise a bold and intimidating 'scare-eye'. When Kade Twist's wife, Andrea Hanley, the chief curator at the Wheelright Museum of the American Indian in Santa Fe, New Mexico, brought home several scare-eye balloons to use to keep birds out of a fig tree in their backyard, they both recognised 'Indigenous medicine colors and iconography – the same graphic used by Indigenous peoples from across South America to Canada for thousands of years'.[42] Traditionally, the scare-eye not only symbolises 'enlightenment' and 'awareness'; Twist has noted that the powerful iconography also conveys a sense of 'watching and accountability', an 'early form of surveillance'.[43] Postcommodity's adoption of 'scare-eye' iconography in *Repellent Fence* 'troubled reason with eyes in the skies', as Bedoya put it, opening an aesthetic portal into heterotemporal time-space that both recognised a 'sovereignty of context' and refused settler colonial geographies and national borders.

Geographies of bordering

> A borderland is a vague and undetermined place created by the emotional residue of an unnatural boundary. It is in a constant state of transition.[44]

The installation of 26 enormous tethered balloons across a heavily militarised international border was not an easy task. It required years of meeting with local communities and engaging with state bureaucracies in both countries (as well as developing a strategy to navigate the activities of cartels and non-governmental authorities in the borderlands).[45] In choosing to tether balloons in the borderlands, Postcommodity directly engaged the relational tensions between air and terrain, time and space, as well as national and transnational and even extra-national sovereignties and power-brokers. Moreover, the simultaneous occupation of airspace by aerostats over two nations not only deterritorialised the physical 'line in the sand' that divides the US from Mexico, the decision to launch balloons with symbolic eyes troubled the atmospheric politics of border surveillance and the regulation of airspace. While the border wall offers the most obvious physical manifestation of militarised national security practices and policies, the airspace above the border is tightly controlled. Yet border zone airspace, like the soil beneath it, is often represented as an area vulnerable to unauthorised incursions.[46] Despite the fact that the US–Mexico border is one of the most heavily surveilled and fortified international boundaries in the world, the perception that its airspace puts national security at risk is not uncommon.

In her work on an emergent 'civic view from above', Hagit Keysar has argued that in a contemporary moment structured by state-regulated No-Fly Zones and aerial surveillance there is a 'tension between the sky as a technology of control and as an open space of experimentation and resistance'.[47] This approach resonates with the work of other scholars and activists who insist that airspace must be understood as a dynamic historical construct. Thus, Alison Williams asks us to recognise airspaces as plural, multi-volumetric areas that are produced through 'human interventions'.[48] It is important to consider the ways that objects like balloons, planes, and drones contribute to the production of airspace as part of an assemblage with human beings, apprehended through a broad array of material objects, elements, infrastructures, practices, and operations. Such assemblages operate in a complex environment in the neoliberal era of the global War on Terror as 'security measures' generate new corporate-governmental alliances. For example, Lisa Parks argues that in the US the 'close collaboration of federal agencies' with 'corporations such as DigitalGlobe, GeoEye, and Google' blurs the lines between 'state, military, and civilian activities'.[49] Thus, airspace can be understood always to be already militarised at least to some degree and mobilised for this moment of intensified capitalist penetration of nation state agencies, policies, and practices.

The US–Mexico border is usually conceptualised geographically – that is, as ground rather than airspace. It is a vast and variegated territory, stretching almost 2,000 miles from the Pacific Ocean at one end to the Gulf of Mexico on the other. The cartographic 'line' that comprises the border is relatively new, and for many years did not require any physical barriers. As EagleWoman tells us, 'In North America, prior to European settlements, there was not a fence to be found.'[50] The territorial border as we are familiar with it today was established firmly by the end of the nineteenth century following wars and disputes between the US, Spain, Mexico, and native inhabitants. While the US CBP was established as far back as 1924 and some dedicated fencing began in the 1990s, it is only after the attacks by al-Qaeda on the US on September 11, 2001 and the accompanying rapid escalation of militarised security on a global scale that the US–Mexico border has become more intensely policed and surveilled. In the years between 2000 and 2017, the budget for the CBP rose from $1.1 billion to almost $4 billion and the miles of walls grew from less than 100 to close to 700.[51] Mountain ranges and rivers had been presumed to be 'natural' barriers between zones of population or property but under the Trump administration even this terrain was ear-marked for 'harder' fortification. The greatest unfenced area is the Rio Grande – a river that runs 1,900 miles, from south-central Colorado to the Gulf of Mexico, with almost 1,000 miles comprising the international border. The river rises and ebbs seasonally and its watershed covers many hundreds of thousands of square miles. Attempts to 'wall' such an enormous river, like the efforts to engineer effective walling of mountain ranges, come at a high cost and may never succeed in preventing human migration.

For many years, the CBP believed that if migration flows could be channelled away from the more densely populated metropoles like San Diego, Tijuana, El Paso, and Ciudad Juárez, the hardships and dangers of river, desert, and mountain crossings would prevent large numbers of people from attempting to move between the two countries. Indeed, CBP adopted this approach as a strategy to isolate border crossers in 'rugged' terrain where it would be easier to track and detain them.[52] Rather than deterring migrants, however, this strategy simply placed more people in danger, resulting in a high number of deaths due to exposure to the elements under extreme conditions.[53] The population that has borne the brunt of this policy of geographic manipulation has been constructed as expendable. Undocumented migrants, in particular, forced by shifting strategies and tactics of 'national security' into unsafe environments, have become subjects of the settler colonial logics of a 'globalised racial divide' that reproduces empire through 'population management, spatial differentiation, and bio-politics'.[54] This calculated weaponisation of the desert terrain itself has created a 'crucible of death and disappearance' in the Arizona–Sonora borderlands, leading to fatalities that have numbered over 10,000 since 1994.[55]

Simultaneously with the strategy of geographical 'prevention through deterrence', CBP continued to invest in automation and electronics to control population flows in the border zone. Iván Chaar-López points out that digitisation and other new information technologies were borrowed from systems originally designed for use in the Vietnam War to 'draw an electronic "line in the sand"' and to develop advanced methods to transform migrants into quantifiable 'illegal aliens'.[56] For a time, a 'virtual fence' seemed to offer a cost-effective alternative to concrete and steel constructions. In 2006, the US Department of Homeland Security replaced older surveillance systems with the Secure Border Initiative Network (SBInet), a programme in line with the US military's so-called 'Revolution in Military Affairs' that sought to create a 'system of systems' to integrate communications, mapping, logistics, and other capacities into an 'always on' electronic frontier. SBInet promised panoptic, real-time surveillance and 'full-spectrum dominance', reducing the need for CBP personnel on the ground, and moving border control into the dispositional atmospherics of satellite sensing, predictive algorithmic computing, datamining, biometrics, and, of course, 'unmanned' aerial observation.

As Geoffrey Boyce has detailed, however, the 'remoteness, composition, and inhabitants' of the mountainous terrain selected for the SBInet pilot programme 'served to inhibit, disrupt, and unravel' operations, 'rendering much of the technology ineffective'.[57] Problems abounded: high concentrations of copper underground disrupted the communications network, radar and ground sensors were triggered by animals and even rainstorms, and extreme heat created mirages that affected visuality.[58] The 'system of systems' still required the labour of border agents, engineers, computing and administrative staff, maintenance personnel, and many other 'human factors', not to mention the 'labour' of undocumented migrants without whom the entire system would have no purpose.[59] While SBInet was finally abandoned in 2010 after expenditures of more than $8 billion dollars, the CBP has continued to expand its aerial surveillance capacity, maintaining a fleet of ten unarmed Predator B drones along with helicopters, light aeroplanes, and aerostats. Reflecting national and global trends, in recent years CBP has been testing small drones to augment border air power, a move which will, demonstrably, extend the conceptualisation and enforcement of the border.[60] Coordinating with US Immigration and Customs Enforcement and local law enforcement, CBP's steady incorporation of predictive algorithmic policing and automated sensing draws from the 'pattern-of-life' analysis utilised in US drone warfare, blurring the division between 'border' and 'domestic interior' of the nation, criminalising and targeting migrants at a significant distance from the geographical 'border'.[61] Yet, despite the 'imperial control fantasy'[62] of 'persistent surveillance' that structures the relentless US national investment in electronic modes of border security, systems like SBInet continue to be stymied by the region's terrain and climate along with the ingenuity and courage of migrants.

At the heart of the symbolic and material 'emptying' of the border zone between the US and Mexico lies the history of dispossession and dispersal of native peoples and the engineered alteration of modes of cultivation and animal habitats. Already a zone of transit, the colonial project removed native peoples from their own places and spaces and resettled them in reservations while instituting racialised and classed relations of property and national identity. By installing *Repellent Fence* across the 'hard' border in the midst of an enormous federal push for virtual fencing and an expanded criminalisation of undocumented border crossing, Postcommodity not only recognised the repellent character of the wall itself (in the sense of repelling migration as well as something innately ugly or evil) but bore witness to the continuities and discontinuities of Indigenous life across times and spaces. Acknowledging the importance of self-determination through freedom of movement as well as dwelling, *Repellent Fence* expanded placemaking into the atmosphere. The balloons occupied airspace even as they held fast to the land, creating a sovereignty of context.

Atmospheric politics in the borderlands

> If you ever want to have a conversation with someone on the other side of the aisle, just show up with balloons.[63]

Balloons are mysterious and evocative objects. As one historian of inflatable art has written, 'The ability to defy gravity, and even to fly, is certainly tied to childhood imagination, but it also persists as a powerful trope for adults, allowing them to imagine alternate realities.'[64]

Inevitably linked in the Western imagination to fantasies of escape from all manner of boundaries and weights, balloons are also material objects that could only be produced in specific times and places. Since their introduction in the late eighteenth century in Western Europe, balloons have signified the achievements of the modern sciences of chemistry, meteorology, and physics even as they have gestured to and borrowed from more traditional, even ancient, methods of flight and ceremony. For example, principles of hot air inflation were known to the Chinese long before the Europeans supposedly 'discovered' flight.[65] As cosmopolitan, Western scientific tools to explore the material properties of the atmosphere and weather, modern balloons almost immediately became marshalled for warfare as well as for philosophical and poetic inspiration.[66] Although their use by the military was limited due to logistics, observation balloons offered new powers of surveillance and strategic advantage, inaugurating an age of aerial reconnaissance. As more people flew in aerostats or read about the experience of flight, ideas about embodiment and sensibility shifted. Derek McCormack has observed that balloons 'hold out the promise of immersion' even as they are 'haunted by something in excess of immediacy'.[67] Balloons produce as well as move through atmospheres, opening elemental spaces to new forms of perception. Difficult to control, floating serenely away from their launch site or fighting against their tether as the wind attempts to move them, balloons inspire both delight and unease.

Due to these inherent properties, conceptual artists, especially in the late 1960s, explored the relationship between gaseous bodies, atmospheres, and materiality by working with balloons. Linked to the protest aesthetics of the era, balloons offered artist collectives such as Utopie in France, Archigram in Britain, Ant Farm in the United States, and UFO in Italy the ability to stage an event quickly and to utilise the structural qualities of inflatables to reject 'architectural rigidity and conformity'.[68] Continuing in a utopian vein, recently the artist Tomas Saraceno has worked with inflatable spheres and solar power to propose replacing the toxic Anthropocene with a 'future *solar-cene*'.[69] For *Repellent Fence*, Postcommodity expanded the scale and complexity of the small, commercial scare-eye balloons by working with the tension in conceptual art between mystique and critique as well as the possibilities of Indigenous ceremonial immersion. The inflation, launching, tethering, and observation of large balloons occupying airspace in a fraught border zone challenged the usual modes of making or receiving 'art'. As Postcommodity members have commented, in their work you are not just looking *at* something, 'you become the thing'. 'You don't just represent/ embody it, you become it'.[70]

Aerostatic flight generates a powerful 'allure', described by Derek McCormack as an 'aesthetics of everyday sublimity'.[71] Central to these compelling qualities of aerostation, McCormack argues, is the way that balloons produce an anticipation of movement: 'They disclose variable conjunctions of affects and forces, whose outcomes are never predetermined, yet whose affects are felt, even in anticipation, as movement registering, and resonating, across, within and between the sensing spaces of bodies: bodies ascending, descending, falling to the ground.'[72] Nothing prevents a balloon from moving in the air, a propensity we experience as 'aerostatic spacing', a mode of 'becoming and being mobile'.[73] *Repellent Fence* enhanced the anticipation of movement by tethering the aerostats, literally tying them down. If the so-called 'free balloon' epitomises buoyancy and lightness and may be best characterised by its propensity to drift, the tethered balloon must always battle the elements to some degree as the winds that carry the free balloon far and wide encounter the material resistance of the tethered balloon's cable and anchor. The coordinated, intensive labour required to tether the large aerostats of *Repellent Fence* to the Sonoran desert contributed to the 'aesthetics of everyday sublimity' generated by the work: filling the balloons with enough helium, moving them by truck to their precisely designated sites, coping with weights that proved to be insufficient in the face of wind forces greater than expected, observing the spectacular launch from both sides of the border, and so on.[74] Thus, the tension of anticipation in this work included the uncanny relational qualities of tethered suspension, here manifested not only transnationally across a walled border but trans-Indigenously as productive of time-space.

Suspension, as Timothy Choy and Jerry Zee have written, moves us to consider 'what it is, in changed times, to be in this air, held and distributed differentially'.[75] Moving beyond generalities, Kristen Simmons has argued that the settler colonial project places 'Indigenous nations and bodies in suspension', positioning them as 'ghostly traces that must be pushed aside'.[76] The atmospherics of settler colonialism 'suffuses all places', she continues, and 'keeps in play the contradictions and ambiguities built into the colonial project'.[77] The suspended aerostats of *Repellent Fence* were restrained from representing utopian, airborne 'freedom'. Instead, they embodied complexities as well as wonders, generating 'multiple openings and entryways' into presence.[78] As Kade Twist put it, 'becoming atmospheric' made possible a reimagining of 'metaphor, expectation, or history' in spatial as well as temporal terms.[79]

An 'atmospheric otherwise'

> Those in suspension arc toward one another – becoming-open in an atmosphere of violence.[80]

Repellent Fence eschewed the purely sublime allure of aerostatic spacing in order to 'stay with the trouble', as Donna Haraway puts it; to tether participants to the complicated politics of the border as well as to open aesthetic portals to the multiform modes of trans-Indigenous contextual sovereignty across time-space.[81] As Andrea Miller has argued, *Repellent Fence* prompts us to consider how the atmospheric itself operates as a 'mode of colonial weaponry', 'fragmenting the air' through practices that range across 'commodification, securitization, and scientific knowledge production' to ceremony.[82] This 'cracking open' of the atmospheric refuses the purely sublime or utopian ahistoricism of most of the contemporary conceptual art that deploys aerostats and reconnects to the insurgent atmospheric politics of some earlier aerostatic projects.[83] *Repellent Fence* troubled the representation of Indigeneity within the temporality and spatial logics of the militarised border, recognising inevitable attachments to the powers of surveillance without acceding to the strict confines of settler colonial temporality.

Repellent Fence sought to make palpable the 'complex Indigeneity' of people from the entire region, beyond, before, after, and during the historical events of bordering. Postcommodity has described the US–Mexico border as a 'very long filter of bodies and goods – a mediator of imperialism, violence, market systems, and violence capitalism'.[84] In the unspooling of such violent and unequal histories in such a site, Postcommodity reconceived borderland airspace as ambiguously repellent as well as repelling, re-animating trans-Indigenous presence as ambiently atmospheric as well as territorially grounded. If the sublimity of aerostation caused cheering on both sides of the border as the balloons were launched, bringing into being a sense of belonging and emergent community, the vigilant and repelling eyes in the sky warned that 'everything is weaponised in our world'.[85] Postcommodity has asserted that their goal is to try to 'disarm metaphorical structure and the economics behind it'.[86] Yet the scare-eyes watch attentively, on alert, demanding accountability, protecting, warding off, and even welcoming, recognising, making identities and communities. As Emily Eliza Scott has noted, *Repellent Fence*'s 'potentially penetrating, if elusive' sentinels can be read as a 'call to hold space for the irreducible and incommensurate even as it decenters us at the same time'.[87]

For four days in 2015, 26 eyes in the skies produced an aesthetic portal through ceremonial participation. Ceremony, as Louise Erdrich writes, 'usually involves a transformation'.[88] Cristobal Martinez used just this term to describe the time-space of *Repellent Fence*:

> One way that I like to talk about the work is to say that those four days are like four days of ceremony. In order to prepare for four days of ceremony, it took eight years of bi-national diplomacy and dialogue. The purpose wasn't to put something in the land that would be permanent, the way the border wall is. What happens after ceremony is that there is a transformation process, and the balloons are a tool for enacting that transformation. After the ceremony the tool goes away, and things have changed.[89]

This 'collective reimagining' produced an 'atmospheric otherwise' that resonates as public memory. Indeed, following the installation, Twist commented that the 'afterlife of the piece is memory'.[90] Always alluring, vigilant, and generative, Postcommodity's eyes in the sky brought into connection past, future, and present struggles for Indigenous self-determination and open borders.

Notes

I have enjoyed discussing many of the ideas in this paper with Andrea Miller. I thank her for sharing her own work and making suggestions for further reading. I would also like to acknowledge that I live and work on the traditional, unceded land of the P'atwin (Southern Wintun) people, and to honour the Indigenous people connected to this place.

1 K. Stewart, 'Atmospheric attunements', *Environment and Planning D: Society and Space*, 29 (2011), 445.
2 The international border runs through the lands belonging to 26 federally recognised Native American nations in the US and eight Indigenous peoples in Mexico. See V. Felbab-Brown, 'The wall: The real costs of a barrier between the United States and Mexico', August 2017, Brookings Institute. www.brookings.edu/essay/the-wall-the-real-costs-of-a-barrier-between-the-united-states-and-mexico/ (accessed 10 March, 2021). See also O. Leon, 'The Tohono O'Odham fight for sacred lands' (20 December, 2019), *The Real News Network*. https://therealnews.com/stories/the-tohono-oodham-nations-fight-for-sacred-lands (accessed 10 March, 2021).
3 M. Irwin 'Suturing the borderlands: Postcommodity and Indigenous presence on the U.S.–Mexico border', *Invisible Culture: An Electronic Journal for Visual Culture* (2017). https://ivc.lib.rochester.edu/suturing-the-borderlands-postcommodity-and-indigenous-presence-on-the-u-s-mexico-border/ (accessed 11 March, 2021).
4 A. M. Potts, *The World's Eye* (Lexington: University Press of Kentucky, 1982).
5 D. Cosgrove, *Apollo's Eye: A Cartographic Genealogy of the Earth in the Western Imagination* (Baltimore: Johns Hopkins University Press, 2001), xi.
6 A. Schmidt-Burkhardt, 'The all-seer: God's eye as proto-surveillance', in T. Y. Levin, U. Frohne, and P. Weibel (eds), *CTRL [SPACE]: Rhetorics of Surveillance from Bentham to Big Brother* (Cambridge, MA: MIT Press, 2002), 22.
7 C. Bernd. 'Large military-grade drones could soon be flying over your backyard', *Truthout* (16 January, 2020). https://truthout.org/articles/large-military-grade-drones-could-soon-be-flying-over-your-backyard/ (accessed 10 March, 2021).
8 See C. Kaplan and A. Miller, 'Drones as "atmospheric policing": From US border enforcement to the LAPD', *Public Culture*, 31:3 (2019): 419–445, and

A. Feigenbaum and A. Kanngieser, 'For a politics of atmospheric governance', *Dialogues in Human Geography*, 5:1 (2015): 80–84.

9 'Postcommodity artist talk + op-ed launch' (11 March, 2017), Walker Art Center, Minneapolis, https://walkerart.org/magazine/artist-talk-op-ed-launch-postcommodity-2 (accessed 10 March, 2021).

10 The term 'survivance' marks the dynamic possibilities of an 'active sense of presence, the continuance of native stories, not a mere reaction, or a survivable name'. G. Vizenor, *Manifest Manners: Narratives on Postindian Survivance* (Lincoln, NE: Nebraska University Press, 1999), vii.

11 K. Simmons, 'Expanse', *Journal for the Anthropology of North America*, 22:2 (2019): 104.

12 A. EagleWoman, 'Fencing off the eagle and the condor, border politics, and Indigenous peoples', *Natural Resources & Environment*, 23:2 (2008): 33.

13 K. Simmons, 'Settler atmospherics', *Cultural Anthropology* 189:32 (2017). https://culanth.org/fieldsights/settler-atmospherics (accessed 10 March, 2021), emphasis in original.

14 R. Bedoya, 'Postcommodity', n.d., *A Blade of Grass*. www.abladeofgrass.org/fertile-ground/the-great-divide-and-the-pronoun-we-2/ (accessed 10 March, 2021).

15 C. Allen, *Trans-Indigenous: Methodologies for Global Native Literary Studies* (Minneapolis: University of Minnesota Press, 2012).

16 M. Rifkin, *Beyond Settler Time: Temporal Sovereignty and Indigenous Self-Determination* (Durham, NC: Duke University Press, 2017), 1.

17 See B. Lindsay, *Murder State: California's Native American Genocide, 1846–1873* (Lincoln, NE: University of Nebraska Press, 2015); B. Madley, *An American Genocide: The United States and the California Indian Catastrophe, 1846–1873* (New Haven: Yale University Press, 2016), and P. Wolfe, 'Settler colonialism and the elimination of the native', *Journal of Genocide Research*, 8:4 (2006): 387–409. When considering the history of murder, displacement, and discrimination against native peoples it is important to keep their own accounts of resistance and resilience in mind; see, for example, G. Vizenor, *Manifest Manners*.

18 M. J. Saldaña-Portillo, *Indian Given: Racial Geographies Across Mexico and the United States* (Durham, NC: Duke University Press, 2016), 67.

19 D. Chakrabarty, *Provincialising Europe: Postcolonial Thought and Historical Difference* (Princeton: Princeton University Press, 2000), 243.

20 See my discussion of wartime aftermaths in C. Kaplan, *Aerial Aftermaths: Wartime from Above* (Durham, NC: Duke University Press, 2018). See also M. Favret, *War at a Distance: Romanticism and the Making of Modern Wartime* (Princeton: Princeton University Press).

21 M. de la Cadena, 'Runa: Human but *not only*', *Hau: Journal of Ethnographic Theory*, 4:2 (2014): 253–259.

22 Postcommodity. http://postcommodity.com/DoYouRememberWhen.html.

23 The city of Phoenix, Arizona lists the ancient Hohokam peoples among the earliest inhabitants of the land. Twenty-one Native American tribes are represented

in contemporary Arizona, 'more than in any other state', including: Ak-Chin Indian Community (Pima and Papago), Cocopah Tribe, Colorado River Indian Tribes, Fort McDowell Yavapai Nation, Fort Mojave Indian Tribe, Fort Yuma-Quechan Tribe, Gila River Indian Community, Havasupai Tribe, Hopi Tribe, Hualapai Tribe, Kaibab Paiute Tribe, Navajo Nation, Pascau Yaqui Tribe, Salt River Pima-Maricopa Indian Community, San carlos Apache Tribe, San Juan Southern Paiute, Tohono O'odham Nation, Tonto Apache Tribe, White Mountain Apache Tribe, Yavapai-Apache Nation, and Yavapai-Prescott Indian Tribe, www.native-languages.org/arizona.htm (accessed 10 March, 2021).

24 M. Goeman, 'From place to territories and back again: Centering storied land in a discussion of Indigenous nation-building', *International Journal of Critical Indigenous Studies*, 1:1 (2008): 23.

25 Goeman, 'From place to territories and back again', 24.

26 Bedoya, 'Postcommodity', *A Blade of Grass*.

27 Sovereignty is a vexed but necessary term in Indigenous peoples' resistance to dispossession and genocide. As Jolene Rickard has argued: 'I was raised to understand my own subjectivity as a citizen of the Tuscarora 'Nation', which is part of the Six Nations or Haudenosaunee. The concept of sovereignty has become a unifying political strategy among the Haudenosaunee that has been instrumental in our ongoing struggles to maintain our communities, land, and traditions. We simultaneously appropriated the European word *sovereignty* and rejected a US legal interpretation of it while creating a uniquely Haudenosaunee understanding'. J. Rickard, 'Visualizing sovereignty in the time of biometric sensors', *The South Atlantic Quarterly*, 110:2 (2011): 467. See also Audra Simpson's notion of 'nested sovereignties', in A. Simpson, *Mohawk Interruptus: Political Life across the Borders of Settler States* (Durham, NC: Duke University Press, 2014), 11.

28 P. Schmelzer, 'Aesthetic portals: A postcommodity primer', *Sightlines* (9 March, 2017). https://walkerart.org/magazine/aesthetic-portals-a-postcommodity-primer (accessed 10 March, 2021).

29 Irwin 'Suturing the borderlands'.

30 J. Barker, *Critically Sovereign: Indigenous Gender, Sexuality, and Feminist Studies* (Durham, NC: Duke University Press, 2017), 7.

31 L. R. Lippard, 'Postmodern ambush', *Afterall: A Journal of Art, Context, and Enquiry*, 39 (2015): 17.

32 S. Ketchum, 'Native American cosmopolitan modernism(s): A re-articulation of presence through time and space', *Third Text*, 12:4 (2005): 357. See also M. Watson, '"Centring the Indigenous": Postcommodity's trans-Indigenous relational Art', *Third Text*, 29:3 (2015): 141.

33 C. Migwans, 'About place: An interview with Postcommodity', *Miamirail* (9 December, 2016). https://miamirail.org/winter-2016/about-place-an-interview-with-postcommodity/ (accessed 10 March, 2021). Raven Chacon has explained that the name of the group puns on the practice of going to the tribal office or 'post', as it is referred to in reservation communities, where commodities like 'butter, powdered milk, cheese, baloney, and rice' are available in generically

packaged form. Cristobal Martinez adds that treaties with the US government resulted in the provision of inadequate and unhealthy commodities. Kade Twist points out that their aim is 'to move beyond the commodity; beyond those relationships initiated by a paternalistic entity'.

34 In addition to Chacon (2009–2018), founding members included Steven Yazzie (2007–2010) and Nathan Young (2007–2015). http://postcommodity.com/About.html (accessed 10 March, 2021).

35 Lippard, 'Postmodern ambush', 25.

36 'Postcommodity artist talk + op-ed'.

37 J. Rickard, 'Sovereignty: A line in the Sand', *Aperture*, 139 (1995): 51.

38 B. Kelley Jr., 'Reimagining ceremonies: A conversation with Postcommodity', *Afterall: A Journal of Art, Context, and Enquiry*, 39 (2015): 30.

39 Kelley Jr., 'Reimagining ceremonies', 29.

40 Kelley Jr., 'Reimagining ceremonies', 28–29.

41 Kelley Jr., 'Reimagining ceremonies', 28–29.

42 'Postcommodity artist talk + op-ed launch'.

43 M. Trecka, 'The implication of a fence: Part one – an early form of surveillance', *Beacon Broadside* (14 June, 2016), www.beaconbroadside.com/broadside/2016/06/the-implication-of-a-fence-part-one-an-early-form-of-surveillance.html (accessed 10 March, 2021).

44 Gloria E. Anzaldúa, *Borderlands/La Frontera: The New Mestiza* (San Francisco, CA: Aunt Lute Books, 1999).

45 'Postcommodity artist talk + op-ed launch'.

46 J. Pappalardo, 'Securing the U.S.–Mexico border – at altitude', *Dallas Observer* (29 July, 2016), www.dallasobserver.com/news/securing-the-us-mexico-border-at-altitude-8538002 (accessed 10 March, 2021).

47 H. Keysar, 'Experimental aerial testimonies from zones of conflict and colonization', *re;publica* (8 May, 2019), https://19.re-publica.com/en/session/experimental-aerial-testimonies-zones-conflict-colonization (accessed 10 March, 2021).

48 A. J. Williams, 'Reconceptualising spaces of the air: Performing the multiple spatialities of UK military airspaces', *Transactions of the Institute of British Geographers*, 36 (2011): 254.

49 L. Parks, *Rethinking Media Coverage: Vertical Mediation and the War on Terror* (London: Routledge, 2018), 102–103.

50 EagleWoman, 'Fencing off the eagle and the condor', 33.

51 C. Penichet-Paul, 'Border security along the southwest border: Fact sheet', National Immigration Forum (11 March, 2019), https://immigrationforum.org/article/border-security-along-the-southwest-border-fact-sheet/ (accessed 10 March, 2021).

52 G. A. Boyce, 'The rugged border: Surveillance, policing, and the dynamic materiality of the US/Mexico frontier', *Environment and Planning D: Society and Space*, 34:2 (2016): 248.

53 The Missing Migrants website records 2,256 deaths of men, women, and children between 2014 and 2019 (over 300 each year, with some years reaching over 400). The numbers are widely acknowledged to reflect an undercount since

many fatalities and serious injuries are not reported to any agency. https://missingmigrants.iom.int/region/americas?region=1422 (accessed 10 March, 2021).

54 T. Vukov and M. Sheller, 'Border work: Surveillant assemblages, virtual fences, and tactical counter-media', *Social Semiotics*, 23:2 (2013): 230.

55 G. Boyce, S. N. Chambers, and S. Launius, 'Bodily inertia and the weaponization of the sonoran desert in US boundary enforcement: A GIS modeling of migration routes through Arizona's Altar Valley', *Journal on Migration and Human Security*, 7:1 (2019): 33.

56 I. Chaar-López, 'Sensing intruders: Race and the automation of border control', *American Quarterly*, 71:2 (2019): 497–498. See also R. C. St. John, *Line in the Sand: A History of the Western U.S.–Mexico Border* (Princeton: Princeton University Press, 2011).

57 Boyce, 'The rugged border', 251.

58 Boyce, 'The rugged border'.

59 Vukov and Sheller 'Border work', 234–235.

60 S. Shankland, 'Trump's border wall could be a virtual barrier patrolled by drones too', *C/Net* (15 February, 2019), www.cnet.com/news/trumps-border-wall-could-be-a-virtual-barrier-patrolled-by-drones-too/ (accessed 10 March, 2021).

61 See Kaplan and Miller, 'Drones as "atmospheric policing"', 427–428.; Vukov and Sheller 'Border work', 227, 229, and A. Miller, 'Atmospheric insurgencies and "aesthetic portals"', in Postcommodity's *Repellent Fence*', conference paper, American Studies Association, Chicago (November 2017).

62 Chaar-López, 'Sensing intruders', 512.

63 Postcommodity.

64 A. Blauvelt, 'Inflated realities', *Perspecta*, 42 (2010): 56.

65 T. D. Crouch, *The Eagle Aloft: Two Centuries of the Balloon in America* (Washington: Smithsonian Institution Press, 1983), 18.

66 C. Kaplan, 'The balloon prospect: Aerostatic observation and the emergence of militarised aeromobility', in Adey, Whitehead, and Williams (eds), *From Above*, 19–40, and Kaplan, *Aerial Aftermaths*, 86–103.

67 D. P. McCormack, *Atmospheric Things: On the Allure of Elemental Envelopment* (Durham, NC: Duke University Press, 2018), 8.

68 Blauvelt, 'Inflated realities', 57.

69 T. Saraceno, S. Engelmann, and B. Szerszynski, 'Becoming aerosolar: From solar sculptures to cloud cities', in H. Davis and E. Turpin (eds), *Art in the Anthropocene: Encounters Among Aesthetics, Politics, Environments and Epistemologies* (London: Open Humanities Press, 2015), 59.

70 'Postcommodity artist talk + op-ed launch'.

71 McCormack, *Atmospheric Things*, 76–77.

72 D. P. McCormack, 'Aerostatic spacing: On things becoming lighter than air', *Transactions of the Institute of British Geographers*, 34 (2009): 36.

73 McCormack, 'Aerostatic spacing', 26.

74 Postcommodity has posted several videos that chronicle the launch and installation of the work: https://youtu.be/SZBNqwNMkQE; https://youtu.be/

KqgrTH7xk-Q. See also *Through the Repellent Fence: A land art film* (2017), directed by Sam Wainwright Douglas. www.throughtherepellentfence.com/ (all accessed 10 March, 2021).

75 T. Choy and J. Zee, 'Condition – Suspension', *Cultural Anthropology*, 30:2 (2015): 211.

76 Simmons, 'Settler atmospherics'.

77 Simmons, 'Settler atmospherics'.

78 Simmons 'Settler atmospherics'.

79 Kelley, 'Reimaging ceremony', 30.

80 Simmons, 'Settler atmospherics'.

81 D. J. Haraway, *Staying with the Trouble: Making Kin in the Chthulucene* (Durham, NC: Duke University Press, 2016).

82 Miller, 'Atmospheric insurgencies', 5.

83 Miller, 'Atmospheric insurgencies', 8.

84 Postcommodity, http://postcommodity.com/AVeryLongLine.html (accessed 10 March, 2021).

85 'Postcommodity artist talk + op-ed'.

86 'Postcommodity artist talk + op-ed'.

87 E. E. Scott, 'Decentering land art from the borderlands: A review of *Through the Repellent Fence*', *Art Journal OPEN* (27 March, 2018), https://artjournal.collegeart.org/?p=9819 (accessed 10 March, 2021).

88 L. Erdrich, 'Sonic spirituality: Louise Erdrich on Postcommodity's ceremonial transformation of LRAD', *Sightlines* (18 April, 2017), https://walkerart.org/magazine/lrad-louise-erdrich-postcommodity-at-documenta-14-nodapl (accessed 10 March, 2021).

89 Migwans, 'About place'.

90 Migwans, 'About place'.

Bibliography

Allen, C. *Trans-Indigenous: Methodologies for Global Native Literary Studies*. Minneapolis: University of Minnesota Press, 2012.

Barker, J. *Critically Sovereign: Indigenous Gender, Sexuality, and Feminist Studies*. Durham, NC: Duke University Press, 2017.

Bedoya, R. 'Postcommodity', n.d., *A Blade of Grass*. www.abladeofgrass.org/fertile-ground/the-great-divide-and-the-pronoun-we-2/ (accessed 10 March, 2021).

Bernd, C. 'Large military-grade drones could soon be flying over your backyard', *Truthout*, 16 January, 2020. https://truthout.org/articles/large-military-grade-drones-could-soon-be-flying-over-your-backyard/ (accessed 10 March, 2021).

Blauvelt, A. 'Inflated realities'. *Perspecta*, 42 (2010): 55–58.

Boyce, G. 'The rugged border: Surveillance, policing, and the dynamic materiality of the US/Mexico Frontier'. *Environment and Planning D: Society and Space*, 34:2 (2016): 245–262.

Boyce, G., S. N. Chambers and S. Launius. 'Bodily inertia and the weaponization of the Sonoran Desert in US boundary enforcement: A GIS modeling of migration routes through Arizona's Altar Valley'. *Journal on Migration and Human Security*, 7:1 (2019): 25–35.

Chaar-López, I. 'Sensing intruders: Race and the automation of border control'. *American Quarterly*, 71:2 (2019): 495–518.

Choy, T. and J. Zee. 'Condition – suspension'. *Cultural Anthropology*, 30:2 (2015): 210–223.

Cosgrove, D. *Apollo's Eye: A Cartographic Genealogy of the Earth in the Western Imagination*. Baltimore: Johns Hopkins University Press, 2001.

Crouch, T. D. *The Eagle Aloft: Two Centuries of the Balloon in America*. Washingto: Smithsonian Institution Press, 1983.

EagleWoman, A. 'Fencing off the eagle and the condor, border politics, and Indigenous peoples', *Natural Resources & Environment*, 23:2 (2008): 33–35.

Erdrich, E. 'Sonic spirituality: Louise Erdrich on Postcommodity's ceremonial transformation of LRAD'. *Sightlines*, 18 April, 2017. https://walkerart.org/magazine/lrad-louise-erdrich-postcommodity-at-documenta-14-nodapl (accessed 10 March, 2021).

Feigenbaum, A. and A. Kanngieser. 'For a politics of atmospheric governance'. *Dialogues in Human Geography*, 5:1 (2015): 80–84.

Felbab-Brown, V. 'The wall: The real costs of a barrier between the United States and Mexico'. Brookings Institute (August 2017). www.brookings.edu/essay/the-wall-the-real-costs-of-a-barrier-between-the-united-states-and-mexico/ (accessed 10 March, 2021).

Goeman, M. 'From place to territories and back again: Centering storied land in a discussion of Indigenous nation-building'. *International Journal of Critical Indigenous Studies*, 1:1 (2008): 23–34.

Haraway, D. J. *Staying with the Trouble: Making Kin in the Chthulucene*. Durham, NC: Duke University Press, 2016.

Irwin, M. 'Suturing the borderlands: Postcommodity and Indigenous presence on the U.S.–Mexico Border'. *Invisible Culture: An Electronic Journal for Visual Culture* (2017). https://ivc.lib.rochester.edu/suturing-the-borderlands-postcommodity-and-indigenous-presence-on-the-u-s-mexico-border/ (accessed 11 March, 2021).

Kaplan, C. 'The balloon prospect: Aerostatic observation and the emergence of militarised aeromobility'. In P. Adey, M. Whitehead and A. J. Williams (eds), *From Above: War, Violence, and Verticality*, 19–40. London: Hurst, 2013.

— *Aerial Aftermaths: Wartime from Above*. Durham, NC: Duke University Press, 2018Kaplan, C. and A. Miller. 'Drones as "atmospheric policing": From US Border enforcement to the LAPD'. *Public Culture*, 31:3 (2019): 419–445.

Kelley, B. Jr. 'Reimagining ceremonies: A conversation with Postcommodity'. *Afterall: A Journal of Art, Context, and Enquiry*, 39 (2015): 27–35.

Ketchum, S. 'Native American cosmopolitan modernism(s): A re-articulation of presence through time and space'. *Third Text*, 12:4 (2005): 357–364.

Keysar, H. 'Experimental aerial testimonies from zones of conflict and colonization'. *re;publica*, 8 May, 2019. https://19.re-publica.com/en/session/experimental-aerial-testimonies-zones-conflict-colonization (accessed 10 March, 2021).

Leon, O. 'The Tohono O'Odham fight for sacred lands'. *The Real News Network*, 20 December, 2019. https://therealnews.com/stories/the-tohono-oodham-nations-fight-for-sacred-lands (accessed 10 March, 2021).

Lippard, L. R. 'Postmodern ambush'. *Afterall: A Journal of Art, Context, and Enquiry*, 39 (2015): 17–25.
McCormack, D. P. *Atmospheric Things: On the Allure of Elemental Envelopment*. Durham, NC: Duke University Press, 2018.
— Aerostatic spacing: On things becoming lighter than air'. *Transactions of the Institute of British Geographers*, 34 (2009): 25–41.
Migwans, C. 'About place: An interview with postcommodity'. *Miamirail*, 9 December, 2016. https://miamirail.org/winter-2016/about-place-an-interview-with-postcommodity/ (accessed 10 March, 2021).
Miller, A. 'Atmospheric insurgencies and "aesthetic portals"'. In Postcommodity's *Repellent Fence*', conference paper, American Studies Association, Chicago, November 2017.
Missing Migrants. https://missingmigrants.iom.int/region/americas?region=1422 (accessed 10 March, 2021).
Pappalardo, J. 'Securing the U.S.–Mexico Border at altitude'. *Dallas Observer*, 29 July, 2016. www.dallasobserver.com/news/securing-the-us-mexico-border-at-altitude-8538002 (accessed 10 March, 2021).
Parks, L. *Rethinking Media Coverage: Vertical Mediation and the War on Terror*. London: Routledge, 2018.
Penichet-Paul, C. 'Border security along the Southwest Border: Fact sheet'. National Immigration Forum, 11 March, 2019. https://immigrationforum.org/article/border-security-along-the-southwest-border-fact-sheet/ (accessed 10 March, 2021).
Postcommmodity. 'Postcommodity artist talk + op-ed launch'. Walker Art Center, 11 March, 2019. https://walkerart.org/magazine/artist-talk-op-ed-launch-post-commodity-2 (accessed 10 March, 2021).
— http://postcommodity.com/DoYouRememberWhen.html (accessed 10 March, 2021).
— http://postcommodity.com/AVeryLongLine.html (accessed 10 March, 2021).
Potts, A. M. *The World's Eye*. Lexington: University Press of Kentucky, 1982.
Rickard, J. 'Visualizing sovereignty in the time of biometric sensors'. *The South Atlantic Quarterly*, 110:2 (2011): 465–482.
— 'Sovereignty: A line in the sand'. *Aperture*, 139 (1995): 50–59.
Rifkin, M. *Beyond Settler Time: Temporal Sovereignty and Indigenous Self-Determination*. Durham, NC: Duke University Press, 2017.
Saldaña-Portillo, M. J. *Indian Given: Racial Geographies Across Mexico and the United States*. Durham, NC: Duke University Press, 2016.
Saraceno, T., S. Engelmann, and B. Szerszynski. 'Becoming aerosolar: From solar sculptures to cloud cities'. In H. Davis and E. Turpin (eds), *Art in the Anthropocene: Encounters Among Aesthetics, Politics, Environments and Epistemologies*, 57–62. London: Open Humanities Press, 2015.
Schmelzer, P. 'Aesthetic portals: A Postcommodity primer'. Sightlines, 9 March, 2017. https://walkerart.org/magazine/aesthetic-portals-a-postcommodity-primer (accessed 10 March, 2021).
Schmidt-Burkhardt, A. 'The all-seer: God's eye as proto-surveillance'. In T. Y. Levin, U. Frohne, and P. Weibel (eds), *CTRL [SPACE]: Rhetorics of Surveillance from Bentham to Big Brother*, 16–31. Cambridge, MA: MIT Press, 2002.
Scott, E. E. 'Decentering land art from the borderlands: A review of *Through the Repellent Fence*'. *Art Journal OPEN*, 27 March, 2018. https://artjournal.collegeart.org/?p=9819 (accessed 10 March, 2021).

Shankland, S. 'Trump's border wall could be a virtual barrier patrolled by drones too'. *C/Net*, 15 February, 2019. www.cnet.com/news/trumps-border-wall-could-be-a-virtual-barrier-patrolled-by-drones-too/ (accessed 10 March, 2021).

Simmons, K. 'Expanse'. *Journal for the Anthropology of North America*, 22:2 (2019): 103–105.

— 'Settler atmospherics'. *Cultural Anthropology*, 189:32 (2017). https://culanth.org/fieldsights/settler-atmospherics (accessed 10 March, 2021).

Simpson, A. *Mohawk Interruptus: Political Life across the Borders of Settler States*. Durham, NC: Duke University Press, 2014.

St. John, R. C. *Line in the Sand: A History of the Western U.S.–Mexico Border*. Princeton: Princeton University Press, 2011.

Stewart, K. 'Atmospheric attunements'. *Environment and Planning D: Society and Space*, 29 (2011): 445–453.

Trecka, M. 'The implication of a fence: Part one – an early form of surveillance'. *Beacon Broadside*, 14 June, 2016. www.beaconbroadside.com/broadside/2016/06/the-implication-of-a-fence-part-one-an-early-form-of-surveillance.html (accessed 10 March, 2021).

Vizenor, G. *Manifest Manners: Narratives on Postindian Survivance*. Lincoln, NE: Nebraska University Press, 1999.

Vukov, T. and M. Sheller. 'Border work: surveillant assemblages, virtual fences, and tactical counter-media'. *Social Semiotics*, 23:2 (2013): 225–241.

Watson, M. '"Centring the Indigenous": Postcommodity's trans-indigenous relational art'. *Third Text*, 29:3 (2015): 141–154.

Williams, A. J. 'Reconceptualising spaces of the air: Performing the multiple spatialities of UK military Airspaces'. *Transactions of the Institute of British Geographers*, 36 (2011): 253–267.

Coda: the life, death, and rebirth of drone art

Arthur Holland Michel

Ever since the drone entered the mainstream, it has confronted us with many complex and unfamiliar questions. Conflict would now be waged from oceans away, and largely in secret; could any such war be just and good? The airspace, previously the exclusive domain of those with either significant resources or significant expertise, would be democratised; could this be a force of liberation, or chaos? Our every move would be watched from above; would our remaining shreds of privacy be eviscerated once and for all by aerial intrusion? These machines would soon even make decisions by themselves, including, eventually, the ultimate decision to take a human life; could we ever trust them?

Obviously, these questions would never be fully addressed through straight research, policy, and journalism alone. Instead, we have had to turn to alternate modes of enquiry and expression to reconcile ourselves with the drone. Foremost among these modes is art that responds to the drone, either by depicting its form or its effects, or by employing the technology itself as the medium of creation. Such works, which collectively we might call 'drone art', have helped build aesthetic, moral, and ethical vocabularies to interrogate the issues that the technology poses, and build a vital *community* around the drone imaginary – a community that has interacted closely with the communities that arose around the other modes of inquiry.

And yet over the course of its relatively short history, drone art has already undergone a profound transformation, precursor to an even more profound set of transformations that it is set to pass through in the years ahead. Why is this? Fundamentally, on the one hand, it is because when art serves a specific purpose – as being a vessel of, or aid to, enquiry into complex questions around the technology – we must accept that once it has served its purpose, its potency is diminished. Additionally, on the other hand, as the subject matter itself evolves, the art that responds to it must evolve too.

To a significant extent, drone art has served many of its original purposes. But the technology is evolving, and eventually it will evolve to such an extent that it will raise new questions that must, in turn, be explored in new art. This pattern of emergence and evolution is not unique to drones, nor is the course of works responding to it unique to drone art. All technologies raise challenging questions. All technologies evolve. Therefore, the arc of drone art is a valuable object lesson for how art about technology emerges, flourishes, evolves, fades and, ultimately, becomes something else.

Drone 'surfacing'

For those who have tracked the drone art movement closely, it is hard not to feel that the genre's golden years have come and gone. Today, drone art in its original community-building form and function has less resonance and prominence in the public debate than it once did.

In the years when the first wave of drone art was at its apex, from about 2010 to 2014, very few people had ever seen a civilian drone in the flesh, or a military drone in image or video. For such a high-profile news topic, drone strikes produced very little actual visual media. The drones themselves were never photographed in action from close range. The effects of their strikes looked no different from the effects of strikes by inhabited aircraft – and thus in their effects they produced a category of imagery to which the public was already inured. Most people I interacted with outside the field did not understand that the word 'drone' encompassed a wide range of different types of aircraft, from Predators and Reapers to quadcopters and Styrofoam hobby kits.

Many of the most prominent early drone artworks were premised around this invisibility. Interventions like James Bridle's *Drone Shadows*, large one-to-one scale outlines of Predator and Reaper drones painted on the ground, and Ruben Pater's *Drone Survival Guide* – a chart of drones in silhouette form reminiscent of a birding guide – served in part to simply fill the gap in our notions of what drones looked like. Their subject, the drone, may have been complex, but their object was intuitive: put a form to the name.

Trevor Paglen's series of photographs of military drones that appear as nothing more than tiny specks against vast, cloud-hatched skies flipped this logic. Instead of making the drone visible, these works captured how drones were literally and figuratively almost invisible. To the uninformed eye, many of Paglen's works from this series are merely pretty pictures of the sky, in the same way that you likely would not be able to spot a drone that's watching you from 30,000 feet above unless you knew what to look for. As such, the pictures illustrate both how and why this invisibility is highly intentional on the part of those operating the drones, and highly problematic for us on the ground.

Other works from the same period pushed this proposition further by making the drone not only visible, but present. Josh Begley's Drone+ app, which was, for a period, banned from Apple's App Store,[1] delivered users a push notification every time a new US drone strike was reported. Begley's Twitter account @Dronestream, meanwhile, tweeted an announcement for each known strike dating back to 2002, when the US first used drones to target individuals outside of declared war zones. Joseph Delappe's *In Drones We Trust*, a participatory project in which the artist distributed small rubber stamps of Predator drones for participants to mark on US currency, sought to achieve a similar effect – putting the drone right in front of not just the willing users of an iPhone app or followers of a Twitter account, but everyone. Delappe's goal was to force citizens all over the country to confront the image of the drone, whether they wanted to or not. In this way, these works sought to counteract the vast unknowability of the drone and its effects by making it entirely inescapable (in the same way that a drone is inescapable to someone on a distant battlefield who finds themselves locked in its crosshairs).

Other works responded to the drone by seeking to situate it within, or against, long-established aesthetic and intellectual traditions, to make the drone visible *culturally*. Consider, for instance, the many paintings that employed traditional artmaking techniques and aesthetics to portray unmanned aircraft, such as Fernando Brizuela's formal drone watercolours and John Stark's *Vampyre*; Mahwish Chisty's miniature drone paintings and Kathryn Brimblecombe-Fox's mystical drone landscapes – which both depict the drone using millennial artmaking techniques and imagery from Pakistan and Australia, respectively; or Teju Cole's 'Seven short stories about drones', which spliced references to drones into the famous opening sentences of seven canonical books – a literary version of appropriating drones to a classical artistic medium that was picked up widely in the popular media.[2] These works strove to impress upon viewers a sense that more than just existing, drones are, and will forever remain, a part of our legacy.

Such efforts to show us all what the drone looks like (or, at the very least, what the gaps it inhabited looked like), to make the drone inescapable, and to convince us that it matters, all operate according to a common underlying, and purposeful, logic. In a post on Reddit in 2012, Begley captured this impulse, explaining that his 'purpose' with his projects was to 'surface this information in new and different ways.'[3] These acts of surfacing serve a variety of functions. On the one hand, there is a practical motivation for surfacing the drone. As Ruben Pater has said of his survival guide, 'To what extent can lawmakers protect citizens if we do not know which drones are or [sic] commercial, armed, or unarmed?'[4] By extension, surfacing was also regarded as something of a pre-requisite to any truly substantive discourse. 'By making visible the invisible', writes Alex Danchev, 'slowly, slowly, [drone art] brings home some truths.'[5] It's hard to debate drones if you don't know what they look like.

When invisibility is so nearly absolute and so intentional on the part of those in power, such acts of making the invisible visible[6] is a radical proposition. Similarly, the mere act of portraying the drone artistically in a new aesthetic or medium (as opposed to, say, journalistically) was received as an assertive, rather than passive, intellectual gesture. But as that invisibility erodes, largely as a result of 'surfacing', so too does the power of the proposition. Today, there is less of a need to surface the drone or convince an uninitiated public that it is important and worthy of attention. It is becoming harder to find people who have never *seen* a hobby drone in the flesh or a Predator drone on TV, even if their understanding of how these aircraft work remains rudimentary. In other words, the needs of the 'community' that drone art rose to meet have changed.

Already in 2014, Bridle remarked that the gap in public understanding of what drones do, what they look like, and what they mean was being filled – and the project was, as a result, becoming less necessary.[7] That year, one survey found that 91 percent of US adults were aware of drone warfare, and even 73 percent were aware of the idea of drone deliveries.[8] The drone's cultural and aesthetic novelty have also worn off. A work that aspires to the condition of drone art today can no longer justify itself simply on the basis of straight portrayal. What was, in 2014, a commentary on the technology is, today, mostly just a picture of an unmanned aircraft. A report of a drone strike is, likewise, just a report of a drone strike – sadly, old news. In 2017, Josh Begley tweeted from the @Dronestream account, 'After 5 years, I think @dronestream is over. Please read this', with a link to an investigation into civilian casualties from airstrikes in the coalition campaign against ISIS in Iraq.[9] Even though there are more drone strikes happening around the world than ever before, the project had ran its natural course, and the community's discourse is richer because of it. The account never tweeted again.

To be sure, many of these works, including Begley's, sought to do more than merely conscientise the public. Their purpose was also to spur social and political action by building assertive commentary on a foundation of surfacing. As Bridle explained in an interview with the Center for the Study of the Drone in January, 2014, 'the Shadows are not really about what the drone looks like; they're about the absence of the drone in the contemporary discourse.'[10] It is only by depicting the drone that one can highlight how little it is seen and how this (mostly intentional) invisibility is ethically dubious.

A more classical instance of drone protest art was JR and Reprieve's *#NotABugSplat* (2014). The work is a giant portrait of an unidentified girl who is reported to have lost several relatives in a drone strike, which was installed on a field in Khyber Pukhtoonkhwa, Pakistan – a region where drone attacks were thought to be common. The idea was to put drone pilots, peering through their flying cameras, face-to-face with a victim of their actions. In a sense, an act of targeted surfacing intended to make reminders of the effects of drone strikes inescapable for those conducting them (just as Delappe's stamps made reminders of the drone inescapable for regular citizens using US dollars). It remains to be known whether any pilots did, indeed, see the installation. But even if not, the work served a secondary purpose of drawing public attention to (and outrage against) drone strikes. In this regard it was wildly successful – the project garnered global attention and acclaim in the popular press.

A number of artists, including Brian Bailey and Heather Layton in their exhibition *Drone Home*, Tamira Sawatzky and Elle Flanders in *Drone Wedding*, Tomas Van Houtryve in *Blue Sky Days*, and James Bridle with his *Drone Shadows*, posit a parallel flipping of the script. By imagining Western citizens living under military drones – and, in the case of Van Houtryve's series, actually submitting a range of unwitting people to a drone's eye in the sky – these works pose the question right to the audience: how would you like to live under drones? Extending this notion further, Adam Harvey's *Stealth Wear* and Hito Steyerl's *HOW NOT TO BE SEEN: A Fucking Didactic Educational. MOV File* offer semi-tongue-in-cheek instructions on how to evade a drone's surveillant gaze, raising the possibility that we will need to take up a range of active measures to remain hidden from the drone's panoptic gaze in the near future. They suggest that in contrast to the secret drone, the human's default mode in a drone-filled age will be one of total naked visibility.

It is difficult to overstate the impact of these works on the public discourse. They have been reproduced so widely – in policy reports, news stories, presentations, and other media – that they have become key signifiers for the ethical quandaries posed by drone technologies. The issues that these works address are more prescient than ever before (drone use, both domestic and foreign, militant and surveillant, is booming) and the artworks continue to feel resonant to the contemporary viewer.

But more recent drone artworks that have attempted to pose these same questions seem to lack that original vital energy and sense of urgency that motivated earlier works. For example, Ai Wei Wei and Herzog and Demeron's *Hansel and Gretel*, a vast installation in the Park Avenue Armory that submitted visitors to a dystopic all-seeing surveillance apparatus in the summer of 2017, was met with a tepid critical response from the reviewers and an intellectual shrug from the audience. When I visited the show, it appeared that most visitors were more interested in the installation's

Instagrammability than the substance of its message. Hundreds of mobile phone cameras were drawn. In each direction I turned, poses were being struck. As one reviewer commented, the installation 'inspire[d] brief awe, then you figure it out, and it is reduced to technology, and fun.'[11] If anything, rather than critique the invisible drone's power to intrude upon our sacred invisibility, the show put into relief the audience's desire to be as visible as possible. It's hard to imagine that this was the artwork's intended purpose.

Drone novelties

A second axiom of art about technology: the act of highlighting the *possibilities* (both positive and negative) of a technology ceases to be so much an *artistic* proposition when the technology bears out the possibilities that the works have speculated. This, too, has eroded some of the poignancy of drone art in its more recent years.

No work better illustrates the passage from possibility to reality, and what it means for art about technology, than Marko Peljhan's *S-77CCR System-77 Civil Counter-Reconnaissance*. This fixed-wing surveillance drone, displayed in a pavilion at Karlsplatz, Vienna in 2004, as a commentary on the possibilities of drone technology for monitoring law enforcement actions (a notion known as 'sousveillance'), was activism art in a strict sense of the term. The project was suffused with an excitement around the possibilities of techno-enabled resistance. But soon after, Peljhan turned the artwork into an entrepreneurial venture and actually began producing a similar drone commercially, for airborne data collection. The project ultimately evolved into a successful business, C-Astral, that sells fixed-wing drones for a range of operations, including military and law enforcement surveillance (but as far as we know not yet for countersurveillance).[12] When the commentary becomes indistinguishable from – indeed, even part and parcel of – the subject of its intervention, its critical potency evaporates. Nobody today would call C-Astral an 'art project'.

While the Peljhan's case is certainly extreme, it is a good allegory for how the drone is increasingly no longer an object of art by default. In the early years of the adoption of civilian drone technology, any video made with a drone, by virtue of being made *by* a drone, was automatically *about the* drone. The Bureau of Inverse Technology's *BIT PLANE* project, from 1999, which flew a camera-equipped drone over several Silicon Valley tech campuses, highlighted the drone's own incredible potential for surfacing other invisible spaces and entities. Even over a decade later, John Vigg's drone aerial photography was received as a credible, sincere celebration of the opportunities that the technology creates (he used a drone to discover that a housing development visible on Google Maps in the middle of the New Jersey Pine Barrens did not, in fact, exist), the artists even going so far as to call it 'a new aesthetic'.[13]

As I have written previously,[14] aeriality is fundamental to the public fear and fascination around drones. It is the reason we find Vigg's new aesthetic so appealing, and also why we find drones so scary. Kathryn Brimblecombe-Fox's paintings depict the sky that her drones inhabit as distant, unreachable, mythical space. Penelope Umbrico's *Sunset Portraits from 12,193,606 Flickr Sunsets on 4/25/13* is a commentary on the grandness and unknowability of the firmament and thus, by extension, of the drones that can access it. Frederick Belzile's *Eyes in the Sky*, an abstracted aerial video from a #NODAPL protest drone, points to a fundamental unknowability and *strangeness* of the aerial perspective. An ongoing project by the drone-flying duo Tushev Aerials, meanwhile, highlights the decorative potential of the vertical perspective. For a period, the artists commissioned rugs displaying aerial shot from their drones, framing this new human capacity in a highly aestheticised medium. Miki Kratsman's 2010 series *Targeted Killing* similarly adopts the aerial perspective – as well as the tools of airborne surveillance – to imagine what the scene of a targeted airstrike looks like in the moments before it occurs.

But today the mythos of the aerial perspective has largely been eroded. Drone aerial photography is so common in TV and film that the journalist and filmmaker Bilge Ebiri has commented we're nearing a 'dronepocalypse' – an over-saturation of the drone's-eye-view in popular media.[15] In a dronepocalypse, one cannot make a commentary on the drone simply by using a drone.

And the same could be said of the mythos of mechanical creatures that inhabit the sky. Even millions of everyday citizens now own drones. Soon enough, drones will be so common that projects like Damn Kim's *First Flight*, which captures the excitement, wonder, and apprehension of first-time drone owners (as seen through the footage from the drone itself) and Suzanne Treister's *The Drone that Filmed the Opening of its Own Exhibition* – a video taken by a drone prowling around a gallery, sparking a whole lot of bemusement from its fellow gallery-goers – simply will not be possible, because the technology will no longer inspire those feelings. Someday, *BIT Plane* will simply be a very old piece of drone footage, especially if viewed outside of an artistic context. Superflux's *Drone Aviary*, which imagined a future in which drones filled the skies over our cities, is likewise quickly seeing its vision turning to reality; once that reality (or some version thereof) fully arrives, the artwork turns from a thought – provoking piece of speculative commentary to a plain prediction of a future that has been for the most part achieved. Such works will be historically interesting, and that is all.

Other works could *only* function at the intersection of broad public excitement about the technology's newness *and* the absence of public familiarity with the technology. Ricardo Dominguez capitalised on that fleeting intersection to great effect when he staged a fake Reaper drone crash on the campus of the University of California-San Diego in the summer of 2012 and then issued a statement from the (also fake) UC Center for Drone Policy and Ethics noting that the 'origin and manufacturer of the crashed drone remains unclear.' The incident captured national headlines, even after the University corrected the record and explained that both the crash and the Center were spurious.[16] By simultaneously surfacing and challenging the drone for a broad audience, the work was a very successful venture, though it has since been largely overlooked.

One drone artwork was able to mine so much poignancy from this intersection that it has actually *shaped* the development of drone technology, a claim that few other works can credibly make. In 2012, the fictive 'low-cost air and space exploration'[17] research laboratory Darwin Aerospace unveiled the *Burrito Bomber*, a drone delivery service for spiriting Mexican wraps right to your doorstep. The project, presented to the world by way of a savvy media campaign was, like *S-77CCR*, pure commentary. But it so fully captured the imagination of the public that soon even leading experts in the field were telling journalists and audiences that unmanned aerial vehicle technology would be delivering Mexican wraps to their homes in the years to come. When Alphabet's (non-satirical) drone delivery programme, Project Wing, conducted tests on the Virginia Tech campus, the drones delivered just one type of dish: burritos.[18] The artwork had built not just a theoretical community imaginary, but an actual reality. When life imitates art, it means that art has, for better or for worse, done its part.

Drone evolutions

As a result of all of these factors, so many drone artworks now function not as active interventions, but as artefacts. And to be sure, in this role they still hold value. As an artefact, the *Burrito Bomber* and its public reception illustrate where the public view of drones stood in 2013, and how it has evolved since then. *First Flight* is no longer about how drones make us feel now, but rather a compelling record of how drones *used to make us feel*. The works of James Bridle, Josh Begley, and Trevor Paglen will similarly point to how the absence of the drone in the popular discourse was profoundly troubling because it was so wide and so empty – and that the secrecy was so absolute that even a peek behind the veil was a gallery-worthy gesture.

Future drone art must therefore draw its potency from new fronts. But what will those sources be? Will artists find new possibilities to push beyond this first wave of works, and new lines of energy in the material? Of course they will, because the drone itself is evolving. For instance, as our fascination with the drone as an aerial creature recedes, a new kind of drone is emerging: the non-aerial drone. And as far as the artists seeking to continue probing the issues around unmanned technology could be concerned, this is an opportunity. Systems such as the US Navy's Sea Hunter, a 130-foot long uncrewed ship – a drone boat – could certainly be held with the same mix of fear, mistrust, awe, and reverence as the Predator. As could Russia's uncrewed nuclear submarine/torpedo, the Poseidon, or Israel's ghost speedboat, the Seagull. After all, humans have feared creatures that live in the depths of the ocean for just as long as they have feared and revered those that come from the sky. Similarly, ground robots could soon be just as controversial as the notion of an armed police drone, as speculated by the street artist Essam[19] in his series of fake NYPD posters that depicted a police Predator drone firing a missile at a fleeing family. (Already in the summer of 2016, a SWAT team in Dallas used a ground robot laden with explosives to kill an armed man who was engaged in a shoot-out with police.) All of these technologies raise new questions that will need to be unpacked – and will pose injustices that will have to be challenged.

As of right now, we have yet to see any significant works of non-aerial drone art, but the stage – so to speak – is very much set for a new wave of works that engage this technology and all the questions it raises with the same vigour as the canonical works of drone art that have shaped our collective relationship with its aerial counterparts. It is not difficult to imagine a dance that choreographs humans alongside ground robots – in the style of the dance troupe Elevenplay's performances that choreographed human dancers under flitting swarms of light-equipped multirotor drones – to interrogate the role that these machines should and should not play in society. Such a performance might fruitfully illustrate, like Elevenplay, how these technologies can extend our reach and multiply our powers – and, in the same gesture, how they can challenge us, threaten us, and put into hard metallic relief our human frailty.

As drone technology creeps to new domains, it is also taking on new roles. When drone art first emerged, drones served only two general purposes: to kill and to *see*. Works such as Morgan Skinner's *Gorgon Stare* – which set video feeds from surveillance and strikes drones alongside clips of first-person-shooter video gameplay – and IOCOSE's *Drone Selfies* (literal selfies taken from a drone hovering in front of a mirror) interact with various forms of what some describe as 'drone vision' (as does Trevor Paglen's work of that same name). But future drones will serve a far wider variety of purposes: delivering goods, stringing power lines, painting walls, and so on. The use of the drone in these ways in the near future will also raise new conundrums about the kind of future that we are, together with them, building for ourselves. Do we want drones to deliver packages to us in thirty minutes or less? Will our cities be more or less welcoming to humans when they are built by machines? What will painters do when they have been displaced by robots? (And so on.) Here too, new opportunities – one might even say needs – for inquiry through artmaking will arise.

The most significant way that drones are evolving is not in their form or function, but in their intelligence. Drones are getting smarter. The implications of artificial intelligence have been a long-running theme in drone art throughout its history. Often, particularly in the genre's earlier years, it was, in a way, an unavoidable theme. In many attempts to use drones as a tool for artmaking, as in the case of *BIT Plane*, Sterling Crispin's *Charon* (an autonomous quadcopter that interacts with a human subject as though it were a machinic dance partner), and Katsu's *ICARUS* (a drone equipped with a spray can for graffiti), the technology's relative lack of refinement suggested how autonomy blurs the lines of authorship. The *BIT Plane* skipped and weaved unsteadily as it flew. Crispin's Charon drone skittishly overcompensates for any disturbance in its balance, giving it the appearance of a nervous dancer. The *ICARUS* was incredibly tricky to operate; at best, KATSU could suggest what he wanted the drone to draw. In Suzanne Treister's *The Drone that Filmed the Opening of its Own Exhibition*, the relatively unsophisticated gimbal-less drone bumps around its gallery like an art critic who has had too much Chardonnay. Roman Signer's *56 Kleine Helikopter*, a video of 56 remote control helicopters flying around in a small room and mostly crashing with each other or the walls, simultaneously conveys the idea of machine intelligence (when the helicopters in the video operate successfully) and machine stupidity (when they collide). The drone in these depictions appears as a genuine thinking, feeling being, endowed of a certain artistic agency that was independent of – and even directly challenged – its creator's intentions.

Somewhat counterintuitively, it is harder to productively mine such themes with these early technologies' more intelligent descendants. Take *ICARUS*. KATSU's early drone graffiti works felt like a true collaboration between artist and recalcitrant machine, but as KATSU continued to improve *ICARUS*' autonomous features, such as its computer vision algorithms and its stabilisation mechanisms, the gap between the artist's intent and what the drone actually produced began to narrow. By 2017, the artist was able to draw clear, legible characters. At the time of writing, his drones can generate figurative pictures that look like they were created by a skilled graffiti artist. They can even autonomously generate a convincing rendition of the artist's signature graffiti tag, a complex figurative skull rendered with a single continuous line. The technology has become so manageable that the artist has even released a version for commercial sale.[20]

This poses a problem for an artist wishing to use an autonomous drone to comment on the questions surrounding machine intelligence. A drone that is smart enough to perfectly execute the artmaking task as dictated by the operator does not blur the line of authorship; it does the opposite. It becomes just another paintbrush, another tool. Nor does it raise particularly challenging questions around the notion of true machine autonomy. Even instructing a drone to perform random acts, to execute a form of artistic agency, to behave randomly and spontaneously, is really just another form of the human artist exercising their own agency, expressed in code. The notion of machine *autonomy*, in the non-technical sense of the term, is lost.

Nevertheless, as autonomous technologies become more advanced, there will be a renewed need for art to guide us through the tricky, complex questions that they raise. Machine intelligence, es expressed in both physical and virtual domains, will subject our lives to forces mysterious and secretive. Indeed, on a daily basis our will is already swayed by algorithms of which we have no awareness, let alone comprehension.[21] The more pervasive and advanced autonomy becomes – be it in the form of intelligent unmanned systems or other autonomous devices – artists will once again be best placed to fill those gaps and furnish a broad public with the aesthetic and intellectual vocabularies necessary to pick apart the questions that those technologies raise. If the short but vibrant history of drone art is any indication, they will surely rise to the challenge. Let us hope they do so soon.

Notes

1 N. Wingfield, 'Apple rejects app tracking drone strikes', *New York Times* (30 August, 2012). http://bits.blogs.nytimes.com/2012/08/30/apple-rejects-app-tracking-drone-strikes/ (accessed 2 March, 2021).

2 A. Danchev, 'Bug splat: The art of the drone', *International Affairs*, 92 (2016), 712–713.

3 J. Begley, 'really appreciate you, Reddit', comment posted to Reddit (12 December, 2012), www.reddit.com/r/worldnews/comments/14qexa/an_nyu_grad_student_is_tweeting_every_drone/ (accessed 2 March, 2021).

4 R. Pater and F. Lorenzin, 'To conceal and to reveal: An interview with Ruben Pater', interview by Filippo Lorenzin, www.digicult.it/news/nascondere-e-rivelare-intervista-ruben-pater/ (accessed 2 March, 2021).

5 Danchev, 'Bug splat'.
6 S. Braeunert and M. Malone (eds), *To See Without Being Seen: Contemporary Art and Drone Warfare*, Mildred Lane Kemper Art Museum, Washington University in St. Louis (2016).
7 J. Bridle and A. H. Michel, 'Interview: James Bridle', interview by Arthur Holland Michel, Center for the Study of the Drone (17 January, 2014), www.dronecenter.bard.edu/interview-james-bridle/ (accessed 2 March, 2021).
8 T. D. Miethe, J. D. Lieberman, M. Sakiyama, and E. I. Troshynski, 'Public attitudes about aerial drone activities: Results of a national survey', University of Las Vegas Center for Crime and Justice Policy (July 2014), CCJP 2014-02. www.unlv.edu/sites/default/files/page_files/27/Research-PublicAttitudesaboutAerialDroneActivities.pdf.
9 J. Begley, 'After 5 years, I think @dronestream is over. Please read this', comment on Twitter (posted 16 November, 2017), www.twitter.com/dronestream/status/931262631381471232 (accessed 2 March, 2021).
10 Bridle and Mitchel, 'Interview: James Bridle'.
11 R. Smith, 'Watch out: You're in Ai Weiwei's surveillance zone', *The New York Times* (8 June, 2017), www.nytimes.com/2017/06/08/arts/design/watch-out-youre-in-ai-weiweis-surveillance-zone.html (accessed 2 March, 2021).
12 M. Peljhan, 'Text accompanying the artwork "Situational Awareness"', in *Ars Electronica Festival Catalogue* (2007), 188–189.
13 J. Vigg, 'Photography in the age of the personal drone', interview by Morgan O'Leary, *Vice* (4 June, 2013), www.vice.com/en_us/article/aej5jg/the-age-of-the-personal-drone (accessed 2 March, 2021).
14 A. H. Michel, 'What we talk about when we talk about the drone', Center for the Study of the Drone at Bard College (25 April, 2013), www.dronecenter.bard.edu/on-the-drone/ (accessed 2 March, 2021).
15 B. Ebiri, 'The dronepocalypse is here – in documentary footage, at least', *New York Times* (8 May, 2019), www.nytimes.com/2019/05/08/movies/drones-documentaries.html (accessed 8 May, 2019).
16 T. Kingkade, 'Drone crashes on UC San Diego campus, revealed as "new media art project"', *Huffington Post* (12 July, 2012), www.huffpost.com/entry/drone-crash-uc-san-diego_n_2258323h (accessed 2 March, 2021).
17 'About', Darwin Aerospace, www.darwinaerospace.com/about.php.
18 M. McFarland, 'Google drones will deliver Chipotle burritos at Virginia Tech', *CNN Business* (8 September, 2016), www.money.cnn.com/2016/09/08/technology/google-drone-chipotle-burrito/index.html (accessed 2 March, 2021).
19 K. Chayka, 'Street artist behind NYC drone posters arrested', *Hyperallergic* (30 November, 2012), www.hyperallergic.com/61192/street-artist-behind-nyc-drone-posters-arrested/ (accessed 2 March, 2021).
20 G. Leung, 'KATSU launches first semi-autonomous smart painting drone', *HYPEBEAST* (30 November, 2019), https://hypebeast.com/2019/11/katsu-tsuru-robotics-katsuru-beta-semi-autonomous-spray-painting-drone-release-info (accessed 2 March, 2021).
21 C. O'Neil, *Weapons of Math Destruction* (New York: Crown, 2016).

Bibliography

Baraona, E., M. Otero, and M. Shoshan (eds), *Drone: Unmanned. Architecture and Security Series*. Barcelona: DPR Barcelona, 2016.

Begley, J. 'After 5 years, I think @dronestream is over. Please read this', Comment on Twitter (posted 16 November, 2017), www.twitter.com/dronestream/status/931262631381471232 (accessed 2 March, 2021).

— 'really appreciate you, Reddit'. Comment posted to Reddit, 12 December, 2012. www.reddit.com/r/worldnews/comments/14qexa/an_nyu_grad_student_is_tweeting_every_drone/ (accessed 2 March, 2021).

Berkowitz, R. 'Drones and the question of "the human,"' *Ethics & International Affairs*, 28:2 (2014): 159–169.

Braeunert, S. and M. Malone (eds). *To See Without Being Seen: Contemporary Art and Drone Warfare*. Mildred Lane Kemper Art Museum, Washington University in St. Louis (2016).

Bridle J. and A. H. Michel. 'Interview: James Bridle'. Interview by Arthur Holland Michel, Center for the Study of the Drone, 17 January, 2014. www.dronecenter.bard.edu/interview-james-bridle/ (accessed 2 March, 2021).

Chayka, K. 'Street artist behind NYC drone posters arrested'. *Hyperallergic*, 30 November, 2012. http://hyperallergic.com/61192/street-artist-behind-nyc-drone-posters-arrested/ (accessed 2 March, 2021).

Danchev, A. 'Bug splat: the art of the drone'. *International Affairs*, 92 (2016): 703–713.

Ebiri, B. 'The dronepocalypse is here – in documentary footage, at least'. *New York Times*, 8 May, 2019. www.nytimes.com/2019/05/08/movies/drones-documentaries.html (accessed 8 May, 2019).

Michel, A. H. 'What we talk about when we talk about the drone'. Center for the Study of the Drone at Bard College, 25 April, 2013. www.dronecenter.bard.edu/on-the-drone/ (accessed 2 March, 2021).

Miethe, T. D., J. D. Lieberman, M. Sakiyama, and E. I. Troshynski. 'Public attitudes about aerial drone activities: Results of a national survey'. University of Las Vegas Center for Crime and Justice Policy (July 2014), CCJP 2014-02. www.unlv.edu/sites/default/files/page_files/27/Research-PublicAttitudesaboutAerialDroneActivities.pdf.

Kingkade, T. 'Drone crashes on UC San Diego campus, revealed as "new media art project"'. *Huffington Post*, 12 July, 2012. www.huffpost.com/entry/drone-crash-uc-san-diego_n_2258323h (accessed 2 March, 2021).

Lange, C. 'Blurred visions'. *Frieze*, 24 May, 2013. www.frieze.com/issue/print_article/blurred-visions/ (accessed 2 March, 2021).

Leung, G. 'KATSU launches first semi-autonomous smart painting drone'. *HYPEBEAST*, 30 November, 2019. https://hypebeast.com/2019/11/katsu-tsuru-robotics-katsuru-beta-semi-autonomous-spray-painting-drone-release-info (accessed 2 March, 2021).

McFarland, M. 'Google drones will deliver Chipotle burritos at Virginia Tech'. CNN Business, 8 September, 2016. www.money.cnn.com/2016/09/08/technology/google-drone-chipotle-burrito/index.html (accessed 2 March, 2021).

O'Neil, C. *Weapons of Math Destruction*. New York: Crown, 2016.

Pater, R. and F. Lorenzin. 'To conceal and to reveal: An interview with Ruben

Pater'. Interview by Filippo Lorenzin. www.digicult.it/news/nascondere-e-rivelare-intervista-ruben-pater/ (accessed 2 March, 2021).

Peljhan, M. 'Text accompanying the artwork "Situational Awareness"'. In *Ars Electronica Festival Catalogue* (2007).

Rothstein, A. '[Longreads] The complexities of drones in art'. *Vice*, 12 November, 2014. www.vice.com/en_us/article/pgqa3k/longreads-the-complexities-of-drones-in-art (accessed 2 March, 2021).

Smith, S. 'Watch out: You're in Ai Weiwei's surveillance zone'. *The New York Times*, 8 June, 2017. www.nytimes.com/2017/06/08/arts/design/watch-out-youre-in-ai-weiweis-surveillance-zone.html (accessed 2 March, 2021).

Vigg, J. 'Photography in the age of the personal drone'. Interview by Morgan O'Leary. *Vice*, 4 June, 2013. www.vice.com/en_us/article/aej5jg/the-age-of-the-personal-drone (accessed 2 March, 2021).

Wingfield, N. 'Apple rejects app tracking drone strikes'. *New York Times*, 30 August, 2012. bits.blogs.nytimes.com/2012/08/30/apple-rejects-app-tracking-drone-strikes/ (accessed 2 March, 2021).

Index

Artworks and literary works can be found under artist's / author's names

EU authorised representative for GPSR:
Easy Access System Europe, Mustamäe tee 50,
10621 Tallinn, Estonia
gpsr.requests@easproject.com

www.ingramcontent.com/pod-product-compliance
Lightning Source LLC
Chambersburg PA
CBHW072039280526
45788CB00006B/2118

* 9 7 8 1 5 2 6 1 7 8 9 8 5 *